To Michelle —
All the Best,

[signature]

More praise for SOULS OF STEEL

"Pat Williams's new book on character couldn't come at a better time. Our country is going through a crisis of character, particularly with our young people. This important and practical book can help turn the tide."
— Herman Edwards, head coach, Kansas City Chiefs

"The message in this book marries with the recruiting philosophy of Notre Dame Football. The most important ingredient for a successful program is high character."
— Charlie Weis, head football coach, University of Notre Dame

"Pat Williams has written many successful books. He has done it again with SOULS OF STEEL, a resource that will help both young and old build good character in their lives."
— David Dombrowski, president, general manager and CEO, Detroit Tigers

"Pat Williams has written dozens of books that have helped people enrich their lives. SOULS OF STEEL may be the best of them all! Pat explains the essence of what makes a great teammate in the clubhouse and the kind of person you want to have as a teammate in life. The more people who read this book, the better off we all will be."
— Ernie Accorsi, former general manager, New York Giants

"SOULS OF STEEL is another 'all net' shot by Pat Williams. A must-read that specializes in building character, but it all starts with love."
— Avery Johnson, head coach, Dallas Mavericks

"Character is the crucial ingredient of success in business, sports, and every aspect of life. I don't care how much wealth and fame you acquire, if you don't have good character, you have nothing. In SOULS OF STEEL, Pat Williams gives us the practical, road-tested principles for becoming men and women of character—and he shows us how to pass the legacy of good character along to the next generation. If you want to influence young lives, you *must* read this book!"
— Drayton McLane, Jr., chairman, McLane Group, and owner of the Houston Astros

"SOULS OF STEEL appeals to me as a major league manager. You will win some games with talented players, but you will never win championships without players who have strong character. This book is destined to serve as a manual to all of us in the character-building business."

—Clint Hurdle, manager, Colorado Rockies

"Many people today recognize the lack of character and integrity in our society, but Pat Williams provides solid plans for actually building these vital qualities into the lives of our young people. Be sure to place this valuable book in the hands of parents, grandparents, teachers, coaches and all who care about fortifying our next generation of leaders."

—Les Steckel, president and CEO, The Fellowship of Christian Athletes

"We live in a world that is extremely challenging, especially to young people. There are influences everywhere, and many are left to drift without the guidance of leaders and mentors of previous generations. SOULS OF STEEL is a book that strikes right at the heart of the issue. Many people believe that good character is for someone else to teach or to convey to children. Pat Williams shares his life and his experiences to personalize this message. He has taken a lifetime of personal and professional experience and shared the importance of this valuable lesson and the impact that good character can have on the lives of people around the world. How and where to start? SOULS OF STEEL helps you start with yourself and your children. A great first step to the world."

—Urban Meyer, head football coach, University of Florida

"Having played baseball professionally, built a championship team in the NBA and raised 19 children of his own, I can think of no one better to discuss character and personal growth than Pat Williams. His life is a testament to the value of courage, hard work and humility, and the imprint great character can make upon those we interact with every day. I have no doubt that you will enjoy this book immensely."

—Mike D'Antoni, head coach, Phoenix Suns

Souls
OF
STEEL

*How to Build Character
in Ourselves and Our Kids*

Pat Williams
WITH JIM DENNEY

NEW YORK   BOSTON   NASHVILLE

Unless otherwise indicated, Scriptures are taken from the HOLY BIBLE:
NEW INTERNATIONAL VERSION®. Copyright © 1973, 1978,
1984 by International Bible Society. Used by permission of Zondervan
Publishing House. All rights reserved.

Scriptures noted NASB are taken from the New American Standard
Bible®. Copyright © 1960, 1962, 1963, 1968, 1972, 1975, 1977, 1995
by The Lockman Foundation. Used by permission.

Scriptures noted KJV are taken from the King James Version of the Bible.

Scriptures noted NKJV are taken from the NEW KING JAMES VERSION.
Copyright © 1979, 1980, 1982, Thomas Nelson, Inc., Publishers.

FaithWords
Hachette Book Group USA
237 Park Avenue
New York, NY 10017

Visit our Web site at www.faithwords.com

Printed in the United States of America

First Edition: February 2008
10 9 8 7 6 5 4 3 2 1

FaithWords is a division of Hachette Book Group USA, Inc.
The FaithWords name and logo is a trademark of
Hachette Book Group USA, Inc.

Library of Congress Cataloging-in-Publication Data

Williams, Pat
    Souls of steel : how to build character in ourselves and our kids / Pat
Williams. — 1st ed.
    p. cm.
    ISBN-13: 978-0-446-57973-5
    ISBN-10: 0-446-57973-4
    1. Character. I. Title.
    BJ1581.W7423 2007
    170'.44—dc22   2007011212

To the late Stu Inman,

longtime NBA executive and dear friend,

and to Ernie Accorsi,

recently retired NFL executive

and my friend of almost fifty years.

These two souls of steel have

modeled character to me for decades.

Acknowledgments

With deep appreciation I acknowledge the support and guidance of the following people who helped make this book possible:

Special thanks to Alex Martins, Bob Vander Weide and Rich DeVos of the Orlando Magic.

Thanks also to my writing partner Jim Denney for his superb contributions in shaping this manuscript.

Hats off to four dependable associates—my assistant Latria Graham, my trusted and valuable colleague Andrew Herdliska, my longtime adviser Ken Hussar and my ace typist Fran Thomas.

Many people helped me with the research for this book. I am grateful to Josh Looney, Jennica Pearson, Bobby Williams, Mary Lynn Nesbit, Michael Williams and Nasreen Malik.

Hearty thanks also go to my friends Rolf Zettersten, Gary Terashita and the capable staff at Hachette Book Group. Thank you all for believing that we had something important to share and for providing the support and the forum to say it.

I especially want to thank the many people from all walks of life who contributed their thoughts and stories to this effort. There were literally hundreds of people who shared their insights with me—so many that I was overwhelmed by their generous and enthusiastic responses. My only regret is that space limitations prevented me from including everyone's input and acknowledging each one by name.

And finally, special thanks and appreciation go to my wife, Ruth, and to my wonderful and supportive family. They are truly the backbone of my life.

Contents

Foreword

BY DICK VERMEIL

Dick Vermeil builds championship character. In 1975, as head football coach at UCLA, he led the Bruins to a Rose Bowl victory over top-ranked Ohio State. Moving to the NFL in 1976, he coached the Philadelphia Eagles to their first Super Bowl appearance, Super Bowl XV in 1981. After a fifteen-year broadcast career with CBS and ABC, Dick returned to coaching with the St. Louis Rams (1997–1999), winning Super Bowl XXXIV in 2000. He later coached the Kansas City Chiefs to a division title. As sportswriter Ray Didinger observed, "All coaches talk about character, but for Vermeil, it was his coat of arms. He believed in it as a way to live and a way to win."

When Pat Williams called and said he was writing a book called *Souls of Steel*, I said, "Man! What a great title!" Then he told me that his new book was all about how to build character in the next generation. I said, "If we ever needed such a book, we need it now!"

Today there are many celebrities, but maybe not enough role models. There are plenty of people who are famous for being famous (or infamous). But how many are known for their character

traits? Young people may not have enough heroes to look up to, people whose character traits are worthy of emulation.

It's hard to raise kids today! In contrast to earlier generations, they are exposed to too much too soon. There is more television violence and more material with sexual overtones than ever before, things that don't reinforce the value of good character development. The world sure seems different than when my generation was growing up, and these differences are not all good.

My dad was not a well-educated man, but he was very wise when it came to teaching the value of hard work, loyalty, discipline, accountability, responsibility, honesty, and pride. He made his living running The Owl Garage. It was called The Owl Garage because he worked most of the night as well. The garage was twenty-five yards behind our house, so we ate three meals a day together. His vivid examples of how to live your life and treat people were always right there in front of me. I got a clear picture of how a man was supposed to conduct his life from a values standpoint 24-7!

Today, dads and moms both have jobs away from home. A lot of kids don't spend as much time around their parents as they used to, so they don't have the role models they once had.

To make matters worse, we as parents are trying too hard to make life better for our children. We buy them computers and iPods, expensive clothes, and even their own cars when they turn sixteen. We've made life easier for them—but not necessarily better.

In *Souls of Steel*, Pat Williams shows us how to truly improve and transform the lives of young people by encouraging their character growth. He draws upon his own experience as a father to nineteen children (four birth children, fourteen by international adoption, and one by remarriage).

Not only that, but he's taken this book to the next level by tracking down literally hundreds of people from all walks of life and asking them for their stories and insights about character. From these hundreds of interviews, Pat Williams has assembled a treasure trove of life-changing principles you can immediately put into practice.

In these pages, you'll also find fascinating, powerful stories about integrity, hard work, self-control, courage, perseverance, humility, love, responsibility, faith, and influence. These are the character qualities that excite me! Maybe I overuse the word *character*, but I believe you win with character players. When I see people of any age demonstrating these traits, they become my heroes! And that's why I think this book is so important. *Souls of Steel* is not a book of theory, but of hard-knocks, dirt-under-the-fingernails reality.

I agree with Pat Williams that we need to reinforce these character qualities in our society—and that's why I think *Souls of Steel* may be the most important book you'll read this year. It's a book to reread, highlight, and savor. I hope parents, grandparents, teachers, coaches, youth workers, and pastors will absorb its insights and apply its truths to their own lives and the lives of those around them.

This book hits me where I live—where I have always lived as a father, grandfather, and coach. It's no secret that throughout my coaching career I've cared deeply about my players as human beings. Even years after they retired from football, I've kept in touch with them and counseled them and encouraged their personal growth. In short, I was interested in them as *people of character*—you might even say, as *souls of steel*. That's why I'm so enthusiastic about this book.

What kind of mark do you want to make on the world? What kind of influence do you want to have on the next generation? Do you want to leave a legacy of character? Then turn the page. Begin the journey.

It's time to change the world—one soul at a time.

PART I

The Steel Rod
of Character

1

Steel Embedded in Flesh

"The measure of a man's character is what he would do if he knew
he would never be found out."

THOMAS BABBINGTON MACAULAY

NINETEENTH-CENTURY ENGLISH POET-HISTORIAN

The summer after my eighth-grade year, I tried out for a sandlot
baseball team. I made the cut and was the youngest player on the
team by far. I felt a strange mixture of elation and self-doubt: *Yes!
I'm on the team—but can I really perform at this level?*

My mother drove me to my first game. My grandmother sat in
front with Mom, while I sat in back. As we drove, we talked about
my prospects with the team. At one point, I said, "If things don't
work out, I can always quit."

My grandmother whirled around, looked me in the eye, and
jabbed her finger in my chest. "You . . . don't . . . quit!" she said.
"Nobody in this family quits!"

I got that message, loud and clear—and I didn't quit.

That was a huge character-building moment in my life. That
early lesson in perseverance served as the foundation for everything else I have accomplished in life. Let me give you one example
of how my grandmother's words have echoed down through my
adult life.

Journalist David Whitley of *The Orlando Sentinel* called June
19, 1986, "one of the biggest days in Orlando history," a day
that "has had an incalculable effect on Central Florida." That was

the day Orlando businessman Jimmy Hewitt announced plans to bring a National Basketball Association team to Orlando. It's the day he introduced an NBA executive from Philadelphia as the man who would hammer that dream into a reality.

That Philadelphia basketball exec was me.

Now, I'm not suggesting that the birth of the Orlando Magic ranks up there with the day Walt Disney decided to build a Florida theme park or the day they squeezed the first glass of Florida orange juice. But ever since that June day more than two decades ago, the Magic has been an integral part of the culture and economy of the greater Orlando region. Pro basketball is big business, and it produces jobs, prosperity, tourism, and tax revenue.

By David Whitley's count, the first twenty years of Orlando Magic history also generated exciting entertainment for 10,497,076 paying fans, who attended 1,422 games and saw 113,065 shots which netted 136,834 points. The 143 players who donned Magic blue jerseys also accounted for 3,400 celebrity appearances at charity functions. The lives of Central Florida youngsters have been dramatically impacted by the millions of dollars distributed by the Orlando Magic Youth Foundation.

I have to tell you: I honestly question whether any of those numbers would have been racked up if my grandmother hadn't jabbed her finger in my chest and said, "You . . . don't . . . quit!"

Understand, I'm not claiming I single-handedly built the Magic organization. It took a lot of people to make Magic happen in Orlando. But in those prehistoric days of the summer of '86, the Orlando Magic "organization" consisted of little more than Jimmy Hewitt, Pat Williams, and a Kelly Girl we hired to type letters and answer the phone. The Kelly Girl and I shared a secondhand desk in a closet-sized office we rented from sports attorney Robert Fraley.

I left a secure, well-paid job as general manager of the Philadelphia 76ers, which won the NBA championship just three years earlier. I'd been managing a team that boasted the legendary Doc-

tor J (Julius Erving) and a youthful Charles Barkley. I was also the sole breadwinner for a family of six children. So the decision to quit my job, uproot my family, and move to Orlando was not an easy one.

The NBA had made no commitment to grant an expansion franchise to the city of Orlando. In fact, the odds were against it. Many more populous markets (including two Florida cities, Miami and Tampa–St. Pete) were competing against us for a new franchise. I was taking a huge personal and professional risk in trying to build an NBA franchise in Central Florida.

In order to convince the league that Orlando was a serious contender, I had to go around town, selling season tickets (at a hundred bucks a pop) for a team that might never exist. I made the rounds of every Rotary, Lions, Kiwanis, Elks, and Odd Fellows club in the area. I gave my sales pitch to people in the checkout line at the health food store and the dentist's waiting room. If you put a fruit cup in front of me, I'd stand up and give a speech.

I worked fourteen- to eighteen-hour days all through the summer and fall of 1986. On October 20, I presented 14,176 season ticket deposits to the NBA board of governors—the highest season ticket base of all the cities being considered for expansion. NBA commissioner David Stern was impressed. Armed with only a few flip charts and graphs, I made my pitch. I heard later, after I left the room, one of the NBA owners said, "Wow! Pat Williams talked for half an hour without notes! Incredible!"

Well, it wasn't so incredible. I had already criss-crossed the Sunshine State umpteen-hundred times, giving that same speech everywhere I went. Believe me, I knew my lines. And the result of that half-hour presentation? As David Stern later told *The Orlando Sentinel*, "All the energy and enthusiasm that was generated" in Central Florida caused the league to "reassess how large a market had to be."

On January 5, 1987, we broke ground for the Orlando Arena, and one week later, I pres‿ ‿d David Stern with a jar of dirt from

the ground-breaking. In April of that year, the NBA board of governors granted an expansion franchise to Orlando. The Magic played its first game on November 4, 1989, at the Orlando Arena. The rest, as they say, is history.

That experience has truly been the fulcrum of my life. Everything I've done since as a writer, speaker, and sports executive has been shaped by the lessons I learned through that marathon experience of turning magical dreams into reality. It took incredible perseverance from a lot of people to get the job done. Many times, when the odds seemed impossible and the goals unattainable, I wondered, *What have I gotten myself into? There's no way this team is ever going to happen.*

But it never occurred to me to think, *Well, if things don't work out, I can always quit.* I honestly believe the Magic organization, the arena, the sports history we've made, and the benefits to the entire Central Florida community exist today because my grandmother glared at me and said, "You . . . don't . . . quit! Nobody in this family quits!"

I'll be forever grateful to my grandmother. She hammered a steel rod of character into my spine that day—and that steel rod has been embedded in my flesh and my bones ever since.

"Character" Versus "Reputation"

I have always looked up to John Wooden as a role model and a hero. Coach Wooden, the "Wizard of Westwood," led the UCLA Bruins basketball team to a never equaled ten NCAA national championships. Without question, Coach Wooden is the greatest college basketball coach in history, which is why I have written a book about his life, *How to Be Like Coach Wooden: Life Lessons from Basketball's Greatest Leader.* Shortly before that book was released, I asked Coach Wooden to reflect on the issue of character—what it is, where it comes from, and how we can maintain it.

"I first became aware of the importance of character," Coach told me, "in my grade school days. From the time I was very

young, my father would say, 'Be more concerned with your character than with your reputation. Your character is what you really are. Your reputation is merely how you are perceived by others.' When I graduated from grade school, my father gave me a piece of paper on which he had written, 'Son, always try to live up to this.' Today, I call his advice 'The Seven-Point Creed.'"

As he said this, Coach Wooden gave me a copy of The Seven-Point Creed. Here's what I read:

- Be true to yourself.
- Make each day your masterpiece.
- Help others.
- Drink deeply from good books, especially the Bible.
- Make friendship a fine art.
- Build a shelter against a rainy day.
- Pray for guidance and give thanks for your blessings every day.

For years, Coach Wooden carried that piece of paper in his wallet. Eventually, the paper wore thin and the words began to fade. So, while it was still legible, he made a copy for himself, plus additional copies to hand out to others. Coach told me his life goal was to live up to that creed.

When I asked Coach Wooden the secret to winning in sports or in life, he told me, "In a word, *character*. Ability can get you to the top, but it takes character to keep you there." And it is Coach Wooden's character that is remembered by everyone who knows him. As NBC sportscaster Bob Costas once observed, "John Wooden is a man of integrity and has always remained true to what he believes."

I asked Coach how he instilled character qualities in the young people he taught and coached. "I required my players and students to treat everybody with respect," he said, "whether it be the custodian or the president of the university. I told them I expected them to always be considerate of others, and I never permitted the

use of profanity." Once, while coaching the Bruins, John Wooden decided not to recruit one of the nation's hottest high school players because he heard the boy speak disrespectfully to his mother. Coach knew that a player who would show open disrespect to his mom would be a bad character risk on the court and in the classroom, and his bad attitude might well infect the whole team.

Sportscaster and Basketball Hall of Famer Bill Walton played for Coach Wooden from 1970 to 1974, during the pinnacle of the Wooden era when UCLA won an NCAA record eighty-eight straight games. Walton credits the team's unparalleled success to Coach Wooden's focus on character. As Walton explains in a tribute to Coach on his Web site, "[Coach Wooden] never talks about winning and losing but rather about the effort to win. He rarely talks about basketball but generally about life. He never talks about strategy, statistics or plays but rather about people and character. And he never tires of telling us that once you become a good person, then you have a chance of becoming a good basketball player or whatever else you may want to do."

Coach Wooden's influence on others has spread far beyond the world of athletic competition. Dr. John Pagel is an oncology specialist and researcher at the Fred Hutchinson Cancer Research Center and Seattle Cancer Care Alliance in Seattle. He specializes in leukemia, lymphoma, and bone marrow transplants. Dr. Pagel told me, "As a kid I grew up watching UCLA basketball, and I once had the privilege of meeting Coach John Wooden. When I met him, he talked about success and how to achieve it, using his famous Pyramid of Success to make the point. I was so impressed with what he had to say I placed a framed Pyramid of Success poster on my wall. I still have it on my bedroom wall today. I have now used the John Wooden Pyramid as a teaching tool for my sons and for the lads in the many youth organizations I am involved in."

Coach Wooden was a teacher and role model of character because his father taught him by word and example, "Your reputa-

tion is merely how you are perceived by others, but your character is who you really are." A politician may have a great reputation for character—until he is caught taking a bribe. An author may have a great reputation for character—until she is exposed as a plagiarist. A pastor may have a great reputation for character— until he is caught in a tryst with the church secretary.

Your reputation is your outer image. Your character is your inner reality. It's possible to live for years behind a façade, with no one suspecting who you really are. You can pretend to have integrity while living a lie—for a while. You might even fool your family and friends.

But the façade eventually crumbles. The dissonance between the *real* you and the *pretend* you will become visible sooner or later. And when your failed character is exposed in the form of ethical corruption, dishonesty, sexual immorality, substance abuse, or moral cowardice, it will cost you. It may cost you your career, your marriage, your family, or even your freedom. It will certainly rob you of your reputation and self-respect.

Don't let that happen to you. Be a person of character. Teach, exemplify, and live out authentic character every day of your life.

Something No One Can Take Away

Brian Roquemore is president and CEO of America's All Stars, Inc., an Orlando-based organization devoted to developing strong character in students from kindergarten through twelfth grade. The organization works with schools and community organizations to promote responsible behavior, academic success, a positive work ethic, and patriotism.

"When I was growing up," Brian told me, "my father had an auto parts store. One of his main employees was a counterman named Arch, who took calls and parts orders from car dealers, gas stations, and independent garages. Arch wrote up the orders, took the items off the shelf, then handed them to me—the delivery driver. I would drive that truck as fast as I could, trying to impress

our customers with our great rush service (and I enjoyed any excuse to drive fast).

"Arch taught me a lot about character—not by what he said but by the way he lived. In the auto parts business, if you send the wrong part, you soon hear about it, usually with a lot of four-letter words. Mistakes were usually the fault of a mechanic who ordered the wrong part—yet Arch graciously took the blame as if it were his fault. He loved his job and was never late to work. He was cheerful and positive, and he never had a negative word to say about anyone. Arch knew everyone in town and everyone knew him.

"A committed Christian, Arch loved America almost as much as he loved his Lord. During World War II, he volunteered for military service. On Valentine's Day 1943, while fighting in North Africa under General George Patton, he was captured by the Germans under the command of General Rommel, the Desert Fox. When the POW camp was liberated by the Russians some two years and three months later, Arch weighed ninety-eight pounds. He returned to the States and received medical care which restored him to his former good health.

"Maybe that was the key to his cheerful and positive outlook on life: Arch had already lived on the brink of starvation and death in a Nazi POW camp. After the war, he was so happy to be alive he didn't let anything or anyone rob him of his joy. Ever since his release, Arch has had an 'attitude of gratitude' for his life and an appreciation for all of humankind."

The boy who used to make auto parts deliveries now heads up an organization devoted to developing character. If you ask Brian Roquemore why he is committed to encouraging young people to live lives of responsible character, he'll tell you: "Watching Arch live his life, seeing his cheerful disposition even when people swore at him or blamed him for their own mistakes—that was a powerful lesson in what's truly important in life. Most of the things we get upset about in life are really not worth the expenditure of

emotion. All that really matters is knowing God, being grateful for each new day, and living out a life of character."

Kevin Mawae is one of the best offensive linemen in pro football today. Playing center for the Tennessee Titans (and previously for the Seahawks and Jets), Kevin has played in six consecutive Pro Bowls and has an impressive "iron man" streak to his credit—177 consecutive games. "Most of what I know about character," Kevin told me, "I learned while growing up in a military family. My dad exemplified character. He demonstrated pride in his job, his uniform, and his family. Later in life, those early lessons in character were reinforced by my faith and spiritual growth through my study of the Bible—God's ultimate guide to good character."

To some people, the center is just the guy who snaps the ball to the quarterback. But the center is actually a leader. He calls out the blocking assignments to the other offensive linemen; he's also responsible for blocking the nose tackles and blitzing defenders. It's a position that requires size, quickness, and toughness—and character qualities, such as courage, determination, and perseverance in the face of adversity. Kevin Mawae has seen plenty of adversity, both on and off the field.

"In May 1996, my brother Scott called me and told me that our older brother, John, had been killed in a car accident. I was in my third year in the NFL at that point, and I wasn't a Christian at the time. John and I were best friends and he was the best man at my wedding. We were close and his death hit me hard. John was baptized shortly before he died, and his death made me think seriously about God. I started reading the Bible, beginning with the Gospel of Matthew.

"Over time, as I searched for answers, I came to faith in Jesus Christ. As my faith has grown, I've seen how important it is to be a person of character. We all have strong areas in our lives, and some weaker ones. My brother's death showed me that life is short, nothing is promised to us, and we need to make every day count for God. That means we have to make the most of our

character strengths, and ask God's help in overcoming the weaknesses in our character. In the end, my character is my legacy. It's what I did with my life, how I dealt with people, and the mark I left behind."

From the Meadowlands, where the Jets play their home games, the New York skyline can be seen in the distance over the stadium walls. On September 11, 2001, two skyscrapers were ripped from that skyline, leaving a smoking hole in the lower end of Manhattan. For days afterward, rescuers dug through the rubble of the towers, hoping to find survivors. Kevin Mawae, then a spokesman for the NFL Players Association, declared that he and his teammates would rather forfeit the upcoming home game against the Raiders than play while the smoke of the city still drifted over their stadium. In response, the NFL suspended play for a week.

Because of his reputation for wisdom and character, players often come to Kevin for advice about football—and about life. "My parents molded my character," he told me. "They modeled what character is all about. They taught me about hard work, keeping your word, and treating others right. They taught me that character means doing the right thing, even if it's the hard thing to do. This world can take everything else away from you, but it can't take away your character."

I interviewed Buck O'Neil, another great athlete from a bygone era, a few months before his death in October 2006. Born in 1911, Buck was the great-grandson of an African-born slave. He became an outstanding first baseman in the Negro American League, playing most of his career with the Kansas City Monarchs. Our phone interview was just a few weeks before he played in the last professional baseball game of his career—at age ninety-four! He told me, "Your character is the one thing that you keep with you all your life, and no one can take it away."

Buck O'Neil was raised under segregation in Florida. At the age of twelve, he worked in the fields, picking celery. It was

back-breaking, sweaty work, and Buck decided there had to be a better way to make a living. After seeing his first game of semi-pro baseball in West Palm Beach, Buck knew he wanted to be a ballplayer.

Though racial segregation kept him from attending high school and playing in the major leagues, Buck never gave in to bitterness. "My generation did the groundwork for the guys who play the game today," he told me. "I don't want anyone feeling sorry for me. Every generation has its part to play. We all have our duty."

That's a word Buck uses a lot when he looks back over his childhood: *duty*. "My parents and my grandmother made sure I knew my duties at school and at home," he told me. "I had an honest day's work to get done in the school room—then I had to come home and work. When I was eight or nine years old, my job was to bring in the water and fill up the tubs so we could do the wash. That was my duty. I loved to play ball, but I also had my jobs to do, and I felt bad if I failed to hold up my responsibilities in the family. Sometimes, I'd come in after dark and my mother would say, 'You've got to quit the game earlier so you can get the water in here before dark.' I had a duty to perform."

That sense of duty and hard work served Buck O'Neil well as a ballplayer. During two decades in the Negro leagues, Buck compiled a .288 career batting average (during four seasons, he batted over .300, posting a career-best .358 in 1947). After playing in the Negro leagues from the mid-1930s to 1955 (a career interrupted by World War II), Buck became a coach and scout in Major League Baseball.

In 2006, Buck O'Neil was nominated for admission to the Baseball Hall of Fame, though he failed to receive the 75 percent of votes needed for induction. After receiving the bad news, Buck went before a crowd of disappointed fans, saying, "God's been good to me. They didn't think Buck was good enough to be in the Hall of Fame. That's the way they thought about it and that's the way it is, so we're going to live with that. Now, if I'm a Hall of

Famer for you, that's all right with me. Just keep loving old Buck. Don't weep for Buck. No, man, be happy, be thankful."

A few days later, at age ninety-four, Buck O'Neil became the oldest player in professional baseball. On Tuesday, July 18, 2006, he stepped up to the plate in the Northern League All-Star Game—his first professional at-bat since 1955. Though he was walked twice, he looked fit and muscular in his red and white Monarchs jersey.

Buck told me, "In the Negro Leagues you had to hang in there. There were so many good ballplayers who wanted to take your job away." It took courage to play baseball during times of bigotry and segregation. "Courage is part of living," Buck told me. "There's always going to be obstacles and troubles out there. You've got to have the courage to stay in there."

Faith in God was always an important part of Buck O'Neil's life. "As a kid I'd go to church three times a day on Sundays," he told me. "I was in church all my life. My faith in God is what got me through."

His first role models were his father, his mother, his grandmother, and a grammar school teacher. "When we lived in Sarasota," he said, "I met Mrs. Emma Booker who ran the Booker Grammar School. She preached character to all her students. So I've had outstanding people in my life who taught me right from wrong. Segregation was wrong and it was hard, but my parents and my teachers taught me something important: people might segregate you, but they can't segregate your character. If you have good character, you have something no one can take from you."

Buck O'Neil was concerned about today's kids. "So many children today only have one parent," he told me. "They don't have what I had. Kids today need all the help they can get from good people. Everyone older than me taught me something. They wanted me to be the best I could be. That's what I want for the kids who are growing up today."

Year after year, whenever Buck attended Kansas City Royals games at Kauffman Stadium, he occupied his own seat—section 101, row C, seat 1, directly behind home plate. After his death, the Royals announced the "Buck O'Neil Legacy Seat Program" to honor him. The public is invited to nominate "heroes of character"—people from any walk of life who have demonstrated outstanding character. Every year, the Royals will choose eighty-one heroes, one for each home game on the schedule, to be honored by a place in the Buck O'Neil Legacy Seat. I know Buck would be pleased.

People Who Stand Firm

In February 2006, my son Bobby and I flew to Houston for the NBA All-Star Weekend. On Thursday the sixteenth, the day before the festivities, Bobby and I went for a jog. Returning to our hotel, we noticed a flurry of activity in front of an office building a block away—reporters, TV cameras, and boom mikes.

We jogged to the corner and saw a man and woman emerge from the jostling mass of reporters and walk to the corner across from us. When the light changed, the couple started across the street—and I recognized the man. "Bobby," I said, "that's Ken Lay!" It was indeed the former CEO of Enron, who was two weeks into a federal trial for securities fraud and related charges. He was walking straight toward us.

I thought, *What do you say to a guy who's facing up to twenty-five years in prison?* I knew Ken Lay once lived in Winter Park, Florida, where I now live—though he moved to Texas long before I came to Florida. And I knew he talked openly about having trusted Jesus Christ as his Lord and Savior. I wondered how this preacher's son, who claimed to live his life on Christian principles, could have ended up embroiled in the biggest corporate scandal in American history.

As Ken Lay and his wife stepped up on the curb beside us, I put out my hand and said, "Mr. Lay, I'm Pat Williams with the

Orlando Magic. I understand you used to live in Winter Park, where I now live."

He took my hand, smiled warmly, and introduced his wife, Linda. We chatted for a few moments about Central Florida before I said, "Ken, I want you to know we're praying for you."

"I appreciate that," he said.

"And I'm standing with him all the way," Linda added.

We said good-bye, and Ken and Linda Lay continued toward the parking garage.

"Dad," Bobby said, "he's really a nice guy."

Yes, he certainly seemed to be. And I couldn't help wondering what went wrong. Did Ken Lay succumb to pressure from stockholders? Was he duped? Did he yield to materialism and the arrogance of power? After all, he was a friend to presidents and one of the highest-paid CEOs in the world. In the fall of 2001, he reaped millions more by selling Enron stock while urging his employees to buy more of the very stock he was unloading. Enron's collapse cost thousands of employees their jobs and life savings. It wiped out a billion dollars in pension funds and at least twenty-five billion dollars in investor holdings. Clearly, someone made some very bad decisions at Enron.

I did pray for Ken Lay throughout the weeks of his trial. I was even pulling for him, hoping he would produce some piece of evidence out of his hat to prove himself innocent. But on May 25 of that year, Ken Lay was convicted of defrauding employees and investors. Sentencing was scheduled for October 23. After being convicted, he said, "We believe God is in fact in control and indeed He does work all things for good for those who love the Lord."

On July 5, while he and his family were vacationing in Old Snowmass, Colorado, Ken Lay suffered a massive heart attack and died.

Who was Ken Lay? He was the son of a Baptist minister and a devoutly Christian mother. He made a profession of faith and was baptized at age twelve. His parents took him to church

every Sunday, and he was active in Sunday school and the church youth group.

To this day, I don't know what to make of Ken Lay—and I'm not going to pass judgment on him. A federal jury had the job of passing judgment on Ken Lay, and after looking at the evidence, they voted unanimously to convict. After the verdicts were announced, one of the jurors said of Ken Lay (and co-defendant Jeffrey Skilling), "I wanted very badly to believe what they were saying, but there were places in the testimony where I felt their character was questionable."

Sometimes people excuse themselves for a moral failure by saying, "It was out of character for me to do that! I was under pressure! The temptation was just too great!" But whatever we do, we do "in character." If I steal, lie, or cheat, I can't say, "That was out of character," because *I did it.* That means *something in my character* allowed me to do it.

We can't excuse ourselves on the basis that we were under pressure or the temptation was too great, because those are the times when character counts the most. You don't need strong character when everything is easy. Good character is the strength to make good decisions even in the crucible of pressure and temptation. A person of good character is honest even when the truth will cost him everything. A person of good character keeps going even when he's ready to collapse. A person of good character is courageous even when defeat seems inevitable.

As the Old Testament tells us, "When the storm has swept by, the wicked are gone, but the righteous stand firm forever" (Prov. 10:25). We live in a world of stormy adversity. Authentic character enables us to stand firm amid the storms of opposition, pressure, and temptation.

Where will the people of character come from? Who's training and equipping them? Who's motivating and inspiring them? Who's setting an example of character for young people to follow? There's no question about it: character doesn't just happen. Char-

acter must be taught, modeled, and constructed anew in every generation. Where are the people of character? It's our responsibility to *be* the people of character, and to *raise up* people of character for generations to come.

I have conducted literally hundreds of interviews with people across the country who are engaged in character-building in one form or another. I have gathered their insights and stories—stories of how the steel rod of character came to be embedded in their flesh. The wisdom they have generously shared with me has changed my life and my outlook as a father, grandfather, leader, teacher, coach, and mentor—and I believe this book will have a profound impact on your life as well.

That's the mission of this book: together, you and I are going to learn how to build the steel rod of character into ourselves, our kids, and the young people we teach, coach, and mentor.

Together, we are going to discover how to forge souls of steel.

2

Parents on the Front Lines

"While we try to teach our children all about life, our children
teach us what life is all about."

ANGELA SCHWINDT
AMERICAN EDUCATOR

Y. A. Tittle, the great NFL quarterback of the 1960s, once called
my friend Bill Glass "the meanest preacher I ever met." Bill Glass
played eleven seasons in the NFL with the Detroit Lions and
Cleveland Browns. In 1964 (in those prehistoric days before the
first Super Bowl), Bill Glass and the Browns beat the Baltimore
Colts in the NFL Championship game, 27–0.

Bill attended divinity school while playing in the NFL, and he
planned to become an evangelist. On one occasion, he visited a
prison to preach to the inmates—and his experience there altered
the course of his life. From that day forward, he had an intense
burden for men and women behind bars.

He retired in 1969 after a long career in which he never
missed a single game, practice, or workout. At the urging of
evangelist Billy Graham, he formed Bill Glass Ministries (now
called Champions for Life). Three years later, he started a prison
ministry. He has spoken in more than a thousand prisons, and
is reputed to have preached to more prisoners than anyone else
in history.

When Bill was in the NFL, he was my hero. Today he's my
friend, and I serve on his board. I once asked him, "Is there a com-

mon denominator among all the prisoners you've met—something they all have in common?"

"Absolutely," he said. "They all have a father problem. Some were abused, others were abandoned, but bottom line, they all hate their fathers. The greeting card companies donate cards to the prisons for Mother's Day and Father's Day. The Mother's Day cards are all snatched up; the Father's Day cards go untouched. What does that say about the way men in prison feel about their dads?"

In July 2006, Chaplain Bernard Fleeks invited me to speak to about sixty young men under the age of eighteen who were incarcerated at the Thirty-third Street Jail in Orlando. After I delivered my message, Chaplain Fleeks did a Q&A session with the youthful offenders. He asked, "How many of you grew up without your dad in the house?"

Fifty-seven of sixty hands went up.

"Okay," he said. "Tough break—but you can't go back and change that. The question is: what are you going to do with the rest of your life? You can sit and mope about how unfair life is—or you can start making better choices. Now, let me ask you: How many of you are in here because a so-called friend got you in trouble and you wouldn't rat him out?"

Again, almost every hand went up.

"Now, how smart was that?" he said. "Your 'friend' is out there living the good life while you're sitting in here, taking his punishment."

Clearly, two common threads ran through the lives of almost every one of these young offenders: First, they grew up without fathers. Second, they succumbed to peer pressure. I left the prison feeling heartbroken for all of those young souls robbed of a father's love, a father's guidance. Young people need fathers to bless them, teach them, and exemplify manly character.

But young people also need mothers to guide them, nurture them, and exemplify the character of godly womanhood. Dr.

Jack Hayford is the founding pastor of the ten-thousand-member Church on the Way in Van Nuys, California, and the author of more than three dozen books and six hundred hymns and choruses. Pastor Jack shared with me a memory of how his mother shaped his early character.

One afternoon, when he was eleven years old, young Jack Hayford was visiting at the home of his friend Chuck. While the boys were looking for things to do, Chuck pulled out a tiny telescope-like object and said, "Look at this. My brother gave it to me." He handed it over and Jack raised it and peered inside. The image he saw was pornographic. The boy didn't want to appear "uncool" in front of his friend, so he laughed—yet, at the same time, he experienced a sense of guilt so strong that it hurt his chest.

The next morning, as Jack was about to leave for school, his mother called him into the kitchen and said, "Jack, I want to ask you a question. Listen carefully, son, because I'm asking you in front of Jesus."

Jack knew that whenever his mother said those words, he was in for a serious discussion. He also knew that whatever she asked him "in front of Jesus," he didn't dare answer with anything but the absolute truth. His parents taught him from an early age "you can never fake it with God." They taught him God loves us more than we know—but His love demands our honesty.

"Jack," his mother continued, "tell me in front of Jesus: what happened at Chuck's yesterday?"

How did she know? Jack wondered.

Then his mother explained that she'd had a feeling, an unexplainable heaviness of heart, when her son came home from Chuck's the previous day. So she prayed for Jack and asked God to show her why she felt that way—and God impressed it on her heart to confront her son and ask for an answer "in front of Jesus."

The boy broke down in tears and told his mother what happened, and he asked her to pray with him. Mother and son prayed

together, and Jack instantly felt his guilt replaced by joy, peace, and cleansing forgiveness.

Jack's mother used those four powerful words, "in front of Jesus," to remind her son that he needed to be a young man of Christian character and integrity. Our kids need both moms and dads of character to teach them what a life of character is all about.

Proud to Be His Son

My friend Richard Lapchick is director of the National Consortium for Academics and Sports at the University of Central Florida. In addition to being a recognized expert on sports issues, Richard is a human rights activist and was named by *The Sporting News* as "One of the 100 Most Powerful People in Sports." Richard gives credit to his dad, Joe Lapchick, for building positive character traits into his life.

Joe Lapchick was a pro basketball player who played with the original Boston Celtics in the 1920s and '30s. After his playing career, Joe coached basketball at St. John's University before becoming head coach of the New York Knicks from 1947 to 1956. During that time, Joe Lapchick made one of his most historic and controversial decisions as a coach: He signed Nat "Sweetwater" Clifton to play for the Knicks, and Clifton became the first African American to play in the NBA.

"I saw my father persevere through a fire storm," Richard Lapchick told me. "After he signed Clifton, things got ugly. They hung my father in effigy from a tree across the street from our house in Yonkers. I heard my dad called horrible names. I knew my dad was right, and I saw him standing tall while people attacked him for doing the right thing. My father taught me that if you don't stand up for justice, you're just getting in the way."

For as long as I have known Richard Lapchick, the great theme of his life has been racial justice. When you hear him tell the story

of his father's courageous decision to tear down the color barrier in the NBA, it's easy to see how the character of the father shaped the character of the son. Richard told me about other ways his father modeled character.

"Again and again," Richard said, "I saw my father doing the right thing, even if he had to pay a price to maintain his integrity. When my dad coached at St. John's, a young Bob Cousy came to him, wanting to transfer to St. John's after his freshman year at Holy Cross. Cousy was a freshman and widely regarded as the finest college player in the nation.

"My father had a chance to coach Bob Cousy at St. John's, yet he advised him to stay at Holy Cross, where he would be coached by Alvin F. 'Doggie' Julian, one of the legendary coaches of the game. Cousy stayed at Holy Cross and the rest is history.

"Four years later, my father was coaching the Knicks and competing against Bob Cousy and the Celtics in Boston Garden. At one point, Cousy scored a layup and the referees didn't see the ball go in because one of my dad's players, Carl Braun, knocked it out from under the rim. The officials were going to let the Knicks bring the ball up the court, and the Boston fans were having a fit because they saw the ball go in. My dad called a time-out and told the referees the Celtics' basket was good.

"Did my dad's honesty pay off? It depends on how you look at it. The Knicks lost a very close game that day. But I think my dad's honesty won a much bigger victory. At his funeral in 1970, several of my dad's players told me about that game and how it was one of the most important lessons they ever learned in life. They knew my father loved to win, but they saw that it was more important for him to do the right thing. For Joseph Lapchick, character trumped everything.

"In 1956, after ten years with the Knicks, Dad returned to St. John's as head coach. I'll always remember one October afternoon when he came home from practice. His normal pattern was that he'd go upstairs to his room, change, and come down to read the

Herald Statesman while having a cup of coffee. That day, when he didn't come down, I went up to see if he was okay.

"I found Dad in his room, crying. I was stunned. It was the first time I had ever seen any man cry. When he composed himself, he shared with me that he found out that his players were not going to class and were getting passed through the educational system. He was horrified on two levels. First, as a devout Catholic, he was saddened that something so unethical could be happening in a Catholic school. Second, on a personal level, he realized that he had spoken to his players about their girl-friends, their summer jobs, and what they were going to do when they were finished with basketball—but he had never asked them about their classroom work. He had simply assumed that they were meeting their academic obligations, and he felt he had personally let them down.

"The next day, Dad went back to the school with his assistant at the time, Lou Carnesecca, and they set up the first mandatory study hall in the history of college sports. They went from a zero percent graduation rate to one of the highest in the country. That's the example of character I carry with me to this day. I'm proud to be the son of Joseph Lapchick. He was a man of character."

A Mother Who Lights a Lantern

David Shedlarz is vice chairman of Pfizer, Inc., the world's largest pharmaceutical company. He told me about the lessons in character he learned from his mother. "To me," he said, "the way people deal with life's unfairness is the ultimate test of their character. My mother's character was tested when, at age twenty-six, she was diagnosed with multiple sclerosis [MS]. She turned that bad news into a growth experience for my two brothers and me.

"My mother's name was Rosalyn. Prior to the diagnosis, she was a woman of nearly boundless energy and drive. By her mid-twenties, she earned a doctorate in biology—and at a time when

few women attained advanced degrees. But then came the diagnosis, and her life was profoundly changed.

"MS is as mysterious as it is devastating. It shears off the outer coating of nerves, short-circuiting the body's nervous system. Today, there are some good treatments, but still no known cure. In my mother's time, there weren't even any treatments. A diagnosis of MS usually meant years of progressive disability and physical decline. She endured this disease from age twenty-five until her passing at age sixty-five.

"The toughest part for Mom was the recognition that she couldn't do what other mothers did. The routines kids take for granted—the home-cooked meals or cheering kids on at sports events—these were soon out of her reach. That really hurt her.

"Mom tried to let us learn our life's lessons on our own. But when she did offer advice, it was worth taking. When I left graduate school and began interviewing for jobs, Mom called to suggest I look at a company called Pfizer. Like most young people, I assumed that if my parents recommended something, I wouldn't like it. But I interviewed and got a job with Pfizer. I told her I would work there for a few years until my 'big opportunity' with another company came. I couldn't bring myself to admit to Mom that I really *liked* working for Pfizer!

"Today, I've been with Pfizer for more than thirty years. Until her passing a few years ago, Mom would call me on my service anniversary date, gently reminding me how wise I was to take her counsel. But her impact on my life goes far beyond my career choice. She left an indelible mark on my character by showing me how to live with resilience and determination when life deals you a bad hand.

"Some people say, 'It's better to light one candle than to curse the darkness.' Mom recognized that when life hurts you, it's normal to cry out in pain. So Mom put it best (as mothers usually do) when she said, 'It's okay to curse the darkness, as long as your next move is lighting a lantern.' "

Today, David Shedlarz "lights a lantern" not only through his work at Pfizer but as a board member of the New York chapter of the National Multiple Sclerosis Society. His mother's example of character is her legacy to David, a legacy he continues.

An Example of Courage and Character

Steve Reed is a pastor and the author of *The Suffering Clause: A Leader's Surprising Secret for Outlasting Tough Times.* "My earliest memories," Steve told me, "are of my parents teaching about character through their words and example. Dad was a pastor and missionary when I was growing up. Our lives revolved around the church.

"We lived in Lima, Peru, during the early 1970s. There was a lot of political turmoil there in those days. At one point, there was a major conflict with a great deal of fighting that involved the police and the military. The whole nation was in a state of fear. The military dictator placed the nation under a curfew and announced that any gathering of more than five people would be considered an unlawful assembly. We had five in our family, so if we got together with anyone else, we'd be violating the law."

The first Sunday after martial law was declared, Steve's family was getting ready for church, just as they had always done—but young Steve was worried about what the government might do. So he went to his father and asked if the government would consider going to church an illegal act.

"Yes," his father said. "We'll be seen as violating the law."

"Do you think anyone else will come to church today?"

"Son," Steve's father said, "I don't know."

So the family drove to church—and all the streets were strangely empty. "When we arrived and entered the church building," Steve told me, "we noticed that our family and a handful of other people were the only ones there. We started the service with singing, and a few more families trickled in. They came by twos and threes. As the crowd grew, the singing became louder and more joyful. After

about an hour, the church was packed like I'd never seen it before. People sang with tears in their eyes.

"After the hymns, the congregation sang the Peruvian national anthem: '*Somos libres seamos! Lo siempre seamos lo siempre!* We're free, yes we're free! Always and forever!' That day, the believers were tested in their courage and their love of God, love of country, and love of one another. They passed the test—and the government left the congregation alone."

Steve looks back on that experience as a great lesson in character and faith. "That experience marked my entire life. It gave me a lifelong desire to live for Christ and to demonstrate the same kind of character and courage my parents showed. Affliction and persecution have a way of bringing out the best in Jesus' followers."

As a pastor and father, Steve Reed makes character development one of his top priorities. "When my middle son, Zach, was about ten or eleven," Steve said, "he was getting into trouble from time to time with a couple of his buddies in school. One day, Zach let his friends talk him into breaking the rules at school, and Zach's teacher called us.

"We confronted Zach and he said that his buddies were the ones at fault. 'They talked me into it,' he said.

" 'Zach,' I said, 'from this point on, you are not a follower. You are a leader. They are not in charge in your behavior. You are. You are to be an influence of your buddies, not the other way around. So if you try to blame anyone else, I won't buy it. You're a leader, so act like one.'

" 'But Dad,' he said, 'I don't want to be a leader!'

" 'Zach,' I said, 'you have no choice. When you're with your friends, you have to lead by example.'

"Well, that was hard for Zach, but he started making strides. Eventually, he invited the boys to attend our youth group at church. They started coming, and within a few months, both of Zach's friends committed their lives to Jesus Christ. I couldn't have been more proud!"

How to Shape Your Child's Character

Paul Weyrich is a political commentator and a cofounder of the Heritage Foundation. In the late 1990s, Mr. Weyrich was diagnosed with a spinal injury that has confined him to a wheelchair. Despite his pain, he continues to work hard for the causes he believes in. He told me, "My father was the best role model I ever could have had. He worked hard, tending a boiler room in the days of coal, then he'd take two buses to get to a foundry where he worked his second job.

"My father never complained about having to work hard. He attended church regularly, even after working all night. He often talked about character and the consequences that befall people of weak character. But most of the time, he taught by example rather than words. He was a man of few words, but when he spoke, I listened.

"I first became aware of the importance of character and integrity when I was about five years old. I had spent a year in a sickbed due to pneumatic fever. When I got well and was learning to walk again, a neighbor kid named Jimmy decided to take advantage of me by trying to entice me into situations that would get me into trouble.

"Two neighbor kids saw what Jimmy was doing and they rescued me from the situation. I was only five at the time, but I remember Henry saying to me, 'Stay away from Jimmy. He has no character.' That made a deep impression on me. I was too young to fully understand what this thing called 'character' was, but I connected doing wrong with a lack of character.

"As a father myself, I have always wanted to be the kind of example my father was. With my five children, I have often discussed the meaning of good character as well as various examples of bad character. Most of the time, I'm sure, they didn't really understand what I was getting at. Then, as they experienced various situations in life, they would come back to me and tell me that the things I tried to teach them then, now made sense.

"My son Steve attended Indiana State University. He lived off-campus and organized a group of guys to help with the rent. When one of them skipped out without paying, Steve came to me and said, 'Dad, I sure know now what you meant by having bad character.'"

Kirk Weaver is the founder and executive director of Family Time Training, an organization that trains parents to teach and model Christian character traits in the home. Kirk and his wife, Kelly, have a daughter, Madison, and a son, McKinley.

"Not long ago," Kirk told me, "Kelly and I were talking with Madison on her bed. She was upset with the kids at school. Some of the other kids were picking on an unpopular student, playing a cruel game that Madison chose not to play. Because Madi wouldn't go along with the other kids' cruelty, she found herself being rejected by her girlfriends. Madi tearfully said, 'I'm trying to be like the coffee beans in Dad's story.'

"Madi was referring to an activity we encourage parents to do with their kids. It's built around three pots of boiling water, with the water representing adversity. We drop a carrot into the first pot, an egg into the second, and coffee beans into the third. What choices will we make in response to the adversity we face in our lives?

"Do we get soft like the carrot when adversity comes? That's the way Peter responded when his friend Jesus was arrested. Peter promised to stand firm with Jesus, but instead he went soft and denied his Lord.

"Does the adversity make us hard like a hard-boiled egg? That's the way Pharaoh responded when God, through Moses, brought down plagues of adversity on the land of Egypt. Pharaoh could have responded by yielding to God's will and letting the Hebrews leave in peace. Instead, Pharaoh hardened his heart and kept the Hebrews in slavery.

"There is a third and godly response to adversity—the response of the coffee beans. The coffee beans represent the example of

Paul. When adversity came his way, Paul didn't go soft, nor did he harden his heart. Instead, he chose to have an influence on his environment. He chose to change the world around him.

"Now here was Madison, facing a situation of adversity and applying a lesson we had taught her more than four months earlier. The lesson had stuck—and had become a major reinforcement for her character.

"Sometimes it seems like we try to teach our kids things and nothing sticks. But they are watching us and listening to us all the time. As parents, we have many opportunities to teach life lessons to our kids, and we need to take advantage of those opportunities God brings our way."

Todd Milano, president of Central Pennsylvania College in suburban Harrisburg, told me about some creative approaches to instilling character in his children. "At the dinner table each night," he said, "we take turns reading a page from the book *A Daily Dose of the American Dream: Stories of Success, Triumph, and Inspiration* by Alan C. Elliott. Each one-page story starts with an inspirational, motivational quote, then presents a real-life story with a character lesson we can learn. These stories are great teaching tools and conversation starters.

"I also believe in using today's technology to teach character. When my son turned fifteen, my wife and I gave him an iPod. He was surprised by the gift, because we allow very little television viewing and we limit video games in our home. We set a condition for his iPod: in addition to the approved music he was permitted to load on it, we also required that he load audio files of character-building, motivational, and inspirational talks, such as Brian Tracy's *The Psychology of Achievement*. An iPod could be a time-waster or a tool for increasing a young person's potential. As parents, we should look for ways to leverage a child's interests for the sake of character."

A Reflection of Character

Jim Ross is vice president for development of Crosswinds Youth Services, an organization that works to strengthen families and provide success opportunities for young people. He told me, "It's one thing to try to live out good Christian character to your kids. But what is truly satisfying is when your kids reflect Christlike character back to you.

"When I worked for Brevard Community College in Cocoa, Florida, I saw this kind of character in my son, who was fifteen at the time. The president of the college, Dr. Maxwell C. King, was a close friend of mine. The board went through a change and decided, in a 3–2 vote, to let Dr. King go. This placed those closest to Dr. King in a difficult situation. The employees at the college were expected to cut off contact with him—but I decided I would not turn my back on a friend."

Jim Ross knew his job was at stake, but he decided that, if asked by the board, he would honestly state that he continued to maintain his friendship with Dr. King. Meanwhile, Jim's son went to him and said, "Dad, I know you're in a tough spot. If people find out you're still in contact with Dr. King, you could lose your job and we'd have to move. Dad, I've made friends at school and I want to finish high school here. I don't want to have to start over at a new school."

"Son," Jim said, "I understand. I'll do my best to keep my job so we can stay here until you graduate."

"Thanks, Dad."

One day, the board called Jim in for a meeting. The board members asked if he continued to have contact with Dr. King.

Jim replied, "Yes, I have."

The board asked when Jim had last spoken with Dr. King.

Jim said, "This morning."

At this, the board members became angry and ordered Jim not to talk to Dr. King again. "That demand," Jim told me, "went against my conscience."

Jim Ross went home and called his son into the living room. After explaining the situation, Jim said, "I'm going to have to tell the board the truth, and it may cost me my job—and if it does, it may affect you. It may mean you'd have to leave your school. Will you think less of me as a father if I lose my job over this?"

His son looked at him seriously and said, "Dad, I'll respect you more if you lose your job by taking a stand than if you kept your job and went back on your values." Jim had never been more proud of his son.

He went back to the board, told them he refused to end his friendship with Dr. King—and he lost his job. "But it was worth everything," Jim Ross concluded, "to see my son put principle ahead of his own self-interest. It was worth everything to see real character reflected in my son's life."

Motivational speaker Denis Waitley writes: "Several decades ago, Madame Chiang Kai-shek who, along with her husband, led the Chinese people in their struggle against the invading Japanese army during World War II, put integrity in a golden nutshell when she said: 'In the end, we are all the sum total of our actions. Character can't be counterfeited, nor can it be put on and cast off as if it were a garment to meet the whim of the moment. Like the markings on wood which are ingrained in the very heart of the tree, character requires time and nurturing for growth and development; thus, day by day, we write our own destiny for, inexorably . . . we become what we do.'"

As moms and dads and grandparents, we are on the front lines in the battle for our children's souls. We light the lantern in the darkness. We show them how to take a bold, principled stand for integrity and fairness. We are on the front lines, in the very thick of the battle.

Fight hard for the souls of your kids.

PART II

Character Is Who We Are

3

Integrity: Every Room
Is Clean

"I hope I shall possess firmness and virtue enough to maintain what I consider the most enviable of all titles, the character of an honest man."

GEORGE WASHINGTON
FIRST AMERICAN PRESIDENT

During his twenty-one-year career as a naval officer, Randy "Duke" Cunningham was a Vietnam War flying ace, a Top Gun flight instructor, and a recipient of the Navy Cross, the Silver Star, and the Purple Heart. A certified American war hero, Duke Cunningham was elected to the U.S. House of Representatives in 1991.

Cunningham resigned in disgrace in late 2005 after pleading guilty to mail fraud, wire fraud, tax evasion, and accepting more than $2.4 million in bribes. He was sentenced to more than eight years in prison and ordered to pay $1.8 million in restitution. Announcing his resignation, a tearful Duke Cunningham stood before reporters and said:

"When I announced several months ago that I would not seek reelection, I publicly declared my innocence because I was not strong enough to face the truth. I misled my family, staff, friends, colleagues, the public—even myself. For all of this, I am deeply sorry. The truth is—I broke the law, concealed my conduct, and disgraced my high office. I know that I will forfeit my freedom,

my reputation, my worldly possessions, and most importantly, the trust of my friends and family. . . . In my life, I have known great joy and great sorrow. And now I know great shame."

It's shocking to see a decorated war hero caught up in scandal and corruption—and it's just as shocking to see scandal and corruption in the scientific community. Hwang Woo-suk was a world-renowned professor of biotechnology at Seoul National University in South Korea. He gained fame after reporting a series of breakthroughs in stem cell research. He published peer-reviewed articles on his research in the prestigious journal *Science* in 2004 and 2005—but in November 2005, *Science* retracted the articles after they were found to be based on falsified data.

But falsified science was only part of Hwang's deception. On May 12, 2006, he was indicted for embezzlement. Korean prosecutors charged that Hwang took $3 million in research funds for his personal use. As the *New York Times* observed in an editorial on the Hwang scandal ("The Collapsing Claims on Cloning," December 17, 2005), "The debacle is a reminder that science depends heavily on the honesty of its practitioners."

We are becoming a culture of cheaters. Writing in the *U.S. News & World Report*, Mortimer B. Zuckerman observes, "Some 2 million Americans are estimated to have illegal offshore bank accounts. The wealthier you are, the less the IRS goes after you because the wealthy can engage high-priced lawyers and accountants. Remember Leona Helmsley's famous comment, 'We don't pay taxes; only the little people pay taxes'? . . . Meanwhile, millions of Americans routinely engage in insurance fraud, cable-TV theft, and software piracy. What's so amazing is that many of these same people see themselves as decent, law-abiding citizens."[1]

Cheating is becoming accepted by the younger generation. In 2004, the Josephson Institute of Ethics found that 62 percent of the nearly twenty-five thousand high school students in its survey admitted they cheated on tests. A June 2005 report by Donald McCabe of The Center for Academic Integrity revealed that 70

percent of university students surveyed admitted to having cheated in their school work during the previous year. About 60 percent admitted to committing plagiarism in their writing assignments.

New technologies have made it easier than ever for students to cheat. They can obtain essays on any subject from the Internet. Students can load test answers onto iPods or other handheld media devices. Cell phones can be used to Google answers from the Internet or text-message answers during an exam. Many students still resort to the low-tech standbys, such as writing the answers on the palm of their hands.

In an article for *Reader's Digest*, writer Gay Jervey quotes a California high school student identified as "Daniel," who said, "If I want to get the better grade, I'm going to cheat to get it. No question. Anyway, in the real world you do whatever you have to do to get the better job. . . . I am competitive, so I'm always trying to find a better way of cheating." Jervey quotes David Callahan, author of *The Cheating Culture* and *The Moral Center*, who said, "We hear so often that we should talk to kids about sex, smoking, drunk driving, but do we ever hear about talking to kids about integrity?"[2]

An Undivided Soul

Integrity is a widely used word—and widely misunderstood. People understand that integrity involves being a "moral" person in some sense, but if you asked the average person for a definition of *integrity*, you'd probably hear a lot of hemming, hawing, and stammering. The origin of the word *integrity* makes the meaning very clear.

The word comes from the Latin adjective *integer*, which means "whole" or "complete." In mathematics, an integer is a positive or negative whole number or zero—a number without any fractional part. A person of integrity is honest and upright. His or her soul is not divided or compartmentalized.

One synonym for *integrity* is *sincerity*—the state of being truth-

ful, genuine, and free of deception or duplicity. The word *sincerity* comes from the Latin *sincerus*, meaning "clean and pure through and through." The Latin sincerus comes from two Latin root words, *sine* ("without") and *cera* ("wax"). Tradition tells us dishonest Roman sculptors would cover up nicks and flaws in their statues with a wax filler. The deception would last only until a hot summer sun melted the wax and exposed the flaw. A sculpture that was pure and flawless was said to be *sine cera*, without wax.

In the same way, a human life that is pure and whole is *sine cera*, without wax. The person who lacks integrity has hidden flaws in his character that will inevitably be exposed by the heat of trial and adversity. Only those who are honest and sincere in their character can stand the heat of a thorough examination of their lives. As the Old Testament tells us, "The man of integrity walks securely, but he who takes crooked paths will be found out" (Prov. 10:9).

People of integrity don't abandon their values and principles under pressure. They know that times of adversity and temptation are precisely when values and principles matter most. They keep promises. They fulfill obligations. They maintain their honor even when it is costly to do so.

Our integrity is the most profound expression of *who we are* as people of character. Integrity is the ultimate expression of our relationship with ourselves, of a vow we make to ourselves as to the kind of person we choose to be. If you compromise your integrity, you may get away with it for a while, but no one gets away with it forever. People who lack integrity are eventually exposed.

Optimize Magazine (*Information Week*'s monthly publication for corporate investment officers) published this succinct description of integrity in its May 2005 issue:

The Ten Universal Characteristics of Integrity
1. You know that little things count.
2. You find the white when others see gray.

3. You mess up, you fess up.
4. You create a culture of trust.
5. You keep your word.
6. You care about the greater good.
7. You're honest but modest.
8. You act like you're being watched.
9. You hire integrity.
10. You stay the course.

"Integrity is the word for our times," says Dr. James C. Dobson, founder of Focus on the Family. "It means keeping our promises, doing what we said we would do, choosing to be accountable, and taking as our motto *semper fidelis*, the promise to be always faithful."

Charles Colson, founder of Prison Fellowship Ministries, told me, "I've been speaking on ethics all over the country. I recently spoke to the officers and non-commissioned officers of the Second Marine Division in Camp LeJeune, North Carolina. After I spoke, I took questions from the floor. An African American sergeant major stood up and said, 'Mr. Colson, we're marines. We live by the creed *semper fidelis*, "always faithful." Which is more important, loyalty or integrity?'

"I thought, *Wow! That gets to the heart of it, doesn't it?* Most of us can think of times when our loyalty to someone may bring us into conflict with our integrity, our commitment to the truth. What then? So I said to the sergeant major, 'Loyalty is a virtue if you are loyal to that which is true. If you give your life and your loyalty to a lie, you'll be destroyed.' So integrity is the prime character quality that every individual needs above all. If we keep our integrity, then all the other character traits, including loyalty, will fall right into line."

When General Richard B. Myers was named chairman of the Joint Chiefs of Staff in 2001, he became the nation's highest-ranking officer and the top military advisor to the president, the secretary

of defense, and the National Security Council. Before his retirement in 2005, General Myers told me, "One of the many leadership lessons I learned early in my air force career was that you must have high credibility in your primary field of expertise first before anyone will want to follow you. Credibility comes from character—and especially from the character trait called integrity.

"I grew up in Kansas. My teachers and coaches were part of the 'greatest generation.' Many of them served in World War II and Korea. They were not boastful about their service; they were simply men and women of quiet integrity. By their actions and through their words, they taught us all that integrity means being true to one's values and standards. It means saying what we mean, and meaning what we say. It means holding fast to our honor, so that we are trustworthy and incorruptible.

"I remember working for my dad in his business for six months while I was waiting to go into the air force. I think those six months shaped me more than any other one experience in my life. My dad taught me how to deal with customers, superiors, and subordinates. He placed honesty and integrity at the foundation of his business practices. He asked me this simple question: 'Are you going to be honest, shade it a little, or be dishonest?' I will never forget that question."

Dictionary publisher Merriam-Webster, Inc., announced that, by far, the most looked-up word of 2005 at its Web site was *integrity*. Clearly, the meaning of this all-important character trait is something inquiring minds want to know!

When my son Michael was nineteen, I took him out to lunch. We had a wonderful, wide-ranging conversation. During our talk, I asked him, "Mike, how do you define *integrity*?"

I watched the wheels turn as he thought about it—then he looked me in the eye and said, "Integrity is honesty with a little oomph."

I laughed. In his own unique and offhand way, Mike stated a profound truth. "You nailed it, pal," I said.

Honesty with oomph—that's integrity.

Taking Off the Superhero Mask

For me, the quintessential model of integrity is Coach John Wooden. He was hired by the UCLA Bruins in 1948, when the school had no on-campus arena and the team had to play home games in a tiny, dilapidated practice facility. Coach recalls, "We were playing and practicing under worse conditions than I had in high school back in Indiana—it was that bad. Finally, the city told us we couldn't play any more games on-campus because of the fire codes."

After the city shut down the on-campus facility, the Bruins played their home games at assorted L.A.-area venues, including Venice High School, Long Beach City College, and Santa Monica City College. Despite having to coach under sub-par conditions, Wooden led his Bruins to a 22-7 record in his first season, and 24-7 in his second. At the end of Wooden's second season, the Bruins went to their first ever NCAA Tournament.

That year, Coach's integrity was put to the test when his alma mater, Purdue, offered him the head coaching position. "I've always believed that when you give your word, you honor it," Coach told me. "Some people today don't think twice about breaking a written contract, but I believe you not only honor your written contracts, but your verbal contracts as well. When I first came to UCLA, the school wanted to give me a two-year contract, but I talked them into a three-year deal. Then, after two years, I had a chance to make twice my UCLA salary, plus a number of extra perks and far better working conditions. Plus, I could get away from Los Angeles. After all, being from the farm, I found L.A. to be a frightening place!"

How could Coach turn down an offer to return home to Indiana, work in a first-class athletic program, while doubling his salary? "I was tempted," Coach recalls, "but in the end it came down to the fact that I had given my word to stay at UCLA for three years. The university gave me permission to break the contract, but in the end I had to keep my word. I turned down the other offer."

In his book *The Essential Wooden*, Coach writes, "You can be honest as the day is long and still be short on character. How? You can be honest and selfish, honest and undisciplined, honest and inconsistent, honest and disrespectful, honest and lazy. For a leader, honesty is a strong start, but you can't stop there. There's more to character than just being honest."[3] Author John Maxwell once said, "When your thoughts, words, and actions are all the same, you are a person of integrity." That's how Coach Wooden has lived his life.

Mark Richt, head football coach at the University of Georgia, told me how another legendary college coach, Bobby Bowden, exemplified integrity. "It was a life-changing experience," Mark said, "to serve as an assistant coach under a man of the caliber and character of Bobby Bowden. As the head coach at Florida State University since 1976, Bobby is not only the winningest coach in NCAA Division I-A football history, but also a role model of strong character and integrity.

"I was coming up the ranks as a college coach, and I had heard a lot of war stories about how coaches need to break the rules and cut corners in order to put together a winning team. I remember how, soon after I took the job at Florida State, Coach Bowden eased my ethical concerns. At one of my first coaches' meetings, he said, 'We will not do anything outside of the rules to recruit a player to our program. I will support everyone on this coaching staff in everything they do—except cheating to get recruits or doing anything else that we all know is wrong. This program is built on integrity.'

"When I heard that, I knew I was in the right place, working under the right head coach. Coach Bowden always demanded integrity of his coaching staff, and he instilled integrity in all of his players."

To be a person of integrity, you must stand for honesty at all times—even when under fire, in extreme temptation, in times of loneliness and solitude, in times of great need, suffering, and want.

If your "integrity" is something you can put on and take off like a suit of clothes, it's not integrity at all. It's just a disguise to hide the person you really are.

Don Davis is a linebacker for the New England Patriots. When I asked Don his views about character, he told me, "I always knew that character mattered. The problem was I didn't understand integrity. I didn't realize that character matters even when no one else is around. I always treated people well and played the part of a man of character in public—but privately I was a different person.

"I was raised in the church and was baptized at a young age. I learned how to talk the Christian language, but I didn't know how to walk the Christian walk. I read a lot of comic books when I was growing up, and all the superheroes wore masks: Batman and Robin, Aquaman, The Flash. The purpose of the mask was to hide their true identities. I had the same problem.

"I grew up wearing a mask on Sunday mornings, but all week long my true identity would show itself. I lived a double life throughout my adolescence, my college years, and my early NFL career. The Bible, in James 1:8, talks about the 'double-minded man' who is 'unstable in all he does.' That was me. I was double-minded and unstable in all my ways.

"In June 1999, the team chaplain asked me if I knew that I was going to heaven. I said yes. We took a look at Matthew 7:21, where Jesus says, 'Not everyone who says to me, "Lord, Lord," will enter the kingdom of heaven, but only he who does the will of my Father who is in heaven.' Then the chaplain asked me, 'Are you doing the will of God in every area of your life?' I had to admit that I wasn't. And that's when I understood that I needed total integrity and character in every area of my life.

"Once I realized that true manhood means accepting the fact that I can't run my own life, I began to allow Jesus to change my heart. It wasn't easy, because I'd been a hypocrite so long. But Jesus began to replace my false character with authentic integrity.

It's not that I've arrived or that I've achieved perfection, but now my goal is to be consistent in every part of my life. I can look at myself in the mirror and I no longer see a guy in a 'superhero mask.' I see the real Don Davis."

I asked Don if there was a key person in his life who exemplified to him what character is all about. "Oh, yes," he said. "For me, Aeneas Williams is that guy."

Aeneas Demetrius Williams is a legendary NFL defensive back (Arizona Cardinals 1991–2000, St. Louis Rams 2001–2004, retired 2005). Over his career, he accumulated a record of twelve defensive touchdowns, fifty-five interceptions, one Super Bowl appearance (the Rams' loss to the Patriots in Super Bowl XXXVI), and eight Pro Bowl appearances.

"He and I were teammates in St. Louis in 2001," Don said. "There are other guys who exemplified good character, but Aeneas, more than anyone else, lives out everything he believes. Whenever I had a problem, I could go to him and he would take me to God's Word for the answer.

"I had been through a divorce in 1998. I rededicated my life to Christ in 2000 and remarried that same year. When I got to St. Louis in August 2001, my ex-wife sent a letter to me at the training grounds. After I read it, I wanted to throw it in the trash. But something in me said that I should take it home and show my wife—it was important for me, as a matter of integrity, not to keep any secrets from her.

"But a battle raged in me over that. The old Don would have thrown the letter away and reasoned, 'It means nothing.' But the new Don, who wanted to live a life of absolute integrity, couldn't accept that. I talked it over with Aeneas and he agreed: no secrets, nothing hidden. So I took the letter home. That was a huge step for me.

"Today, God has given me a new role and a responsibility. Now I am a guy people look up to, just as I looked up to Aeneas when we were teammates. I'm quick to tell guys that God can change

their lives, just as He changed mine. God can replace hypocrisy with integrity if we will surrender our hearts and lives to Him."

Don and his wife Yanette have two daughters, Dominique and Denay. I asked him if he had any strategies for instilling character in his own children. "One of my daughters gave me a good analogy of integrity," he said. "From time to time, I tell her to clean her room and she'll do it. I go in and check her room and, at first glance, it looks nice and clean. But if I examine more closely, I often find that she's taken everything that was strewn on the floor and tossed it into the closet and under the bed. All you have to do is open the closet door or look under the bed and the mess is still there. So even though the room seems clean at first glance, it's not clean.

"That's how people are with their character. That's how I once was. If you have genuine integrity, you don't just hide the bad stuff of your life under the bed or behind a closet door. You clean house! If you're a man or woman of character, there are no secret areas. You give God total control of every area of your life—and then the whole room is clean."

Don's right. A person of integrity is the same person at all times, whether alone or in a crowd, whether in church or in the locker room. Every room of his life is clean and tidy, through and through. As David wrote in Psalm 15:1–2, "O LORD, who may abide in Your tent? Who may dwell on Your holy hill? He who walks with integrity, and works righteousness, and speaks truth in his heart" NASB.

All or Nothing

The greatest model of integrity who ever lived was Jesus of Nazareth. Even His enemies had to admit He was a morally flawless man. In Mark 12, His enemies in the corrupt religious establishment sent people to trip Him up with flattering words so they could arrest Him and do away with Him. "Teacher," they said, "we know you are a man of integrity. You aren't swayed by men,

because you pay no attention to who they are; but you teach the way of God in accordance with the truth" (v. 14).

And in Luke 23, before Jesus was to be crucified, He stood before the Roman governor, Pontius Pilate, and the governor questioned Him intensely, looking for some reason to execute Him. In the end, Pilate had to confess, "I find no guilt in this man" (v. 4 NASB). Pilate knew that Jesus was a man of absolute integrity, a morally perfect man.

Unfortunately, you and I can't be perfect. We make mistakes and violate our integrity from time to time. When we fail, we must have the integrity to admit it, ask forgiveness, and set it right. When we violate our integrity, we have to demonstrate some different character qualities: responsibility ("that was my fault"), honesty ("I sinned"), and humility ("please forgive me").

The psalmist David writes, "Then I acknowledged my sin to you and did not cover up my iniquity. I said, 'I will confess my transgressions to the Lord'—and you forgave the guilt of my sin" (Ps. 32:5). And the apostle James adds, "Therefore confess your sins to each other and pray for each other so that you may be healed" (James 5:16).

We have to acknowledge that our character is constantly under construction. We never stop finding hidden corners of our lives that need cleaning. There's not much you and I can do to make ourselves younger, smarter, or more—but we can *choose* the kind of character we will have.

As people of integrity, we wouldn't think of "fudging" on our 1040s or "appropriating" office supplies from work—not a laptop computer, not even a paper clip. As people of integrity, we wouldn't think of keeping a wallet we find in the street or the extra change the clerk mistakenly gave us; that's someone else's money, not our windfall. As people of integrity, we would never download music or movies from a file-sharing Web site to avoid buying a CD or DVD—that would be stealing.

Integrity is an all-or-nothing proposition. We either have it

or we don't. As business guru Tom Peters writes, "There are no minor lapses of integrity." Ninety-five percent integrity won't do. It's 100 percent or nothing. We can't build integrity in the next generation if we don't have it ourselves. Our kids and grandkids may not listen to what we say, but they watch what we do—and if our lives lack integrity, they'll spot it for sure.

Parents Who Model Integrity

How do we model integrity to the next generation? I asked that question to leaders in various walks of life. Jon Daniels, athletic director at Bethany College in Lindsborg, Kansas, told me he learned integrity from his father's example.

"I was a young boy," he said, "and I went with my father to the bank to get a check cashed so we could go on a small vacation. The teller counted out way too much money—at least a hundred dollars. My father quietly tried to get the teller's attention without her supervisor knowing she'd made a mistake. Finally, the teller caught on and took the money back, and we left the bank. That incident took place about forty years ago, but I remember it vividly. I think of my father's example of integrity whenever I face a decision where my character is on the line."

Dr. Prediman K. Shah is director of cardiology at Cedars-Sinai Medical Center in Los Angeles. He's made many key discoveries in the field of atherosclerosis and coronary heart disease, and has published over 250 scientific papers and abstracts. Dr. Shah told me, "My parents have been my role models for such character traits as hard work, compassion, loyalty, and integrity. They instilled these values in me by preaching what they practiced, and practicing what they preached.

"When I was about ten years old and living in India, I went to buy bread from a local baker. I gave him some money and he gave me back the change. After leaving the bakery, I realized that the baker had given me twice the change that was due. I went home and told my father, and he sent me back to the bakery to return the

excess change. The baker was pleasantly surprised and gave me an extra loaf of bread as a reward.

"This simple but profound experience taught me a lesson that has stayed with me ever since: be scrupulously honest, even in such small matters as the change from buying a loaf of bread. This lesson also magnified my respect for my father."

Jerry "Slim" Kindall was head baseball coach for the University of Arizona Wildcats for twenty-four seasons, retiring with a record of 860-580-6. He coached the Wildcats to three national championships. Jerry's playing career in the majors spanned nine seasons with the Chicago Cubs, Cleveland Indians, and Minnesota Twins. The University of Arizona home field is named Kindall Field in his honor.

"I grew up in St. Paul, Minnesota," he told me. "The key person in my life was my father, Harold Kindall. Dad worked two jobs as he and my mother raised three rambunctious boys, of whom I'm the oldest. Mom suffered from multiple sclerosis, a chronic inflammatory disease of the central nervous system that produces muscle weakness, fatigue, pain, and impaired coordination. She was in a wheelchair, yet she ministered lovingly to us from a heart full of godly love.

"We were a blue-collar family, and we lived from paycheck to paycheck. The pressures on Dad were enormous, due to Mom's medical condition, a heavy mortgage, and other concerns. Dad worked from 4 p.m. to midnight, six days a week, for Great Northern Railroad. His second job was from 8 a.m. to 2 p.m. at the Royal Shade and Awning Company.

"Even with all he had to do to make ends meet, Dad found time to do the heavy lifting at home—washing clothes, cleaning house, cutting the grass, shoveling snow, and so forth, until his three boys were old enough to take over the chores. I saw great character in my father, plus a deep faith in Jesus Christ.

"The most memorable example of my father's integrity occurred in 1954, after my freshman year at the University of Min-

nesota. I was invited to work out with a Major League Baseball team for three days, and Dad and I both went to the ballpark. After I worked out with the team and they saw what I could do, the owner, general manager, and chief scout invited me to sign a contract. They offered me more money as a rookie ballplayer than my dad made in five years.

"The problem was that Major League Baseball set a limit in those days of four thousand dollars to sign a young player. Also at that time the 'bonus rule' was in effect, which meant that a team that signed a player to a contract in excess of four thousand dollars had to keep the player on the forty-man roster for two seasons, and couldn't send him to a farm club.

"But the team had ways of getting around these rules. Most of the money would be paid 'under the table'—and much of it was designed to buy my father off. He could pick any car, and it would be delivered to him. His mortgage would be paid off. There would be other inducements, all illegal. They told my dad, 'Don't worry! All the clubs do this!'

"Dad said, 'I'm a Christian man, and my wife and I raised Jerry in a Christian home. I can't accept this, nor do I want my son to think I even entertained this option for a moment. We're leaving—now!' Dad never stood taller in my eyes than the day he turned down those enticements and returned to his fourteen-hour days of hard-but-honest work."

Lessons in Integrity

Dr. Caroline Whitson is president of Columbia College in South Carolina. She is a former member of the national board of directors of America's Public Television Stations. "By word and example," she told me, "my parents taught me that work is valuable and that money is secondary. The real purpose of work is to make the world a better place.

"They made a strong impression on me as a child by telling me the story of my grandfather, Ross Bagby. He was the postmaster in

a small Missouri town in the 1920s and '30s. One day, during the Great Depression, he was notified to take post office funds out of the local bank. The bank was failing and would close the next day.

"My grandfather withdrew the post office funds, but left his own money in the bank. He believed it would be wrong for him to benefit from 'insider' knowledge that his neighbors didn't have. My parents told me his story was written up in the local newspaper, saying, 'Did you ever know a Bagby to do less than his best?' That kind of integrity is rare today, but that story has always inspired me to seek absolute integrity in my own life."

Dr. Ken Whitten is senior pastor of Idlewild Baptist Church in Lutz, Florida. He told me how he and his wife, Ginny, taught integrity to their four children. "We homeschooled our children for several years," he said, "preparing them and teaching them godly character traits before sending them out into the world. Our family standard is that our children may only watch movies rated G or PG. People sometimes ask what's wrong with a PG-13 rating. Sometimes nothing—but I've seen that what was once rated R is often rated PG-13 today. What one generation does in moderation, the next generation does in excess.

"Our oldest, Tara, graduated from Florida State University in Tallahassee. During her junior year, her English professor announced that for their midterm exam they would report to class the next day, watch a movie, and be tested afterward on the theme of the film. After class, Tara went to the professor and asked about the rating of the film.

"'It's rated R,' he said. 'Why?'

"'Could I please do other work for my midterm? It's against my principles to watch R-rated movies.'

"The professor replied, 'Tara, you're almost twenty-one, you're away from home, and it's time to grow up. A little language and nudity won't hurt you. So no, I won't allow you to do an alternate assignment. You choose: watch the movie—or take a zero on your midterm.'

" 'In that case,' Tara said respectfully, 'I'll take a zero.' She turned and started to leave.

" 'Tara,' the professor said, 'just a moment—what sort of alternate assignment did you have in mind?'

" 'I thought I could write a paper.'

"The professor said, 'Okay, I'll take a ten-page report on any subject you choose, due tomorrow.'

"Tara wrote a report called 'Proverbs 31: A Godly Woman' and turned it in the next day. When the grades for the midterm were posted, she was the only student to receive an A."

Sometimes, integrity means standing up for your own dignity and personhood. Rob Evans was the head coach of men's basketball at the University of Mississippi ("Ole Miss") from 1992 to 1998, and at Arizona State University from 1998 to 2006. Rob told me that the number one model of integrity in his life was his father.

"When I was eight," he said, "my dad worked for a janitorial service and cleaned lawyers' offices. My three brothers, ages nine, ten, and twelve, and I helped him clean at night. One night, while we were cleaning up in an office, the attorney and a few of his friends came in.

"The attorney was a bullying kind of guy who liked to push people around. He said to my dad, 'Oscar, get over here.' My dad just kept cleaning. The attorney said, 'Get over here now or you're fired!' My dad set his office keys on the desk and said to the four of us, 'Come on boys, let's go.'

"When we were outside, I asked my dad, 'How can you quit this job? Don't we need the money?'

"He said, 'Son, your dignity and your integrity are nonnegotiable.' He wanted me to know that no amount of money was worth compromising your human self-worth. That was an important lesson in character. The attorney tried to demean my dad. But Dad maintained absolute control and dignity. He looked big in my eyes, and the attorney, who thought he was such a big shot,

looked small. That was a huge lesson for me in what it means to maintain your character and integrity at a high personal cost.

"When I was head basketball coach at the University of Mississippi in 1995, we were struggling to build the basketball program. I often thought of my dad's example of character and integrity, and I wanted to be worthy of the standard he had set. We were winless in our first five games in the Southeastern Conference—and then a total disaster happened: five players, including three of our starters, broke a team rule. I suspended all five for our next game against Auburn.

"Auburn was ranked eighteenth in the nation, and we were going up against them with a record of zero conference wins and only seven players available. But I told my players that we could go into that game with our heads high and win. I'm not sure if I believed it myself, but those seven young men must have because they went onto that court and won the game. After the game, I remembered what my dad had taught me: Dignity and integrity are nonnegotiable."

Gene Hooks recruited me to play baseball at Wake Forest University in the fall of 1958, and he's been a good friend ever since. Before his retirement, Gene devoted nearly four decades of his life to Wake Forest as a student athlete, coach, and most of all, director of athletics from 1964 through 1992. The baseball stadium at the campus in Winston-Salem, North Carolina, is named in his honor. I've always viewed Gene as a great model of integrity, so I asked him where he learned this character trait.

"I was just a boy of nine or ten," he told me, "when I learned a life lesson in integrity—and I learned it the hard way, by doing wrong and living with the regret of it afterward. At the time, I had a job delivering sales circulars for the Belk department store in Rocky Mount, North Carolina. It was during the Great Depression and we were poor, like everyone else in our neighborhood. We delivered the circulars in the more affluent neighborhoods early in the mornings.

"In those days, milk was delivered to the front steps by the milkman at about the same time we delivered the circulars. One house I delivered to always received both regular milk and chocolate milk. I had never tasted chocolate milk in my life! After a few days of passing that house and seeing the chocolate milk on the doorstep, I couldn't stand it any longer! I snatched the chocolate milk and drank it.

"The people who lived in that house missed their chocolate milk and the milkman knew he had delivered it. I heard people talking about the missing chocolate milk, but no one ever asked me about it and I never owned up to it. The theft of the chocolate milk was on my conscience for years afterward. I knew I never wanted to feel that guilty again, so I made up my mind to be a man of integrity. So, in some ways, my character was shaped by guilt.

"But in a more positive sense, my mother and father were the role models who truly shaped the person I am. They were strong Christians—honest, hardworking people of faith. Neither of them went to college, but they were well-read and well-educated. They had a wonderful sense of values, and I always wanted to make them proud of me. They set a high standard for integrity, and I've tried to live up to that standard."

Ideas for Shaping a Child's Integrity

How, then, do we encourage young people to become people of unyielding, uncompromising, steel-hard integrity? Here are some ideas and insights that have emerged from my interviews:

1. *Set an example of absolute integrity.* Your kids are watching you all the time. If they catch you in an unguarded moment, talking about how you "fudged" on your taxes or "borrowed" some items from the office, then you are telling them, loud and clear, that dishonesty is okay. You're letting them know that your talk and your walk do not match. Be an example. Be a person of integrity, through and through.

While this book was being written, I had lunch with my friend

and speaking coach, Alfonso Castaneira. He's the founder of Dreamgineering, Inc., a coaching and consulting enterprise that helps top executives improve their public speaking and leadership skills. Alfonso told me he was recently shaving in front of the bathroom mirror when he noticed his little son standing next to him. The boy had uncapped a toothpaste tube, smeared his lower face with toothpaste, and was using the bottom edge of the tube as a "razor" to scrape off the toothpaste.

"I looked at my son," Alfonso said, "and I looked at myself in the mirror. He was stretching his neck to shave under his chin exactly as I was, and mimicking everything I did to perfection. I tell you, Pat, that was the turning point in my life as a father. I realized the influence I had on my boy. What a responsibility! If I want him to become a person of character and integrity, then I have to be exactly what I want him to be."

Todd Shaw, president of On-Track Ministry, is a chaplain in the popular motorsport of karting, or competitive kart (formerly "go-cart") racing, which is sponsored worldwide by the World Karting Association (WKA). Todd recalls a lesson in integrity he learned from the example of his father. "My father, M. B. Shaw, is a man of faith and integrity," Todd told me. "He taught me many lessons about character. His life was an open book, and he often let me into his world so that I could learn from his experiences.

"One time, a group of men approached him and wanted him to run for a city council seat. They promised to front all of his campaign expenses. They were some of the most wealthy and influential men in our community, and they visited our house many times, trying to convince my dad to run. In the end, he said, 'Thanks, but no thanks.'

"I remember feeling disappointed. I had thought it would be exciting to have my dad on the city council. I asked him, 'Why did you say no? Don't you want to be on the council where you can help the people of our town?'

"'Todd,' he said, 'those men wanted to use me. I have a good

name in this community, and I want to keep that good name as long as I can. Those men thought they could buy my campaign and then they would own me. Todd, it's not worth losing my name and my integrity in order to get a political seat.' Watching my dad wrestle with that decision, then hearing him explain it in terms of his integrity, was a powerful lesson in character."

2. *When teaching your kids about integrity, don't rely on words alone.* Make a vivid and visual impression on your kids. The visual sense is the most powerful of all the senses. The nerve pathways from eye to brain are *twenty-five times larger* than the nerve pathways from ear to brain. Why? Because the eye receives and transmits much more information than the ear. It transmits images, motion, gestures, and facial expressions. If you want to make a memorable impact on your children, make your message *visual.*

Jeff Rickey, dean of admissions at Earlham College, told me, "When I was ten years old, my father mowed the backyard in such a way that the letters of my name stood out. He showed it to me and told me how important my name was, how it stood for who I was, and how I needed to cherish, value, and protect my name with my words and actions. Then, to show me how quickly a good name could be destroyed, he pushed the mower across my name and mowed it out of existence. The visual power of that lesson remains etched in my mind to this day."

3. *Let kids experience the natural consequences of violating their integrity.* Natural consequences tend to be the best way to make the "punishment" fit the "crime." If the child commits an infraction related to bicycle use, then natural consequences would involve taking the bicycle away for a period of time. If the child abuses his computer privileges, then take away those privileges for a while.

Todd Shaw recalls a time when his grandfather allowed him to learn a lesson from the natural consequences of his actions. "I grew up on a tobacco farm," he told me. "One time, when I was

a boy, I rolled my own cigar from some of the tobacco we grew on our farm. I selected the biggest, brightest, most golden leaf of cured tobacco I'd ever seen. I cut all the stems out, then rolled it to make my own handmade cigar. I put that cigar to my lips as if I was a Wall Street big shot smoking a fine Cuban Cohiba. Just then, Granddaddy King walked by.

"'Todd!' he said. 'What are you going to do with that cigar?'

"'Oh, nothing, Granddaddy,' I bluffed. 'Ain't she a beaut?'

"'You're not planning to smoke it, are you?'

"'Oh, no!' I said. 'This is just for looks.'

"My grandfather walked on and I thought I had fooled him. Later that evening, I went behind the barn with my cigar, lit it up, and took a big, deep drag on it—and I learned something that my grandfather already knew but didn't warn me about: you can't smoke straight tobacco. It's too hard and pure. Before it can be smoked, it has to be treated and toned down. I felt like I was inhaling burning rocket fuel. My mouth, sinus cavities, and lungs lit up like the sky on the Fourth of July—*POW!*

"After supper that night, Granddaddy King came up to me and said, 'How was that cigar?' I dropped my head, ashamed that he had been wise to my lies all along.

"'Not too good,' I said.

"My grandfather nodded and walked away. He didn't have to pound the message home. He knew that the cigar had delivered a more powerful moral to the story than any words of his could add—and I had definitely learned a lesson in honesty and integrity."

4. *Give young people time to stop and think about their actions.* Don't impose consequences in the heat of an angry confrontation, because both you and your kids are more likely to overreact. If you come up with an overly severe punishment in the heat of the moment, your kids will know you won't follow through on it. Give your kids and yourself time to think things through and arrive at a thoughtful resolution to the matter.

Scott Harding, executive director of National Relief Network, told me, "I've always told my children that honesty and integrity, two of the strongest traits of good character, can never be taken from you. If you compromise those traits, it's because you've consciously chosen to do so.

"When my kids violate their integrity in some way, I've always tried to give them an opportunity to stop and think about their actions. This way they can act rather than react. I'll ask the question, "What would Jesus do in this situation?" or "What do you think you should have done?" or "What do you think will be the outcome of this choice?"

"Sometimes you have to point out consequences of their choices that may not have occurred to them because they lack the life experience to see around that corner. Our job is to teach and coach and help them think about their choices and learn lessons in character.

"When we, as parents, ask a toddler to do something and the toddler refuses, we count to three. Why? To give the child a chance to think about the outcome of disobedience. As children get older, we have to continually find ways to give children a chance to think about outcomes. This is a tremendous way to instill good character."

5. Teach your kids that it's never too late to right a wrong. We all make mistakes. The true test of character lies in whether we correct our failings—or cover them up.

When my kids were younger and all under our roof, my message was simple: "All I want is the truth. Be honest with me. If you did something wrong, own up to it and things will be much better. Cover it up and it will only get worse." I think that's the cry of every parent.

Our kids need to know that honesty is always the best policy, even when they've made a huge mistake. We need to tell them, "If you get out in the real world and people doubt your word one time, you're in trouble. If they doubt it twice, you're through.

You'll have to pack up your possessions, move across the country, start over again, and hope nobody finds out."

Gordon Gund is a sports entrepreneur who has been an owner of such teams as the NBA's Cleveland Cavaliers and the NHL's San Jose Sharks. A civic-minded Cleveland native, he purchased the Cavs in 1983 to keep the team from leaving the city. Born in 1939, Gordon suffered permanent blindness in 1970 due to retinitis pigmentosa. Because of this condition, Gordon has never seen a game played by the teams he has owned. He is the cofounder and board chairman of The Foundation Fighting Blindness.

"My father and mother were my character role models," Gordon told me. "They always placed a high premium on integrity and trust, and they lived and taught the Ten Commandments. My father displayed an extraordinary work ethic; my mother suffered from cancer during the last ten years of her life, yet she was always upbeat and joyful, never complaining about her pain.

"When I talk to young people about character, I often talk about the 'second mistake.' We all make mistakes of all kinds, and the first mistake can often be a learning experience. How we deal with that first mistake reveals the kind of character we have. Do we go back and fix the first mistake—or do we make a second mistake by trying to cover up the first?

"I sometimes tell the story of when I was a teenager, following my freshman year in college. I went fishing with friends in northern Maine, and there I met a guide and ranger named Frank. He befriended us and I quickly came to like and admire him. He knew all about fishing and living in the woods, and I learned a lot from listening to him.

"At the end of the week, Frank persuaded a friend of his to let me use a rowboat to fish a stretch of the river. While maneuvering the rowboat upriver, I snapped one of the oars. When I returned that evening, I didn't tell Frank about the broken oar. He asked me about the boat and if I had any problems with it, and I said, 'No, no problems.' I felt stupid about the broken oar and didn't want

to admit how inept I felt. Breaking the oar was my first mistake, and it was a fixable mistake. Lying was my second mistake—and it was much worse because it violated my integrity.

"That night, during the drive home, I agonized over the lie I told. It was all I could think about. The next morning, I phoned Frank and told him the truth. I said I had broken the oar and I promised to pay for it. At that point he told me he already knew about the oar. His trust in me had been shaken—but I was grateful to hear that he was willing to accept my apology, though it was late in coming.

"Frank and I became good friends, and for years thereafter we fished and hiked the Maine woods together. My second mistake nearly cost me this wonderful friendship. When you make that first mistake, don't make a second mistake. The cover-up is always worse than the first mistake."

6. *Take advantage of "teachable moments."* A teachable moment is an event in your daily relationship with your child that can serve as an object lesson for instilling character. Brian Roquemore is president and CEO of America's All Stars, Inc., a national organization which seeks to encourage outstanding character in young people. Brian and his wife, Elaine, are parents of five children.

"Elaine and I are always looking for 'teachable moments' we can use to instill integrity in our kids," Brian told me. "One of those moments came when my two youngest sons and I were visiting the community pool. We found fifty-four dollars in cash wrapped in a supermarket receipt. My sons and I asked everyone at the pool if they lost some money, then we asked around the neighborhood. Most of the people we asked said, 'No—but why ask around? Don't be stupid! Just keep the money!'

"We called the phone number on the supermarket receipt and asked the store manager if any of the cashiers cashed a check and gave someone that sum of money in change. The cashiers checked their registers and one of them turned up the check and gave us the name of the individual who wrote it.

"We went to the address and knocked on the door and presented the cash to a startled-looking young couple at the door. 'How did you find us?' they asked. When we explained, they couldn't believe we would go to such lengths to return their money when we easily could have kept it.

"On our way home, the boys and I talked about the lack of integrity demonstrated by the people who said we should keep the money. To them, it seemed normal and smart to keep the cash. Finding the rightful owner, they said, was 'stupid.' But to us, finding the rightful owner was the only thing to do. It was a simple matter of following the Golden Rule and doing to others what we would want others to do toward us."

7. Affirm kids when they make integrity-based choices. Children want to feel good about themselves. They are proud of themselves when they display integrity and other character qualities—and especially when the grown-ups in their lives affirm them for their good character.

Karen Armon is CEO and founder of Alliance Resources, LLC, an executive coaching and consulting company based in Littleton, Colorado. I asked Karen if she could share any strategies for encouraging integrity in young people. She said, "I vividly remember that glow of satisfaction I felt as a child when I knew I had done something honest and right, something that demonstrated integrity.

"My parents gave me fifteen cents allowance every week when I was in the third grade. That doesn't sound like much today, but in those days you could buy three candy bars for fifteen cents, or a considerable amount of penny candy. The local drugstore was halfway along my route home from school, so I often stopped there to spend my allowance. The drugstore owner was a family friend, and he was always very kind to me.

"I had my candy money carefully budgeted so it would last through Friday. One particular Friday, I stopped at the drugstore and took my time making a selection. There were so many candy

bars to choose from and I only had a nickel to spend. After several minutes, I took my selection to the counter. 'That'll be seven cents,' the owner said.

"My mouth dropped open. Seven cents! They used to be a nickel! Seeing my shocked expression, he explained that the prices had just gone up. 'Tell you what,' he said. 'I'll give it to you for five cents today. Just remember, Karen, that this candy bar will be seven cents next time, okay?'

"To me, it wasn't okay. If the price was seven cents, it wouldn't be right for me to pay five cents. I said, 'I'm going to ask my mom to give me two cents advance on next week's allowance. I'll bring back your two cents right away.'

"He said, 'You don't have to do that. We can make this our deal for this week.' But I couldn't do that. I dashed home with the candy bar, but I couldn't eat it because it wasn't really mine yet. I still owed the druggist two cents!

"Arriving home, I explained the situation to my mother. She gave me the two cents and I hurried back to the drugstore. 'Here it is,' I said, 'just like I promised!' I placed the two pennies on the counter.

"I remember the look on the druggist's face. He seemed choked up with emotion over those two pennies! 'Thank you, Karen,' he said. 'You really do what you say you're going to do, don't you?'

"'Yes,' I said, 'I do.' I walked out of the store and the candy bar was finally mine to eat—the best I ever tasted."

When Lorenzo Romar, head basketball coach at the University of Washington, was coaching at Pepperdine in the early 1990s, he took his entire staff to visit Coach John Wooden at his condo in Encino. "We spent four hours with Coach," Romar told me. "The next day, he called me and said, 'One of your coaches lost some change from his pocket, and I found it in my sofa. I want to get it back to him.' A few days later, an envelope arrived in my office with seventy-five cents in change in it. When a person has

that much integrity in the small things, you know he has absolute integrity in the big things as well."

Sports marketing entrepreneur David Paro, founder of Deep Alliance Marketing, told me he first learned the importance of integrity at age eight, while playing Little League baseball. "It was an important game," David told me, "and I came up in the bottom of the last inning with two outs and my team down by two runs. We had a runner on first base.

"I hit the ball pretty well to left center and it got by the out-fielders. The runner from first scored. As I rounded third, bent on scoring the tying run, I was confident I could make it. My teammates, however, screamed, 'Slide! Slide!' I slid home. Looking up through the cloud of dust, I saw the ump call me out! Game over—and we lost.

"I didn't dare argue the call—not when the umpire was my own father. Had any other ump made that call, the game would be long forgotten today. But because the umpire was my own dad, the memory of that moment is very strong. Dad could have called me safe at home, and he wouldn't have gotten much of an argument—it was that close. But he *called* me out because I *was* out. He called it as he saw it.

"That lesson in winning or losing fairly was a cornerstone for my character throughout my early life. I never doubted that Dad wanted me to succeed, whether in baseball or in life, but he wasn't going to endorse anything but absolute integrity in my pursuit of success. That lesson in integrity guides me to this day."

A Legacy of Integrity

Those who have integrity are whole people. Their public reputation is matched by their inner reality. Their souls are not divided or compartmentalized. They are people of authentic character, through and through. If you look in the "closets" or under the "rugs" of their lives, you won't find any dirt or mess there. Every room of their lives is clean and tidy.

The psalmist wrote this description of a person of integrity: "Who may ascend into the hill of the LORD? And who may stand in His holy place? He who has clean hands and a pure heart, who has not lifted up his soul to falsehood and has not sworn deceitfully" (Ps. 24:3–4).

Bestselling author Laurie Beth Jones notes that when she asks "adults to choose a core value that most represents who they are or want to become, many will choose the word 'integrity.' I often joke that they probably copied the word from their neighbors' notes because it is such a popular word. In one of my training seminars, I asked the fourteen people who had chosen 'integrity' as their core value to write their personal definitions of the concept. None of them could.

"I believe it is wise for us to consider the root of the word 'integrity,' and what it means in a dictionary, as well as what it means to us. Integrity is the quality or state of being complete, unbroken, whole, entire. The state or quality of being in perfect condition . . . of being of sound moral principle, upright, honest and sincere. The root word is the Latin *integer,* which means 'untouched, whole, entire.' "

In a magazine interview, evangelist Billy Graham was asked how he would like to be remembered when his life is over. Graham replied that he would be content to have his life summed up with this simple epitaph: " 'A sinner saved by grace; a man who, like the Psalmist, walked in his integrity.' I'd like people to remember that I had integrity."

That's the legacy I want to leave to the next generation. That's the way I want to be remembered. I just want people to say of me, "The rooms of his life were clean. He had integrity."

4

Diligence: Nothing Beats Hard Work

*"The heights by great men reached and kept
Were not attained by sudden flight,
But they while their companions slept
Were toiling upward in the night."*

HENRY WADSWORTH LONGFELLOW
AMERICAN POET

In 2006, the ABC news program *20/20* broadcast a segment on high-achieving people who work sixty, seventy, or more hours per week—people who maintain high-pressure, fast-paced schedules in order to achieve success. One of the people profiled was Cynthia McKay, founder and CEO of LeGourmet Gift Basket, Inc., of Castle Rock, Colorado, a business owner who works eleven- and twelve-hour days seven days a week—and who is on twenty-four-hour call for her clients in every time zone around the globe. McKay told the interviewer her long hours were "absolutely my choice" because "I love being at work."

When I interviewed Cynthia McKay for this book, she told me, "I was profiled on ABC's *20/20* as a workaholic—and before the show even ended, my email box filled with over seven hundred hate mails."

Hate mail? Why would so many people take the time to write hate mail to someone who works hard and loves her work? Isn't Cynthia McKay's strong work ethic a *good* thing? After all, she

creates a valuable service for her clients and generates jobs for her employees. A significant percentage of her company's profits go to support an impressive list of nonprofit organizations: PAALS for Life (which provides animal companionship to the elderly), The Salvation Army, the American Red Cross, Jerry's Kids, Big Brothers–Big Sisters, plus a host of animal shelters and animal rescue organizations, several of which Cynthia herself founded.

I ask you: Does Cynthia McKay deserve hate mail for all of her many hours of hard work—or a Nobel Prize? Why do so many people hate those who work hard?

On September 28, 2006, the *Times* of London, Great Britain's "newspaper of record," published a short article by Malcolm Burgess headlined "Five Reasons to Hate Workaholics." Though Burgess's tongue was in his cheek, he was satirizing the actual views of many people, including all the people who sent hate mail to Cynthia McKay. Let me list some of the reasons Burgess gives:

- "These driven people like to set the benchmarks for the rest of us." In other words, hardworking people make slackers look bad by showing that achievement and excellence *are* possible. People with a strong work ethic expose the laziness and poor work ethic of everyone else.
- "Workaholics like to impress us with their BlackBerries and claim, with martyred looks, that there's never a second when clients can't contact them." In other words, slackers think diligent, hardworking people are just showing off.
- Hardworking people are "the inspiration for, and authors of, those essential management tomes our boss thinks we should have read." True enough! And I'm proud to be one of those hardworking authors who writes about the value of hard work!
- Hardworking people make everyone else "feel guilty" because they wish to have a "(a) minimal lunch; (b) social life; (c) sex life." What a sour grapes rationalization!

Most of the hardworking people I know—people like myself who labor sixty to eighty hours a week—tend to be well-nourished, physically fit, socially active, sexually satisfied human beings. Most of the people I've met who have a poor work ethic tend to be as lazy with the rest of their life as they are in their professions. They are often overfed couch potatoes who do not live their lives in a meaningful way.

Diligence—a strong work ethic—is one of the most important of all the components of good character. Those who work hard not only produce success and achievement for themselves, but they contribute to a successful, abundant economy. They create wealth and jobs that benefit employers, investors, workers, and retirees on pensions. They pay the taxes that make our society strong and secure.

One of the most underrated benefits of hard work is it creates wealth which funds the charitable institutions of a compassionate society. If it weren't for the hardworking people in our society, there would be no money to provide for disaster relief, help for the homeless, shelters for abused women and kids, or research to cure cancer, Alzheimer's, and AIDS.

People who work hard take responsibility for their own lives—and the world they live in. They are people of maturity and character who generate their own success instead of sitting back and complaining about the unfairness of life. A strong work ethic doesn't just happen. The value of hard work must be taught at an early age and instilled by both word and example. Young people need to hear that diligence is a virtue and laziness is a sin.

Some Christians mistakenly think work is a "curse," an evil effect of the fall of man. But Scriptures tell us work is God's gift to the human race. Genesis 2:15 tells us the Lord God placed Adam, who was then unfallen, in the Garden of Eden "to work it and take care of it." It is not work itself that is a curse of the Fall; rather, Genesis 3:17–19 tells us that, after sin entered the world, the ground became cursed, producing thorns and weeds, so that

God's gift of meaningful work was transformed into sweaty, back-breaking toil.

Though we no longer live in the Garden of Eden, work is still a blessing and a gift—and a solemn responsibility. Those who work hard are aware of the brevity of life and the need to accomplish our life's work while life still remains. Solomon, in the Old Testament, writes "Whatever your hand finds to do, do it with all your might, for in the grave, where you are going, there is neither working nor planning nor knowledge nor wisdom" (Ecc. 9:10).

The apostle Paul tells us hard work is a holy act of worship to our Lord, who will reward us in eternity for the work we do on earth. He writes, "Whatever you do, work at it with all your heart, as working for the Lord, not for men, since you know that you will receive an inheritance from the Lord as a reward. It is the Lord Christ you are serving" (Col. 3:23–24).

The Bible promises prosperity and satisfaction to those who work hard. "Lazy hands make a man poor, but diligent hands bring wealth" (Prov. 10:4). "The sluggard [or slacker] craves and gets nothing, but the desires of the diligent are fully satisfied" (Prov. 13:4). "Do you see a man skilled in his work? He will serve before kings; he will not serve before obscure men" (22:29). "He who works his land will have abundant food, but the one who chases fantasies [such as get-rich-quick schemes or playing the lottery] will have his fill of poverty" (Prov. 28:19) [*brackets mine*].

When slackers see people getting ahead by working hard, they take time out from watching TV to send hate mail to the "workaholics." But people of character don't have time to send hate mail to anyone. They're too busy working hard, contributing to society, and winning God's approval to feel resentment toward others.

"I Hope You Like to Work Hard..."

On a rainy Sunday in February 1965, I arrived in Spartanburg, South Carolina, to take an assignment as general manager of the Spartanburg Phillies baseball club. I pulled up in front of the big

redbrick home of Mr. R. E. Littlejohn, the prosperous owner of a successful petroleum tanker company and co-owner of the Spartanburg Phillies. I went to the door and knocked, and was greeted by Mr. Littlejohn's wife, a gracious Southern lady whom everyone in town knew as "Sam."

"Come in," she said. "I'm sorry Mr. R. E. isn't here. He was called out of town unexpectedly." She offered me refreshments and we talked for a while. Near the end of our conversation, Sam said to me, "You'll never work for or even meet another man like Mr. R. E., no matter how long you're around."

I later learned these were not the overstated sentiments of an adoring wife. When I met Mr. Littlejohn a day or two later, he did indeed turn out to be a unique man—and one of the greatest men I've ever met. I am a Christian today because Mr. R. E. Littlejohn showed me what it means to live for Jesus Christ. My admiration for this man is so great my oldest son, James Littlejohn Williams, is named in his honor.

Mr. Littlejohn taught me everything I need to know about how to be successful in life and how to experience lasting satisfaction and meaning in life. Under his wise leadership and mentorship, I managed the Spartanburg team for four years, from 1965 to 1968. Mrs. Littlejohn was right: I have never met anyone else like her husband—not before and not since.

Here's an amazing fact about Mr. Littlejohn: he bought his first car, a Model T Ford, with his own hard-earned money when he was eleven years old. Where did an eleven-year-old get that kind of money? He earned it by working in a mill after school and all day long during the summer. So it's not surprising that one of the first lessons I learned from Mr. R. E. Littlejohn was the importance of hard work. The day I met him, he told me, "I hope you like to work hard, because there's a lot of work to be done here."

He was right. Opening day of baseball season was just two months away, and the ball field, Duncan Park, was suffering from years of neglect. The grandstands needed painting and the rest-

rooms were filthy beyond belief. But the ballpark was located in a beautiful green park and I knew it could be a real showplace with some hard work and tender loving care.

For the next two months, I worked eighteen-hour days, seven days a week, and did much of the grunt-work myself. I cut the grass, hammered thousands of nails, slapped paint on the outfield walls, and hosed down and repainted the restrooms. When I wasn't sprucing up the ballpark, I was running around town, selling advertising, getting player uniforms mended, getting programs and tickets printed, and brainstorming promotional ideas.

The season opened—and attendance quickly skyrocketed from 30,000 the previous year to over 114,000. Our wild new promotional ideas—from watermelon-eating contests to nighttime skydivers—made headlines across the country. At the end of my first year, I was named Executive of the Year in the Western Carolinas League. Two years later, *The Sporting News* named me Minor League Executive of the Year.

What I learned from Mr. R. E. Littlejohn as a twenty-five-year-old baseball executive is still true today: if you want to get anywhere in life, nothing beats hard work.

The late Jim Valvano was head basketball coach at North Carolina State University, where he coached his team to an NCAA National Championship in 1983. He once said, "At the beginning of every basketball season, there are over three hundred Division I basketball coaches. Every one of them wants to win a championship, but only one can win. Just because you work hard doesn't mean you'll succeed. But if you stop working hard, you don't have a shot of succeeding."

A few summers ago, the Magic organization honored one of our employees, Jack Swope, for his twenty-five-year career in the NBA. The event was held at the beautiful Isleworth Country Club near Orlando. It was a blistering day—95 degrees with 100 percent humidity. While driving on the club grounds, I noticed a man running in the opposite direction, shirtless, his skin glistening,

moving at a very brisk pace in spite of the heat. I thought, *That's not who I think it is!*

I turned my car around and drove back the other way. As I passed the man and got a second look (while trying not to gawk), I thought, *Sure enough, it's Tiger Woods!* I was doubly amazed, because I knew Tiger had just won a golf tournament the previous day in another part of the country. This meant he flew into Orlando late at night and went out the next day for a punishing workout. But that's why he's the best. He's always outworking everyone else. That's what the great ones do.

Willing to Bus Tables and Set Up Chairs

When I speak before audiences, I often ask this question: "Do you know what the two most important words in the English language are?" Answer: *What else.* People of character and diligence, are always asking themselves, "What else? What else can I do? What else can I offer? What else can I contribute?" Those who don't think "what else" just do what's required of them—no more. But the person who thinks "what else" goes the extra mile, gives the extra measure, and always delivers value and excellence.

Charles T. Menghini, DMA, is president of VanderCook College of Music. I met him when he performed the national anthem on the trumpet at a game between the Orlando Magic and the New York Knicks. He recently told me how he learned a strong work ethic at an early age.

"I grew up in a small town in the upper peninsula of Michigan," Dr. Menghini said. "My father was a self-employed wholesaler of candy, tobacco, and paper products. He was the salesman and my mother was the bookkeeper. When I was in junior high and my brother went off to college, I helped stock shelves and make deliveries in the family business. Dad taught me that if we weren't successful in our business, we wouldn't eat.

"One of my responsibilities while working in the warehouse was rotating the stock—that is, making sure the old candy and

tobacco products were sold first to prevent spoilage. While stocking the shelves, I had to make sure the labels were all turned out so they could be read. This attention to detail seemed unnecessary to me. After all, ours was a wholesale delivery business, not a retail store. Rarely did customers come to our place of business and see our shelves.

"My father explained that excellence and professionalism are always important. We should take pride in our work at all times. Even though our customers didn't usually come to us, we wanted to make a good impression on those who did. If we kept our shelves stocked with an attitude of excellence, that same attitude would carry over into everything we did. Diligence, he told me, is synonymous with good character.

"I eventually realized that my dad didn't just sell candy and gum. He sold service. He would call on his customers at the same time every week—the time of his arrival never varied more than ten minutes or so. If he gave you his word about a product, a price, or a delivery time, you could take it to the bank. In a real sense, he was selling his dependable character."

I asked Dr. Menghini if he had any stories about his dad that illustrated his work ethic. "Oh, yes," he replied. "This took place when I was an adult and my dad was in his mid-eighties. My wife and I traveled to the upper peninsula to visit my parents on Easter weekend. My dad had recently purchased a new car, and when we arrived, my wife and I noticed that the car was dirty from the snow and slush of the winter season just past.

"I decided to give my parents a gift for Easter—the gift of my time. I decided to treat my dad to a surprise car wash. So my wife and I took Mom and Dad for a ride in their new car. I drove—and we went to the automatic car wash. It wasn't a drive-through, but the kind where you deposit a lot of quarters and the machine dispenses warm water and an array of soaps and sprays. You do the work of actually washing the car.

"My wife and I did all the spraying and scrubbing while Mom

and Dad watched. My wife and I exchanged glances that said, 'Dad must be pleased with the way his car is starting to sparkle!' Afterward, we drove the car home. I turned off the engine and I heard Dad get out on the passenger side. I opened my door and got out of the car—

"And promptly got hit in the face by a towel! Even in his eighties, my dad could pitch a perfect strike. I laughed, knowing exactly what he was going to say next.

"'Dry the doors!' he said. 'If you don't want to do the job right, then you should leave it dirty!'

"Dad was right. Even in early spring, it freezes overnight in the upper peninsula of Michigan—and wet doors would freeze tight. I felt like I was back in the warehouse, making sure all the labels faced the same way. Even in his mid-eighties, Dad's message was the same: Excellence in all things. Take pride in your work. Diligence is synonymous with good character."

If people learn the value of hard work when they're young, they'll live out a lifestyle of diligence and excellence for the rest of their lives. Tom Schumacher is president of Disney Theatrical Productions. After spending five years on the staff of the Los Angeles Music Center's Mark Taper Forum, he joined the Walt Disney Company in 1988. Tom produced the world premiere of Disney's Broadway musical *The Lion King*, which garnered six Tony Awards, including Best Musical.

"I learned about character and hard work," he said, "from my grandfather in California, my dad's father. He survived the San Francisco earthquake [of 1906] then moved to L.A. to go into the film business. He was a decent and righteous man who taught me the importance of giving back more than you take from your community. When I was in college busing tables in a restaurant for $2.25 an hour, my grandfather kept stressing to me the importance of giving back, paying your way, and volunteering to help others.

"I talk to young people a lot and I tell them this story: At age fourteen or so, I was a volunteer technician and stagehand at a

children's theater in San Mateo, California. We'd work all night sometimes, building scenery and sets and getting things ready for the performance. A lady on the staff, who was about twenty-two or so, would drive quite a distance to take me home from the theater. I asked her, 'How can I pay you back?' She said, 'One day you'll drive someone else home.'

"That principle stuck with me all these years. You can't always pay back, but you can give back and contribute and set an example of service to others. And it's not all about money. You can give back with your time, love, and energy.

"I've been working since I was fifteen and I've had many different jobs. At one point, I was a custodian at a dance studio and would work until ten thirty or eleven at night, sweeping the floor and cleaning mirrors. I'd moan to my dad about how hard I had to work. One day, Dad said, 'Tom, if you think you're too big for the job, the job is too big for you.'

"I've never forgotten that lesson in maintaining an attitude of humility toward my work. All work is honorable, and we should never think we are above serving others by working hard. Not long ago, we were getting ready for a rehearsal of *Tarzan* on Broadway, and I was the one setting up the chairs. The cast was eating lunch in the cafeteria and I was cleaning up their tables afterward.

"I get young people working for me in their early twenties who have never worked in a restaurant before. Not having to work hard has not helped some in this generation. It's a character-building thing to bus tables and learn the value of serving others and working hard."

I agree with Tom Schumacher's observations about serving others through our humble diligence and commitment to excellence. I also think it's appropriate that a man with Tom's work ethic is president of Disney Theatrical Productions, because his is a Disneyesque mind-set—as Art Linkletter will attest.

Art Linkletter is a radio and TV personality who was also one

of Walt Disney's closest friends. He wrote a wonderful foreword for *How to Be Like Walt*, my book on the life and values of Walt Disney. When I interviewed Art Linkletter, he told me how he first met Walt.

"It was 1940," he told me, "and I was working at a local radio station in San Francisco. Walt had come to introduce his new motion picture, *Fantasia*. I arrived early for the press conference, and found the place empty except for one fellow who was busily arranging chairs. I said, 'When is Walt Disney supposed to arrive?' He grinned and said, 'I'm Walt Disney.' I said, 'You are? Why are you arranging chairs?' He replied, 'Well, I like to have things just so.' That was quite an introduction, because it gave me a glimpse of the kind of person Walt was."

Indeed! Though he was the head of a major Hollywood studio, Walt Disney wasn't too self-important to set up chairs. That's how people of character view hard work: No job is too big for them because no job is too small. As Dr. Martin Luther King Jr. once said, "If a man is called to be a street-sweeper, he should sweep streets even as Michelangelo painted, or Beethoven played music, or Shakespeare wrote poetry. He should sweep streets so well that all the hosts of heaven and earth will pause to say, 'Here lived a great street-sweeper who did his job well.'"

"The Job Was *Way* Bigger than I Was"

Sammy T. Mah recently became president and CEO of the World Relief Corporation of the National Association of Evangelicals following a twenty-seven-year career with General Motors. He told me about a time he thought a job was too big for him—and the discovery that changed his mind.

"I used to work in my dad's restaurant in New York City when I was four years old," Sammy told me. "I would stand on a chair with my sleeves rolled up, washing huge piles of dishes by hand. The stainless steel basins were big enough for me to swim in. I was paid ten cents a night, which would buy me a couple of ice cream

cones with gumballs in the bottom of the cone. I don't recall ever breaking a dish—though my dad may recall otherwise.

"My parents were always in the restaurant business, either working for someone else or running their own restaurant. My two younger brothers and I spent a large part of our early childhood in the workplace. Mom and Dad liked having us around—not only to keep us out of trouble but to teach us lessons about character and hard work.

"I remember the excitement when my dad asked if I would like to help him work. I couldn't wait to do what the grown-ups were doing. From starting as a dishwasher, I moved my way up the 'corporate ladder' to food preparation and short-order cooking. I chopped and peeled tons of vegetables, made thousands of egg rolls and wontons, and sliced and diced truckloads of meat. I enjoyed hanging out with Dad and the cooks, watching how the kitchen functioned, and how each person carried out his part.

"Much of my character growth was learned the hard way. I recall one day when my dad had fried hundreds of egg rolls in preparation for the dinner rush. The outside shell of a deep-fried egg roll is like bubble wrap. That day for some reason, I felt an irresistible urge to take a pencil and poke the bubbles on each egg roll!

"My dad was furious when he saw the egg rolls with their bubbly shells broken. I tried to make up a story to cover up my misdeed—but then I saw the disappointment in his eyes. This was the first talk Dad ever had with me about the importance of accepting responsibility for my actions (it was, unfortunately, not the last).

"Working in the restaurant business for twelve years taught me the value of family, integrity, and hard work. My parents often put in twelve or more hours a day, yet they always had time for their kids. They ran their businesses with absolute integrity. My parents also provided a great deal of free food to the needy and homeless.

"The character qualities I learned in my parents' restaurant business were the key to success in my career at General Motors.

There I helped launch new engine programs that powered millions of GM cars and trucks. While at GM, my wife, Lorelei, and I were frequently involved in short-term mission projects with our kids, Nicole, Andrew, and Victoria.

"Our dream was that I would one day retire from GM and we would go around the world, building youth camps with our many missionary friends. Around Thanksgiving 2004, a friend suggested I check the Web site of a recruiting firm that worked with not-for-profit organizations.

"I wasn't ready to retire or change careers, but I checked the Web site. I found that World Relief was seeking a president/CEO. I knew the organization, so I downloaded the position profile—all nine pages! I decided the job was *way* bigger than I was—and I decided against pursuing it. That night, I tossed and turned as God nudged at me to be obedient. Finally, I got up in the middle of the night, typed up an email, attached my resumé, and applied for the position. I slept much better after that.

"Months later, I received a clear call from God to leave General Motors to head up a not-for-profit organization (if you own GM stock these days, then you may think it's a not-for-profit organization as well!). Though the job still seems a lot bigger than I am, I'm often reminded that 'we are God's workmanship, created in Christ Jesus to do good works, which God prepared in advance for us to do' [Eph. 2:10]. Ever since I was four years old, I've worked at jobs that were bigger than I was, and God has been preparing me throughout my life to take on ever bigger challenges."

The Power of an Uncompromising Work Ethic

Jack Stallings has coached basketball at Georgia Southern, Florida State, and Wake Forest. He has been a good friend ever since he was my coach at Wake Forest. When my father was killed in a car accident shortly after I graduated, Jack drove to Delaware to be at the funeral. Today, he's retired from coaching and teaching, and

lives in Statesboro, Georgia. Jack told me how he learned diligence through early involvement in sports.

"When I was a ninth grader," Jack said, "I was invited to play on the high school baseball team. The team was 'coached' (to use the term loosely) by a teacher who 'drew the short straw' and didn't want the job. He 'coached' the team with as little effort as was humanly possible, and every player knew it. Since we were not going to learn anything about baseball from our coach, all we could do was try to learn from the more experienced players.

"The following year, our coach was replaced by a young assistant football coach who had little knowledge or interest in baseball. A few days after the start of baseball practice, a businessman in town heard of our plight and went to the high school principal. He offered to coach the baseball team on the condition that 'you keep that idiot football coach away from me.' The principal agreed, and the next day, Mr. S. E. 'Rip' Tutor came to our practice and started teaching us the game of baseball. We had him as our high school coach and American Legion team coach for the next three years.

"Born in Rockingham, North Carolina, in 1913, Rip Tutor was a hardworking man who operated his own textile mill at age twelve. He had wanted to play Major League Baseball, but a shoulder injury in an amateur boxing match put an end to that dream. He later became a talent scout for such MLB teams as the Baltimore Orioles, the Anaheim Angels, and the Atlanta Braves. He was still actively scouting for the Braves when he passed away in 2004 at age ninety-one—and our high school team had the amazing privilege of being coached by him!

"From the start of practice until dark, he'd talk to us about hard work, perseverance, and responsibility—not only in baseball but in our schoolwork and daily lives. A few of the guys, with typical teenage arrogance, ignored the wisdom Rip offered us, but most of us listened and improved our work habits. We were very successful at the high school level and in American Legion baseball, playing for the state championship twice.

"Rip Tutor had a huge impact on my character. He taught me that success in baseball is not a result of how hard you play the game, but how hard you work in practice to improve your skills. I learned from him that a pre-game pep talk is a waste of breath, but a pre-practice pep talk can produce real improvement in player performance.

"On road trips, I always sat near Rip so I wouldn't miss a word he said. He didn't talk about winning as much as he talked about the work you have to do to 'be in a position to win.' He talked about preparing yourself so you can take advantage of any situation that arises. He often said, 'In baseball, you win some, you lose some, and some get rained out—but you have to dress out for every game.' In other words, don't sit around and hope for a lucky break. Work hard, practice hard, and play every game to the best of your ability. Do that and you can hold your head up high no matter what the scoreboard says. It all comes down to diligence: those who work hard in practice tend to win more games than those who don't."

Jack Stallings was the same kind of motivating force in my life that Rip Tutor was in his. Jack learned his work ethic from a great and hardworking teacher—and I learned much of mine from Jack.

My writing partner, Jim Denney, once worked with the legendary Eagles and Packers defensive lineman Reggie White on his best-selling autobiography, *Reggie White: In the Trenches*. They called Reggie the "Minister of Defense" (due to his prowess as a defensive end and his outspoken Christian faith as an ordained minister). He was a menace to quarterbacks, recording 198 sacks, including nine consecutive years in the NFL with ten or more sacks per season.

Reggie died unexpectedly at age forty-three in 2004 due to a cardiac arrhythmia triggered by chronic lung disease, complicated by sleep apnea. During 2005, three teams Reggie played for retired his number 92 jersey—the University of Tennessee Volunteers, the Philadelphia Eagles, and the Green Bay Packers. Jim recalls the time he met Reggie at the NFL legend's Tennessee home in the spring of 1996.

"When I met Reggie," Jim told me, "I knew he was the most physically powerful human being I had ever met. He literally seemed indestructible. I couldn't have been more stunned the day after Christmas 2004 when I heard that Reggie White had died.

"Reggie showed me his private training room behind his Knoxville home. You'd walk past the Olympic-size indoor pool and arrive at a spacious, well-equipped workout room with a huge Stairmaster. Reggie set the Stairmaster to maximum resistance and put himself through a grueling workout. As he pumped the Stairmaster, I felt the concrete floor vibrate under my feet. I could imagine only two people in the world who could do a workout like that—and the other one wears a cape and a red S on his chest.

"Most people are only aware of how hard Reggie White worked on the football field. But I saw a side of Reggie that most people never saw. I saw him in the off-season, sweating and straining and preparing his body to play games still months away. Reggie had an unbelievable work ethic. He was totally committed to being the best at what he did.

"After his workout, we sat down and he talked about where his work ethic came from. 'During my junior year at the University of Tennessee,' he said, 'I got hurt a lot. I sprained my ankle in a game against Duke, then sprained another ankle against Alabama, then I got an elbow injury and a pinched nerve in my neck. I wanted to make All-American, I wanted to be the best, but I didn't have a good work ethic. I wasn't focused on conditioning and training. Football is a punishing game and my body couldn't take it because I hadn't spent enough time in the weight room.

"'My senior year, I did more weight-lifting and I built my speed and endurance with sprints and laps. As my work ethic improved, my game improved, and I wasn't injured as often.

"'Two months after I started playing NFL football in Philadelphia, I broke a rib. This was in 1985. It was around that time that I saw the Monday night game when [Washington Redskins quarterback] Joe Theismann was sacked by L. T. [New York Giants

linebacker Lawrence Taylor]. Joe's career was ended that night by a compound fracture—and he was in pretty good shape when he took that hit! Man, that really scared me. I thought, *Whoa, my career could be over in a whiff, just like Joe's!*

"'So I doubled up my workouts and made up my mind that I was going to work harder than anybody else and be in better shape than anybody else in the game. I'm sure that's how I've managed to avoid any career-busting injuries.'

"That's where Reggie's work ethic came from," Jim concluded. "That's why I saw him working out every day, even in the spring, when most NFL players are taking it easy and getting fat. Reggie worked hard, all year round. Another thing Reggie told me that day was that the Packers were going to the Super Bowl in January and they were going to win it. 'Make sure that's in the book,' he told me. 'The Packers are going to win it all.' Well, Reggie's prediction was in the book when it came out in October 1996, and on January 26, 1997, the Packers did in fact win Super Bowl XXXI, defeating the New England Patriots in the Louisiana Superdome—and Reggie collected a Super Bowl record three sacks in that game. That's the power of an intense work ethic."

How to Raise Diligent, Hardworking Kids

So how do we promote character traits of diligence and hard work in our kids? Several people I interviewed offered their ideas, experiences, and suggestions. Here's what I learned from them:

1. *Expose your kids to work at an early age.* Dr. Riley P. Green III, director of administration at Alabama Baptist Children's Homes and Family Ministries, told me, "My dad was my role model of character and hard work. As a circuit court judge for twenty-seven years, he went to work every day. For twenty of those years, he drove the same 1969 Plymouth Valiant, a car without air-conditioning. Many days, he and his court reporter would leave town and drive forty-five miles to the next county to conduct court. Dad worked hard and scrimped on his own comforts so my

sisters and I would have what we needed and could get a college education.

"The importance of diligence became real to me when I got a newspaper route at age fifteen. I had seventy-six households on my route. Dad told me it was important that I put the papers where the customers wanted them. At his suggestion, I went to each home, introduced myself, and asked, 'Where would you like your paper?' Most customers wanted it on the front porch, not at the end of the driveway.

"Most news carriers made it easy on themselves and tossed the papers on the driveway. It bothered me that I had to work harder and take more time to put the papers up on the porch—but I was obligated to fulfill my customers' requests.

"One day, I thought, *Why knock myself out? I'll just toss the papers on the driveway.* I did this for several days and received complaints—and I knew I'd made a big mistake. I learned a lesson in diligence and returned to my original commitment to honor my customers' wishes."

2. *Involve your kids in sports.* Dr. Al Mawhinney is formerly the academic dean at the Reformed Theological Seminary in Orlando. "Like many other teenage athletes," he told me, "I learned the value of hard work from my coaches on the football field, in the wrestling room, and on the track. Kids learn hard work through athletic competition. You can't achieve any goal in sports without hard work and preparation. The correlation between effort and progress is so obvious that kids readily grasp the lesson: the more laps you run in practice, the better your stamina and the faster your speed. Kids also see that the hardest-working athletes win praise from the coach. If you want to teach diligence, send your kids out for sports."

3. *Instill a mind-set of excellence.* Again, Dr. Al Mawhinney offers some insightful observations. "My father was an Irish immigrant with an eighth-grade education—and he was the wisest man I knew. He modeled upright character and hard work every

day while I was growing up. He usually worked more than one job to provide for his family.

"On Saturdays, I went with him to help him clean a church outside Philadelphia. In the front of the church were several white pillars, twenty feet tall. One afternoon, we were finishing up and I was tired and looking forward to going home. Dad said, 'We're not finished. Those pillars aren't clean.' They looked clean to me—but Dad got out the tall ladder and climbed up to wash the tops of the pillars.

"I thought my old man had lost his mind. As I steadied the ladder for him, I called up, 'No one will ever know you cleaned the top of those things!' He smiled down at me and said, 'I'll know. God will know. And now you'll know too.' I was too young to understand the wisdom in those words. But today I understand that hard work isn't just a means to making a living. Hard work is a virtue that pleases God. God worked hard for six days, and He created the universe— then He rested. We were created in God's image, and we were made to work hard and pay attention to excellence. Dad knew it, lived it, and taught it with his example, his smile, and his gentle words."

4. *Teach kids to do the job until it's done right.* Dr. Lisa D. Mc-Nary, assistant professor of management at the College of Business at Lamar University told me that, while growing up, she had a close relationship with her father.

"When I was about six years old," she said, "Dad assigned me the task of cleaning the kitchen sink. I whisked through my chore in practically no time at all, and was soon off having fun. When my dad saw me playing, he asked if I finished cleaning the sink. I said, 'I'm all done.' He said, 'Let's take a look at the sink.'

"We looked at the sink together and Dad showed me that I had not done a good job cleaning the area around the drain. He was calm and gentle, but he firmly established his expectation for how the job should be done. He pointed out in detail the dirty places and told me how he expected the sink to look when it was *really* clean. Then he left me to finish the job on my own.

"The sink-cleaning episode became a metaphor for my own personal work ethic. Never again did my dad have to ask me to do a job over. If I wasn't sure I understood all the specifics of an assignment, I asked for clarification at the outset—and then I did the job until it was done right."

5. *Encourage kids to write a personal mission statement.* Dr. McNary told me, "Businesses and charities have mission statements to define the kind of organization they aspire to be. People, too, should have a mission statement to define the kind of people they aspire to be. Such a statement can serve as a compass to help a person stay on-track through life.

"I learned this idea from my graduate studies mentor, W. Edwards Deming, the noted quality-management expert and author of *Out of the Crisis*. When he encouraged me to write a personal mission statement, I began with a long, flowing treatise. Dr. Deming read it then suggested I cut it down until it reflected what he called 'the essence of your being.' I cut it several times, and each time he'd say, 'It's still too long. Make it more concise.' I ended up with a simple statement that continues to be my personal mission statement today: 'Be kind; do my best; and seek joy in life.'"

6. *Give kids entrepreneurial opportunities.* Todd Shaw, president of On-Track Ministry, told me, "It's one thing to give kids chores. All kids should have chores to do around the house. In our household, we don't pay children to do household chores. I think paying kids to wash dishes or take out the trash sends the wrong message, since these are just household duties that need to be done as a part of family life.

"But we can also give kids special jobs and opportunities that resemble real-life careers. In those situations, kids should be rewarded so they will make that connection between hard work and earned rewards.

"When I was a boy on the farm, I was never paid for chores—and believe me, there were many chores to do! But my grandfather did pay me to work in the field to bring in the crops.

"One day, my grandfather took my education to the next level. He sat me down and said, 'Todd, I can pay you twenty dollars a day to work for me—or I can let you farm your own land.' Of course, if I farmed my own land, my income was not guaranteed, but would depend on a number of factors including my own hard work.

"I chose to farm my land. My grandfather gave me one acre and fronted the cost of the seed and labor until I brought in my first crop. After I sold my first crop, I'd pay him back. I'll never forget how proud I felt to pull the tractor onto the field at the beginning of the harvest. I was an elementary school kid overseeing grown men who were working for me. I made sure they did a thorough job. After the first harvest, my grandfather came up to me and said, 'Todd, there's no greater feeling than to do a job well.' He was right. It was a great feeling.

"The big day came when we took our crop to market and I got to see the fruit of my labor sold by the auctioneers. I cashed in the sale ticket and the lady at the teller window handed me a check for about three hundred dollars. I thought it was enough money to retire on!

"I took my grandfather out to lunch, feeling like a wealthy entrepreneur. Then he handed me a bill for the labor, seed, and fuel. Pop went my bubble! But my grandfather was teaching me that in the real world, you don't show a profit until you've deducted your expenses. I continued to plant that acre for years to come. I tithed to the Lord and bought my own school clothes, bicycles, and other things I needed. My parents and my grandfather taught me the value of hard work—and that the first portion always goes to God."

7. *Set high standards and expectations.* Todd Shaw told me, "As a chaplain in competitive sports, I often counsel young people. I always encourage them to expect more of themselves than they think they can do. I challenge them to invest an extra measure of effort in their jobs, then see if that extra effort doesn't pay dividends. Some examples of advice I offer:

"One: Arrive early. Don't try to clock in right on the dot. Ar-

rive ten minutes before you're scheduled to begin. I guarantee the boss will notice—and you'll stand out.

"Two: Always do more than is expected. Find things to do without being asked. Look for ways to improve your performance, bring more profit to the company, and make your boss's life a bit easier.

"Three: Always deliver more than you promise. Make sure your word is gold. Don't make excuses—build trust.

"Four: Give your employer a full day's work—and then some. Don't be a clock watcher. Be the last one out the door.

"This isn't just some grown-up giving advice. These are the rules I was taught by my father and grandfather, and they are the rules I've tried to live by throughout my life. The first job I applied for off the farm was at a taco restaurant. The owners put out a call for minimum-wage workers and got more people than they needed. They put everybody on a trial basis to see who would work out and who would wash out.

"I was nervous because I had no restaurant experience. Some of the other workers were lazy and sloppy. I heard some say, 'I've got more experience. They'll keep me on.' In the end, those people lost out. Sure, they had more experience—but they lacked a work ethic. Hardworking guys like me made the team, while the guys with more experience were cut.

"It may have been a minimum-wage job, but I worked at it as if I owned the place. As a result, I received steady raises—and every pay increase made me want to work even harder to make sure I earned it. The manager liked having a hard worker on his crew, and he rewarded me to keep me around. Years later, I opened my own restaurant—and I knew exactly the kind of employee to look for: young people who were just like I was—not people with padded resumés, but people with a good work ethic."

8. *Set a good example of diligence.* Dr. Chad McEvoy, assistant professor of sports management at Illinois State University, told me, "I learned the character quality of hard work from my mother. When I was in junior high school and my younger

brother in elementary school, my father left my mother for another woman. As Mom dealt with the painful emotions of being abandoned, she committed herself to shielding my brother and me from the effects of the divorce.

"Mom felt strongly that our education shouldn't be disrupted, not only because we attended excellent schools, but because we needed as much stability in our lives as possible. Her teaching salary alone couldn't cover our expenses, so she worked on her master's degree evenings and weekends so she could move higher up the pay scale. She took speed-reading classes, then earned extra income by teaching speed reading to others. My brother and I saw Mom working hard, studying hard, and always making time to fulfill both parenting roles for us.

"Whenever I feel overwhelmed with work commitments, I only need to remember my mother's example. No challenge I face is harder than what she did. As a college professor, I try to exemplify hard work to my students and motivate them to excellence. As a parent, I want to be the kind of inspiring role model to my kids my mother was for me."

Raising People of Character and Diligence

I spoke at a luncheon in Minneapolis a number of years ago. Afterward, a man came up to me and said, "May I give you a ride to the airport?" I agreed, and in the car he said, "I need to talk to you about my son. He's in the eighth grade and loves basketball."

"Well, that's great," I said. "Is there a problem?"

He said, "He wants to play basketball at the University of Minnesota. He wants to know *now* that he can get a scholarship."

I wasn't sure I'd heard him right. "Your son wants a guarantee now, while he's in the eighth grade, that a basketball scholarship will be waiting for him when he starts college?"

"Exactly," the man said. "You see, he doesn't want to do all of that work—all the practice and conditioning and so forth—only to find out he can't get the scholarship."

"Sir," I said, "let me explain how it works: College coaches do not offer eighth graders scholarships in the hope they will be motivated to make the team. The work comes first, then the scholarship—but only if he's good enough. There are no guarantees."

When I arrived home, I told that story to my seventeen-year-old daughter Karyn. Then I said, "Karyn, is this how your generation thinks?"

"Dad," she said, "I'm sorry to tell you this, but yes, many of them do."

How tragic! Diligent work is essential to success—and to good character. You can't build your own good character, nor coach and teach good character to others, without a willingness to work hard. Todd Shaw told me a parable that sums up this principle.

"There was once a farmer working hard in the fields with his sons," Todd said. "A neighboring farmer noticed how hard the man and his boys were laboring, and he stopped by the fence and said to the man, 'You know, you don't have to work your boys that hard just to raise a crop.'

"The hardworking farmer replied, 'I'm not trying to raise a crop. I'm trying to raise men.'"

So it is with you and me. We should not view work merely as a means to making a living. We are building lives and building character. Most of all, we are building a generation of young men and women who will carry on the character-building tradition long after we are gone.

We are working hard to construct a legacy that never dies.

5

Self-Control:
Secure Against Attack

"I count him braver who overcomes his desires than him who
conquers his enemies; for the hardest victory is over self."

ARISTOTLE
GREEK PHILOSOPHER

It's known as "The Drug Draft."

The 1986 NBA draft brimmed with talent, size, and the promise of brilliant pro basketball careers to come. Most of that promise went unfilled. Some of that wonderful promise literally and tragically died.

I'm talking about a young man named Len Bias. He was a six-foot-eight-inch, 210-pound All-American forward from the University of Maryland. During his college career, Len Bias was considered one of the most exciting and amazing players in the game. Many fans and commentators said he was potentially as great an NBA talent as Michael Jordan. Bias was the second pick overall, chosen by the Boston Celtics. Boston's head coach, Red Auerbach, saw Bias as the man who would continue the Celtics' dominance far into the 1990s.

But less than forty-eight hours after he was chosen in the draft, Len Bias lay dead in a dormitory room on the University of Maryland campus. After ingesting what were said to be large quantities of cocaine, he was sitting on a sofa, talking to one of his Maryland

teammates, when he experienced a massive seizure and a fatal cardiac arrhythmia.

The death of Len Bias led to a heightened awareness of drug abuse in college sports and demands for drug testing. The tragedy also impressed all of us who were involved in recruiting players to the NBA that we needed to be focused on a player's character as well as his ability. A lot of us in management became much more thorough in checking out a player to know whether or not he had the character trait of *self-control*.

At the time of the Len Bias tragedy, I was the outgoing general manager of the Philadelphia 76ers, preparing for the move to Orlando to begin building the Magic organization. I traded away our rights to the number one draft pick to Cleveland, so the 76ers didn't have much of a part to play in the first round of the '86 draft.

As it turned out, few of the highly touted first-round draftees in the talent-heavy class of '86 went on to basketball greatness. The number one pick, Brad Daugherty, was a major star for a few years, but his career with the Cleveland Cavaliers was cut short by injuries.

In fact, the careers of half of the top fourteen draft picks in '86 were shortened or adversely affected by substance abuse. All were talented players with exciting potential—and all of them squandered their chance at fame and fortune because of a lack of self-control.

Self-Control: A Matter of Life and Death

One of the most important character traits we need to build into our own lives and the lives of those we influence is self-control—the ability to master our pleasure-seeking impulses for sex, substances (tobacco, drugs, alcohol, food), and spending (including gambling). Those who are self-disciplined and self-controlled are not slaves to bad habits or rash impulses.

Dr. H. James Quigley Jr. is operations director for the Center

for Sustainable Energy at Bronx Community College in New York. He told me his father, the Reverend Harold J. Quigley, taught him the meaning of character and self-control.

"My father was a dedicated activist," he told me. "He risked his life for the sake of justice during those terrible years in the 1960s, when many civil rights leaders were being persecuted and murdered. He was often threatened because of his work on behalf of school integration, fair housing practices, and equal employment opportunities. I admired his courage.

"When I was eight or nine, I had a friend whose father drove a taxi cab. My friend, being loyal to his father, was antagonistic toward a competing taxi company—we'll call it 'Smith's Taxi.' Since I wanted to support my friend, I once called out, 'Smith's Taxi's no good!' as a 'Smith's' driver held the door for a passenger.

"I was standing on the front steps of our house at the time, and everyone knew that the house where I stood was the manse of Rev. Quigley, the Presbyterian minister. The owner of Smith's Taxi called my father and complained that I was defaming his business.

"My father called me in and told me this sort of behavior would not be permitted. He took me in the family car and we drove straight to the offices of Smith's Taxi. We went up to Mr. Smith and my dad made me apologize and promise not to do it again.

"I was humiliated—but I realized then and there that actions have consequences. I had acted impulsively, and my father taught me the need for self-control. From then on, I usually stopped to think about the consequences when I was tempted to do something that might cause harm or embarrassment later. It was a crucial early lesson in self-control."

Self-control is the ability to manage one's own behavior, resist impulses, and replace destructive habits with positive and healthy ones. The Scriptures tell us, "Like a city whose walls are broken down is a man who lacks self-control" (Prov. 25:28). In other

words, a person without self-control is defenseless and easily conquered by his impulses.

People who lack self-control often lack the ability to withstand feelings of sadness, sorrow, or anxiety, so they anesthetize their emotional pain with alcohol, drugs, food, sex, compulsive spending, or compulsive gambling. They turn to these substances or behaviors as a substitute for healthy ways of coping with stress and anxiety.

People with poor self-control are a danger to themselves and others. They take foolish chances, act impulsively, behave selfishly, drive carelessly, and make decisions based on feelings instead of reason and moral principles. They run red lights, gamble away paychecks, engage in promiscuous and unsafe sex, and have unwanted pregnancies. Self-control is not merely a matter of good character. It's also a matter of good health and good relationships. It may even be a matter of life and death.

The Traitor Within Us

On June 7, 1981, fourteen Israel jet fighters streaked away from Etzion Air Force base in the Negev Desert, flew over Jordan, crossed the northern tip of Saudi Arabia, and penetrated Iraq. There they bombed and destroyed a structure housing a French-built nuclear reactor.

Publicly, the United States criticized the attack. Privately, however, the U.S. thanked Israel for stopping Iraq from developing a nuclear weapons capability. Ten years later, after the successful conclusion of Operation Desert Storm (which liberated Kuwait from Iraqi occupation), then–Defense Secretary Richard Cheney presented a gift to the Israeli air force commander, General David Ivry. The gift was a satellite photo of the destroyed reactor site. Cheney inscribed the photo, "For General David Ivry, with thanks for the outstanding job he did on the Iraqi Nuclear Program in 1981, which made our job much easier in Desert Storm."

The secret Israeli plan that led to the destruction of the Iraqi re-

actor was called "Operation Sphinx." It was carried out by several teams of Israeli intelligence operatives from the Mossad, Israel's version of the CIA. How did Israeli intelligence officers learn the secret location of the Iraqi nuclear complex? They learned it from a man named Butrus Eben Halim—a man who lacked self-control.

Halim was an Iraqi physicist working with French scientists on the design of the Iraqi reactor. Mossad agents learned that Halim, who lived in Paris with his wife, was involved in an affair with a French prostitute. The Israeli agents used Halim's relationship with the prostitute to extract information from him. Iraqi dictator Saddam Hussein's dream of a nuclear-armed Iraq went up in smoke because of one man's lack of self-control.

Life is a battlefield. The forces of lust and temptation are at war with your soul and mine. In his book *Wild at Heart*, John Eldredge (founder of Ransomed Heart Ministries) observes that there is a traitor within each of us—a traitor much like the Iraqi physicist Halim. If we let our guard down, that traitor will yield to lust and temptation—and he will surrender the fortress of our souls to the enemy.

Eldredge writes, "Stand on what is true and do not let go. Period. The traitor within the castle will try to lower the drawbridge but don't let him. . . . As Thomas à Kempis says, 'Yet we must be watchful, especially in the beginning of the temptation; for the enemy is then more easily overcome, if he is not suffered to enter the door of our hearts, but is resisted without the gate at his first knock.' "[1]

In her intensely personal book *Stone Cold in a Warm Bed: One Couple's Battle with Pornography*, Kathryn Wilson writes, "Pornography creates a misguided representation of what the most important relationships in life are supposed to be like. For some, these unhealthy expressions of sexuality are a means of escape; for others they are a form of self-medication. . . . Pornography separates and isolates by destroying relationships. It puts distance between us and others, between us and God. It attacks the human

spirit through shame, sexual addictions and profound confusion as to what 'normal' sexuality really is. In the end, it destroys our capacity for intimacy."[2]

In the Bible, we see that even one of the greatest heroes of the Old Testament, King David, struggled with the same kind of temptation that surrounds us today—and when he yielded to temptation, the results were disgrace, humiliation, and even murder. King David's sin began with the temptation of voyeurism.

The account in 2 Samuel 11 tells us, "In the spring, at the time when kings go off to war, David . . . remained in Jerusalem. One evening David got up from his bed and walked around on the roof of the palace. From the roof he saw a woman bathing. The woman was very beautiful (11:1–2)." David was not where he should have been, doing what a king was supposed to do. That's how many of us place ourselves in a position to compromise our character: we have too much time on our hands, and we put ourselves in the wrong place at the wrong time, doing what we know is the wrong thing to do.

David didn't have cable TV or the Internet—but he was still able to view what he knew he shouldn't. He went up on the roof of his palace and watched a woman bathing below. Perhaps he told himself, *Why not look? All guys look. What harm can it do?* But David's first act of compromising his self-control was only the first step down a slippery slope.

After watching the woman bathe, he couldn't stop thinking about her. He went from looking to lusting, then from lusting to possessing. He sent messengers out to bring the woman to the palace—and there he had sex with her. The woman, Bathsheba, was married to Uriah, one of King David's loyal warriors—and Uriah was out on the battlefield, where David should have been. Later, when Bathsheba became pregnant, David had to cover up his sin—and to do so, he had Uriah killed.

King David's "harmless" voyeurism led him step by step to adultery and murder. Once we compromise our self-control, we

never know where we will end up. A little crack in your character may be all it takes to destroy your life, your reputation, and your family.

God loved David too much to allow him to remain unrepentant in his sin, so He sent the prophet Nathan to David to confront him with his guilt. When David's sin was exposed, he repented and God forgave him—but the natural consequences of David's sin haunted him for the rest of his days. David paid a terrible price for his lack of self-control.

Sexual temptation is all around us. It pervades the culture we live in, and it saturates our human nature. Even if we could remove ourselves from our sex-drenched culture and go hide in a desert cave, we couldn't remove the tendency to sin from our hearts. As Jesus said, "For out of the heart come evil thoughts, murder, adultery, sexual immorality, theft, false testimony, slander. These are what make a man 'unclean'" (Matt. 15:19–20).

How, then, do we become people of character and self-control in a world where anything goes?

A Strategy for Self-Control

Character must be absolute. Any tiny gap in the armor of our character could bring about our total destruction. Here, then, is a strategy for maintaining the character trait of sexual self-control in times of temptation:

1. Remind yourself that there is always a price to pay for sexual sin. You may try to convince yourself that a little lust, a little voyeurism, a little "Internet sex" is a "victimless sin." You may say, "It's not as if I'm actually cheating on my spouse." Oh, really? Would your spouse agree? Sexual sin harms our most important human relationships. It can cost you your reputation, the trust and respect of your family, and your self-respect.

Sexual sin also hinders your prayer life and harms your relationship with God. Paul, in Romans 14:12, warns, "So then, each of us will give an account of himself to God." If you had to look

God in the eye and give an accounting for your life right now, what would you say?

2. *Rely on God's power through prayer.* In his book *Experiencing Spiritual Breakthroughs*, Dr. Bruce Wilkinson observes that temptation is always strongest when experiencing emotional stress. He discovered that a simple prayer to "The Comforter," the Holy Spirit, was a powerful way to break the grip of temptation on his soul. He calls this prayer "The Three-Minute Temptation Buster." There is nothing magical about this particular arrangement of sentences, but if you make this appeal to God's Spirit from a sincere heart, He will answer your prayer: "Dear Holy Spirit, You've been sent to me to be my personal Comforter. I am in desperate need of comfort. I don't want to sin. Please comfort me. In Jesus' name, Amen."

Dr. Wilkinson says that the first time he prayed that prayer in a time of stress and temptation, he checked his watch to see how long it would take for God's answer to come. "Slowly," he writes, "I became aware of something—I was comforted. My soul felt soothed and no longer in pain. When I turned back toward that temptation, I discovered it had miraculously slithered into the darkness, far away from my senses. I was free." He adds he has prayed that same prayer every time he is tempted and has always found that the Holy Spirit removed the temptation in three minutes or less.[3]

3. *Make a commitment to yourself, to God, and to a trusted person who will hold you accountable.* Commit yourself to sexual purity, fidelity, and self-control. You may want to write this commitment down and sign it. A written commitment won't immunize you against the attacks of temptation, but it may strengthen your resolve.

Christian author, counselor, and radio host Dr. James Dobson recalls how his own commitment to his wife, Shirley, helped strengthen his self-control during a crucial time of stress and conflict in his life:

Shirley and I had been married just a few years when we had a minor fuss. It was no big deal, but we both were pretty agitated at the time. I got in the car and drove around for about an hour to cool off. Then when I was on the way home, a very attractive girl drove up beside me in her car and smiled. She was obviously flirting with me. Then she slowed down, looked back, and turned onto a side street. I knew she was inviting me to follow her.

I didn't take the bait. I just went home and made up with Shirley. But I thought later about how vicious Satan had been to take advantage of the momentary conflict between us. . . . That is typical of his strategy. He'll lay a trap for you, too, and it'll probably come at a time of vulnerability.[4]

4. Remove all sources of temptation from your life. Most of us think we can coexist with temptation, and even flirt with it. But the Scriptures tell us to *flee* temptation. The apostle Paul wrote to his "spiritual son" Timothy, "Now flee from youthful lusts and pursue righteousness" (2 Tim. 2:22 NASB). Paul also wrote to the Christians in Corinth, "Flee from sexual immorality. All other sins a man commits are outside his body, but he who sins sexually sins against his own body" (1 Cor. 6:18).

Now, when Paul wrote to the Christians in Corinth, he was writing to people living in a pagan city where male and female prostitution was approved of as a sacrament of worship at the great temple to the goddess Aphrodite. Sexual immorality was rampant all around the church in Corinth, so the culture there was not unlike the culture you and I live in. Paul's message to those Christians—and to you and me—is *flee temptation.*

What does that mean in practical terms for you and me in this high-tech, one-click Internet age? It means we should do whatever it takes to guard our character. If we need to pull the plug on the

cable TV, we should do it. If we need to yank out the Internet, we should do it. These gadgets are not necessities—they're toys and conveniences. If they are tempting you to compromise your character, they might even destroy your life and soul. If you can't handle the temptation, get rid of them.

Jesus Himself put it this way: "And if your eye causes you to sin, pluck it out. It is better for you to enter the kingdom of God with one eye than to have two eyes and be thrown into hell" (Mark 9:47). Obviously, Jesus was using an extreme metaphor to make an important point for your life and mine: remove the things from your life that cause you to sin. You don't have to gouge out your eye to keep from sinning. All you have to do is pull a cable out of the wall! If that's what it takes to keep you from sinning, then do it. Turn off the TV and the computer, and spend more time building healthy relationships with family, friends, and God.

5. *Cleanse your mind and soul with Scripture.* The psalmist writes, "I have hidden your word in my heart that I might not sin against you" (Ps. 119:11). Here are some passages of Scripture on which you can meditate to strengthen your character against the attacks of sexual temptation:

- "I will set before my eyes no vile thing." (Ps. 101:3a)
- "You have heard that it was said, 'Do not commit adultery.' But I tell you that anyone who looks at a woman lustfully has already committed adultery with her in his heart." (Matt. 5:27–28)
- "The eye is the lamp of the body. If your eyes are good, your whole body will be full of light. But if your eyes are bad, your whole body will be full of darkness. If then the light within you is darkness, how great is that darkness!" (Matt. 6:22–23)
- "Therefore do not let sin reign in your mortal body so that you obey its evil desires. Do not offer the parts of your body to sin, as instruments of wickedness, but rather offer yourselves to God, as those who have been brought from death to life; and offer the parts of your body to him as instruments of righteousness. For sin shall not

be your master, because you are not under law, but under grace."
(Rom. 6:12-14)

- "Finally, brothers, whatever is true, whatever is noble, whatever is right, whatever is pure, whatever is lovely, whatever is admirable—if anything is excellent or praiseworthy—think about such things." (Phil. 4:8)
- "When tempted, no one should say, 'God is tempting me.' For God cannot be tempted by evil, nor does he tempt anyone; but each one is tempted when, by his own evil desire, he is dragged away and enticed. Then, after desire has conceived, it gives birth to sin; and sin, when it is full-grown, gives birth to death." (James 1:13-15)

6. *Be accountable to a few trusted people for your lifestyle of self-control.* Seek out a fellowship and Bible study group in your church so you can meet weekly to share your struggles, support each other, and hold each other accountable in an atmosphere of confidence and trust. If your church doesn't offer such a group, consider starting one with a few other friends. Ideally, your accountability group should be built on a foundation of covenants you agree upon together. Here are some suggested covenants:

A covenant of your time: You all agree to make it your number one priority to meet regularly at a set day and time.

A covenant of your honesty: You agree to speak the truth to each other, to answer honestly when you are asked about your own life, and to give your honest response to what others in the group share.

A covenant of confidentiality: Nothing said in the group shall ever be shared outside the group. This covenant is necessary to trust.

A covenant of prayer: You promise to support one another daily in prayer. When people in the group share their prayer requests, you agree to pray for those requests every day.

A covenant of mutual accountability: You mutually agree to allow others to ask you tough, realistic questions about your character and your behavior. Some of those questions may include:

- How are you doing in your walk with God and your prayer life?
- Are you experiencing any problem areas of sin, lust, or temptation?
- What spiritual battles are you fighting right now? Are you winning or losing the battle?
- How is your marriage? Would your spouse agree with your answer?
- How is your relationship with your children?
- Are you moving forward in your spiritual growth and character growth? Moving backward? Just coasting?
- Is there anything going on in your life that makes you feel angry? Defeated? Discouraged?
- Is there anything in your life that makes you feel inadequate and overwhelmed?
- Is there anyone in your life you hate or resent? Someone you need to forgive? What's holding you back from forgiveness?
- What would you like us to hold you accountable for this week? How can we best pray for you this week? What one or two things would you like us to check in with you about next week?

When you talk about your own struggles with temptation, you don't have to go into lurid detail, but be honest. Ask someone in the group to check in with you every so often during the week to see how you are doing with your commitment. Behavior observed is behavior changed. So let others into your life to observe your behavior—and I guarantee you will see growth in your character and your self-control.

Raising Self-Controlled Kids in an Out-of-Control World

Young minds today have been heavily infected by the culture of this post-Christian, postmodern world. When you talk to them about such values as character and self-control, they look at you without comprehension. Their views on morality have been strongly influenced by the media culture and their non-Christian peers and teachers. Today's postmodern youth question whether

such things as objective truth or moral absolutes even exist. They commonly believe it's perfectly valid to make up your own God and your own morality.

Many young people today make an arbitrary distinction between sexual intercourse and "outercourse," such as mutual masturbation and oral sex. They are being misled (often by sex-education classes at school) into thinking that "outercourse" is "safer sex." Our kids are often only warned to protect themselves against HIV, the virus that causes AIDS—yet they are given little or no information about the most common sexually transmitted virus, the human papilloma virus (HPV).

The Centers for Disease Control (CDC) estimates that twenty million people were infected by HPV in 2005. The disease is easily transmitted by any genital contact, even if no intercourse takes place, and there is no cure. Condoms provide little or no protection. The only way to avoid HPV is to avoid sexual activity, period. The number of Americans infected by HPV in the United States every year is estimated to be between 2.5 and 6 million, 74 percent of whom are between the ages of fifteen and twenty-four. The disease can cause cancer in both men and women. (Genital HPV Infection—CDC Fact Sheet, Department of Health and Human Services, Centers for Disease Control and Prevention, retrieved at http://www.cdc.gov/std/HPV/STDFact-HPV.htm)

In her book *Sex Has a Price Tag*, Pam Stenzel writes about speaking to an audience of middle schoolers in Ohio. "After the assembly," she says, "a sixth-grade girl went to the school counselor's office and reported that she'd been taking money to perform oral sex on high school boys on the bus. . . . I met with the counselor, the girl, and her mother. I encouraged the mom to take her daughter to a doctor and have her tested. The mother's response was, 'It was only oral sex, she'll be fine.' I carefully explained the dangers and possible consequences of what had been taking place. The mother wasn't convinced. Three weeks later, I got a call. The mother had finally taken the daughter in to get

tested. The girl tested positive for both herpes and gonorrhea of the throat."[5]

Clearly, we have a big responsibility as parents to protect our kids from these threats—and the way to protect them is not by passing out condoms, but by helping them build souls of steel—armor-clad character that is self-controlled and temptation-resistant. That means we have to give them the facts about sexual activity—and the fact is, the only truly "safe sex" is monogamous, committed sex within marriage.

We need to armor-plate their souls by teaching them to resist the many temptations posed by our sex-drenched, porn-glutted society. We need to know what our kids are doing on the family computer. All computers should be out in a high-traffic, visible, open family area, where online activity can't be hidden. We need to check our kids' Web pages on such sites as LiveJournal, Xanga, or MySpace. We need to know who they're talking to in chat rooms or on instant-messaging services like AIM and ICQ, where they are often subjected to obscene language, hate speech, X-rated images, sexual flirting, and more.

Are you checking your kid's Internet use? And no, I'm not talking about a filtering program (there's no such thing as a kid-proof filter!). I'm telling you that you should *spy* on your kid and know *exactly* what he or she is doing on that Pentium-powered one-eyed monster. Put a monitoring program on the computer that enables you to view exactly what your child sees, reads, and sends out over the Web.

You may say, "I can't invade my child's privacy!" I say, "What privacy?" Your children aren't entitled to privacy on the computer you bought, or on the Internet connection you pay for. Their minds, hearts, and souls are at stake, and *you* are responsible for what your kid gets into online—so you have a responsibility to know what's going on.

Seven Steps to Building Your Child's Self-Control

Dannah Gresh is a speaker and author of the bestselling book *And the Bride Wore White* (Moody Publishers, 2004). She tells the story of how she was driving her minivan one day with her baby strapped into the car-seat behind her. The radio was on and she was listening to Dr. James Dobson's *Focus on the Family* broadcast. The subject of the show: How to talk to your children about sex. Dr. Dobson asked his guest, "What's the most common question a young girl will ask her mother about sex?"

The guest said, "She'll ask, 'Mom, did you wait?'"

Dannah Gresh pulled her car to the side of the road and wept. For ten years, she had repressed a time in her teenage life she had regretted since. "My heart's desire was, is, and always will be to live a lifestyle of purity," she later recalled, "but in high school I detoured from that pursuit long enough to get tangled up by lust." She knew if her daughter asked if she waited, her honest answer would be no.

That evening, she went home and, in a three-hour conversation, confessed to her husband what she had never told any other person. After she finished, she wished she had done so sooner. She felt her husband Bob's embrace and God's forgiveness—and that moment was the beginning of a new ministry in her life.

A few weeks later, she spoke to a dozen teenage girls from her church on the subject of moral purity. Within a couple of years, she wrote her first book, *And the Bride Wore White: Seven Secrets to Sexual Purity*, and was speaking to groups of teenage girls all across the state. Today, Dannah Gresh speaks at Pure Freedom Events for teen girls, mother-daughter events, conferences, and churches around the country.

Her goal is to give teenage girls the insights and awareness they need to live virtuous, self-controlled lives. Dannah Gresh believes many girls who get morally off-track actually *want* to live a lifestyle of purity. "The problem when I was a teen," she recalls, "was

not that I did not want to live a life of purity. It's just that no one was telling me *how* to do that."[6]

The Scriptures set a standard of absolute sexual purity for God's people: "But among you there must not be even a hint of sexual immorality, or of any kind of impurity, or of greed, because these are improper for God's holy people" (Eph. 5:3). But how do we encourage our kids to develop the kind of character that will enable them to live pure, self-controlled lives when they are surrounded on every side by a polluted, out-of-control culture? Here are some suggestions for armor-plating the character of our kids in these morally dangerous times:

1. *Teach the truth about abstinence.* This means we should teach kids to abstain from sexual activity—and we should teach abstinence in positive terms. The abstinence message is not (as many opponents of moral education claim) "just say no to sex." Abstinence is about waiting until sex is the right and healthy decision.

Few of those who criticize abstinence education would say we should let children eat sweets and fried foods whenever they feel the urge—yet they believe kids should be free to satisfy their sexual urges as long as they use "safer" sex practices (the word "safer" has come into vogue because there simply are no truly "safe" ways to have promiscuous sex). Just as there are health benefits from abstaining from unhealthy foods and gluttonous behavior, there are health benefits that result when we abstain from unhealthy and immoral sexual expression.

So we shouldn't merely tell kids, "Don't have sex." We should tell them how wonderful sex is when it is saved for marriage, where it is not only safe but emotionally and spiritually fulfilling. According to a comprehensive review of research conducted by David Popenoe and Barbara Dafoe Whitehead of The National Marriage Project, married couples report a higher degree of sexual satisfaction than unmarried people. It stands to reason. In marriage, you experience sex as God intended it to be expressed, with-

out guilt, awkwardness, and worries about sexually transmitted disease.

2. *Teach girls to dress modestly.* Immodest dress tends to go hand-in-hand with lack of sexual self-control. According to the Medical Institute for Sexual Health, girls are more at risk for early sexual activity when they appear older than their true age. Today, very young girls are encouraged to wear makeup and revealing clothing that makes them look older—and blatantly sexual. Through TV shows, movies, magazines, music videos, and peer pressure, these girls are being repeatedly told they need to look "sexy" and "hot."

Vicki Courtney, author of *Teenvirtue* and *Your Girl: Raising a Godly Daughter in an Ungodly World*, observes, "There is a tremendous pressure that the culture puts onto girls to grow up way too fast. It cultivates their sensuality to attract guys—whether it's through the things they wear, or through their behavior. The outfits they wear just scream for attention."[7]

Bare midriffs, belly rings, low-rider jeans, short skirts, spaghetti straps, short-cropped tops, and other style statements are designed to draw attention to the erogenous regions of a girl's body. Girls are made to feel unattractive if they don't display a "pretty hot and tempting" body image. Some of those girls may compensate for feelings of inadequacy by developing an eating disorder, such as anorexia or bulimia. Other girls may compensate for poor self-esteem by becoming sexually active. They achieve a false sense of validation when boys are sexually drawn to them.

As parents, we need to help our teens understand that modesty in attire is a positive choice—a character choice. Girls can dress fashionably and stylishly without sacrificing modesty.

3. *Teach boys to flee temptation.* Self-control is a boy's issue as well as a girl's issue. Our sons need to understand they are responsible for their own character, self-control, and moral purity—even if girls send out a tempting visual message.

This is an increasingly difficult issue for boys today. Even at

church on Sunday mornings, all too many girls dress in ways that create major lust temptation for teenage boys. We need to help our sons understand that while it is not a sin to be tempted by a girl's immodest dress, he does need to resist that temptation. Don't let your sons feel they are alone with that struggle. Tell them it's normal for his eyes to be attracted to a beautiful girl, and there is no shame in that.

But at the same time, they need to commit themselves to a lifestyle of self-control and purity. If a young man's thoughts become fixed on the girl's body and he lets his mind wander toward sexual fantasies, he's crossed the line from temptation to lust. He needs to make the same commitment Job made: "I made a covenant with my eyes not to look lustfully at a girl" (Job 31:1).

Suggest to your son that, when he is with a girl, he should focus his attention on her face, her eyes, her voice, her personality, her ideas and interests—not her body. Also, suggest that if he feels tempted toward lust that he pray for the girl he's thinking about; it's hard to have sinful thoughts about a person while praying.

4. Teach boys and girls about the power of visual temptation. Males are visually wired for sexual arousal. Girls often don't realize the message their immodest attire sends out to boys. They think they are being stylish and "cool," and they are often not even aware of the physical cravings they may be triggering in the young male minds around them. When a boy sees an attractive girl, he's going to have an automatic, involuntary response. True, he's responsible to maintain self-control, even when he's visually tempted—but girls also need to be aware of the effect a glimpse of thigh, midriff, or cleavage can have on a normal, healthy male adolescent.

If a girl wants to be known for her character, she should not dress to emphasize her erogenous zones. If a boy wants to be known for his character, he should keep his eyes and thoughts under control.

5. Keep the lines of communication open. The best sex educa-

tion is character education, and it begins at an early age. When talking to your kids about character, self-control, and sex, engage them in a dialogue—don't just lecture. Do as much listening as talking, and find out what they are thinking, hearing, and learning about their own sexuality from various sources, including the media and their peers. Your kids will be much more likely to open up and talk to you if they know you really listen.

Talk about your own struggles at their age. You don't have to share all the gory details or disclose anything that would diminish your child's respect for you. You need only say enough to show you understand, and that your child isn't alone in the struggle to live a self-controlled life.

6. *Pray.* Some people use prayer as a last resort after all else has failed: "Well, I guess there's nothing to do now but pray." I urge you to make prayer your *first* resort. Pray daily for wisdom in parenting your kids. Pray that your children seek God and build godly character in their lives. As you pray for your kids, I believe you'll be surprised at how often God will change your kids' attitudes and behavior by the power of prayer alone, without you having to do or say a thing.

Under Control or Out of Control?

We've talked about the character quality of self-control primarily in regard to drugs and sex. These same principles, however, apply to all areas of our lives and the lives of our kids. The character trait of self-control is crucial to living a balanced, healthy, and morally pure life so we do not become slaves to unhealthy habits or unhealthy impulses.

The Scriptures tell us, "Do not join those who drink too much wine or gorge themselves on meat, for drunkards and gluttons become poor, and drowsiness clothes them in rags" (Prov. 23:20–21). A self-controlled person does not overindulge in alcohol or food, but lives a lifestyle of moderation. He is not controlled by his lusts and appetites, but maintains control over himself.

In the Scriptures, we also learn about another form of self-control. Paul writes, "But godliness with contentment is great gain. . . . If we have food and clothing, we will be content with that. People who want to get rich fall into temptation and a trap and into many foolish and harmful desires that plunge men into ruin and destruction. For the love of money is a root of all kinds of evil" (1 Tim. 6:6, 8–10).

The love of money takes many forms. Some people are "shopaholics." They spend money and acquire things as a way of anesthetizing their emotional pain or calming their anxiety. The shopping mall does for them what a bottle of gin does for an alcoholic or what a one-night stand does for a sex addict. Some even go on shopping binges, swiping their credit cards to the melting point in order to forget their mounting debts! They are out of control.

For others, the love of money takes the form of a gambling addiction. Some are compulsive players of the state-run lottery. Others go to Nevada, Atlantic City, or Native American casinos. Still others gamble at home over the Internet. Therapists who treat addictions say a gambling addiction is very much like drug addiction or alcoholism. Gambling addicts find they can't control their compulsions. They are in denial about the severity of their addiction. They are constantly chasing a "high" (in the form of a big win) and preoccupied with their addictive behavior. They gamble to escape their pain, shame, and low self-esteem.

There are often deep psychological issues associated with a lack of self-control. To say that a person with an addiction "lacks good character" may be a gross oversimplification of that person's issues. Yes, engaging in habitual or impulsive substance abuse, sexual immorality, gluttony, and overspending is a character issue—but it's usually a symptom of deeper issues, many of which may be rooted in childhood pain or shame.

That is our challenge as people of character. Paul repeatedly told his friend Titus to teach self-control—and set an example of self-control: "Teach the older men to be temperate, worthy of

respect, self-controlled. . . . Teach the older women . . . [and] the younger women . . . to be self-controlled and pure. . . . Similarly encourage the young men to be self-controlled. In everything set them an example by doing what is good" (Titus 2:2–7).

And the apostle Peter makes the same appeal: "Therefore, prepare your minds for action; be self-controlled" (1 Pet. 1:13). Those who are controlled by habits, impulses, and lusts leave themselves wide open to the enemy. Those who live self-controlled lives are secure against attack.

John Fox, head coach of the NFL's Carolina Panthers, tells his players that "it's hard to succeed in this league without having a passion for it. It's not about fame, it's about the kind of man you are. It means having discipline in all facets of your life. If something is not right in one area of your life, it carries over to other areas. Some people claim they can hide a problem, but it eventually impacts their work.

"I tell my players that this is a very short-lived career. It's four for forty: What you do the next four years determines what you do for the next forty. If you really attack these four years and invest and commit to them, you'll be rewarded for the next forty years. It's a simple lesson to comprehend: You're going to get out of it what you put into it. It's more than simply having the talent. You must have the *discipline*."

Is your life under control—or out of control? What kind of legacy of character and self-control are you leaving to your kids?

PART III

Character Is How We Respond to Adversity

6

Courage: Doing the Thing You Fear

"Courage is contagious. When a brave man takes a stand, the spines of others are stiffened."

BILLY GRAHAM
EVANGELIST

Robin Gerber is a noted speaker and author of *Leadership the Eleanor Roosevelt Way*. She told me, "I grew up in Skokie, Illinois, in the 1960s. There, in that working-class suburb on the northwest border of Chicago, my parents joined a community with many other Jewish families. My mother had a monthly card party in the evening with her women friends.

"One of these ladies was Sylvia Melamed, a quiet woman with kind eyes. She was distinguished from the other mothers by her accent. One of her two sons was my age, and sometimes I went across the street to their gray brick house where Sylvia always seemed to be sewing and baking. She made extra money repairing other people's clothes.

"Most of the time I was banished to my room during my mother's gatherings. The house was small, and the women didn't want children listening in on their conversations. But occasionally I would be called in to listen to a story told by Sylvia Melamed. She would pull up her sleeve and show us the numbers on her arm. Then she'd talk about the family she once had—a husband, children, parents, all killed by the Nazis.

"Sylvia had survived the worst of concentration camps because she was a skillful seamstress. She sewed gloves and hats for the German troops. She met her husband in the camp, and together they built a new life and family in America.

"At a time when I was just becoming aware of the adult world, these stories moved me. What did it take for this woman, who seemed so fragile and gentle, to survive such horror? How had she remade her life after such grief? I realized the answer lay in her character, in the faith it takes to cling to hope when all is hopeless; in the courage it takes to overcome the deepest sorrow and build joy."

In these perilous times, who would deny we need people who will battle injustice, endure threats and opposition, and take a lonely stand for truth? Today, more than ever before, we need people of courage like Sylvia Melamed. We need more souls of steel.

Courage Is Founded on Character

What is courage?

Courage is not fearlessness. Courageous people know fear, yet they do the thing they fear because it's the right thing to do. The character trait of courage involves a willingness to take risks, endure pain, suffer setbacks, and struggle against obstacles in the pursuit of a worthwhile goal.

Again and again, the Scriptures call us to be courageous. God told Israel through Moses, "Be strong and courageous. Do not be afraid or terrified because of them, for the LORD your God goes with you; he will never leave you nor forsake you" (Deut. 31:6). And three times in Joshua 1, God commanded Joshua, "Be strong and courageous."

Jesus told His disciples, "In the world you have tribulation, but take courage; I have overcome the world" (John 16:33 NASB). And Paul told the Christians in Corinth, "Be on your guard; stand firm in the faith; be men of courage; be strong" (1 Cor. 16:13).

John N. Howell is associate head basketball coach at Oviedo

High School, a public school in Seminole County, Florida. He told me about the courage of one of his players.

"Matt Stilwell is a star shooter for our varsity team," Coach Howell told me. "Two years ago, when he was on the JV team, we were at the University of Florida Team Camp, playing Gainesville High. One of their players got under Matt as he was driving to the basket. Matt went down, and as soon as he landed, he looked at me. When I got to him, I saw that his arm was broken. When we got Matt to the hospital, the doctor told us Matt had broken both bones in his forearm and they couldn't be set without surgery. That procedure would keep Matt out of action for up to six months.

"It was a crushing blow for Matt, because he lived to play. He asked to stay with the team through the rest of the weekend, so he spent the next day cheering from the bench with his arm in a temporary cast. You could see the pain on his face, but he never complained.

"Later, Matt was examined at Jewett Orthopaedic Clinic in Orlando, and the doctor said the arm could be set without surgery, using a new procedure that would cut the recovery time in half. Matt agreed. So they set the arm. While Matt was healing, he attended every camp, every weight room session. He worked on ball handling and form shooting. Even with his arm in the cast, he ran up and down the floor to stay in shape.

"He returned to *the game* on time and in great physical shape. He was our leading scorer and rebounder from the shooting guard position—and a great leader by example. His demonstration of courage through pain inspired everyone on the team to play harder even when playing hurt.

"Two years after breaking his arm, Matt was playing in a big district showdown game when he was undercut again and landed on the same arm. I dashed out onto the floor and could see he was in a lot of pain. He thought he had broken it again, and he asked me, 'Why, Coach?'

"After the trainers checked him out, however, they had good

news: it was only a sprain. They iced Matt's arm and said he could play if he felt up to it. He went back in the game, playing hurt, and got two huge rebounds, playing primarily with one arm. Having Matt in the game enabled us to pull out the win—not only because of the way he played but because of the way his courage fired up the team. Matt has the kind of character and courage I would love to instill in every one of our players."

Another coach at Oviedo High School, head wrestling coach Tom Coffman, is a retired U.S. Army lieutenant colonel with nearly twenty-two years of service, including combat time as a company commander during Operation Desert Shield and Operation Desert Storm. "In the army," he told me, "character matters most. We send young soldiers into harm's way on our word, so our word had better be backed by character. A soldier's courage and confidence in the field is based in large part on his trust in the integrity of his leaders.

"As a company commander in Desert Shield and Desert Storm, I was in charge of leading 120 soldiers. I was trained in the army ethos which gives us a foundation of knowing the right thing to do in every situation. I knew that if I filtered every decision through that standard, my character would never come into question.

"Shortly before we were deployed to the Middle East, a couple of soldiers came to me in private. They told me they were scared. Well, that's a natural reaction to the situation they were in. That's what you'd expect from a kid just out of high school, getting ready to deploy to the far side of the world and take on unknown risks to defend our great nation. We didn't know what dangers the enemy had waiting for us, and there was no timetable for our return. I was twenty-nine years old myself, just seven years into my military career, and this would be my first time in a combat situation.

"When those two soldiers came to me with their apprehensions, I looked them in the eye and told them I was scared too. But I told them we had trained better and harder than any unit, and I was confident we'd be okay. They bought in to what I told

them and they left feeling better. Why? Because they trusted my character, the character of our unit leaders, the character of our training. They knew that our esprit-de-corps was built on character. Because they trusted the character of their leaders, those young men left with a big boost in their courage and confidence.

"We moved out and spent seven months in the desert during that conflict—and we brought home every solder we deployed with. The character of our leaders and the courage of our soldiers enabled me to lead 120 soldiers into harm's way and bring them home safely."

The Courage of Our Convictions

One of the most important forms of courage we need today is the courage to speak up and confront difficult issues. Silence, they say, is golden—but sometimes silence is cowardly. We can't consider ourselves people of character if we don't have the courage of our convictions. When the truth must be said, we need the courage to say it.

Christina Storm is the founder of an organization called Lawyers Without Borders, a group of volunteer lawyers who provide pro bono legal service to worthy projects and causes around the world. In January 2000, she and her husband were operating a small Hartford, Connecticut, law firm when she suddenly had a vision for using the Internet to create a global network of attorneys who could be mobilized to provide legal assistance for defendants, serve the needs of nonprofit organizations, help with conflict resolution, provide neutral observers for closed trials, and so forth.

She recalls, "I said to myself, 'This is not what I intended to do with my life. I meant to do international law.'" The moment the idea formed in her mind, she took out a credit card and registered the Internet domain name that popped into her mind: www.law yerswithoutborders.org. Then she got on the phone and started building her lawyer-to-lawyer network. Today, LWOB has a membership of over eight hundred lawyers, a headquarters in Hartford, and a good working relationship with the United Nations.

Christina has even placed herself on the front lines of the action.

For example, while working in East Jerusalem, she was detained at gunpoint during a Palestinian Intifada uprising—something that never happened to her while she was in private practice in Hartford.

I asked Christina Storm when she first realized that character matters. She said, "When I had children and realized their behavior was a reflection of my character, I knew that this was an issue I had to take seriously. Of course, I was taught the importance of character throughout my early years. I remember my grandmother telling me again and again, point blank, 'Your character is all that matters.'

"To be a person of character, you have to take a stand for your ideas. In order to do anything worthwhile, you have to defy the naysayers. When I began to promote Lawyers Without Borders to my colleagues in the legal profession, a prominent attorney told me my idea would never work. He was a professor of international law, and some people would have been discouraged to hear an 'expert' pronounce their idea unworkable.

"But my instincts told me it was a much-needed idea that could do a lot of good in the world. I followed my instincts, believed in my own ability and judgment, and remembered my grandmother's mantra, which has always been a source of inspiration and courage: 'Never say never!' Lawyers Without Borders helps people and organizations around the world today because I listened to my grandmother instead of the 'expert.'"

Thomas M. Doran, a professional engineer and partner with Hubbell, Roth & Clark, Inc., told me that character and the courage to speak up are sometimes found in people you might not expect. "My brother-in-law, Danny," he said, "has Down syndrome, a genetic disorder associated with impaired cognitive ability. I first met Danny thirty years ago when my wife and I first began dating.

"There was a time when one of my in-laws' neighbors was thought to be physically abusing his wife. Because this man was otherwise friendly and popular in the neighborhood, no one said anything to him about it. No one would speak up. Once, when this man came to the house for a visit, Danny approached him

and without any hesitation said, 'You shouldn't hit your wife. It's wrong. Don't do that anymore.'

"Everyone in the room was stunned—especially the offender, who reacted with contrition rather than belligerence. Some might say that Danny, with his condition, didn't know what he was doing. But I've known him for thirty years, and I'm certain that he was more aware of what he was doing—and what needed to be done—than the rest of us. By courageously saying what needed to be said, he modeled character that humbled the rest of us."

Never Too Young to Be Brave

You never know how young a child may be when called upon to demonstrate courage. Executive coach Karen Armon is CEO and founder of Alliance Resources, LLC, in Littleton, Colorado. She told me about an incident that demanded all her courage when she was seven years old.

"As the eldest child of five girls," she said, "I was expected to be an example for my siblings. I took this responsibility seriously. One Saturday morning, we were preparing for a Fourth of July outing at the park. Our cousin was staying with us at the time, so there were five kids in the home, ranging in age from two to seven.

"Mom sent us out to the car to wait while my father finished his coffee. The two-year-old, Debbie, jumped into the front seat of the Oldsmobile and the other four of us piled into the back. We goofed around, enjoying the sun, excited about the outing.

"Suddenly, the car started rolling backward down the inclined driveway. Though the engine was off, Debbie had somehow knocked the gearshift into reverse or neutral. As the car quickly gained momentum, all of us in the backseat began screaming.

"Someone had to do something, so I climbed over into the driver's seat. I didn't know anything about driving a car, except that I had seen grown-ups press on that wide pedal when they wanted to stop. So I pressed both feet against the brake pedal, wedged myself against the seat for leverage, and pushed with all

my might. Within a few seconds, the car came to a stop halfway down the driveway.

"I could see the gearshift position marked 'park' and I tried to shove the lever into that position, but it wouldn't go, no matter how hard I tried. In the seat behind me, the kids were frozen with panic.

"I yelled, 'Get out of the car! Go get Dad—quick!' Then, remembering the two-year-old next to me, I added, 'Take Debbie with you!'

"The kids opened the back doors and jumped out, and one of them grabbed Debbie just as she was beginning to cry. 'I'll be okay,' I said, trying to sound brave. 'Just get Dad!'

"I couldn't see over the dashboard, but I could hear the kids yelling as they ran into the house. I was all alone with both feet jammed against the brake pedal, and I was getting tired and scared. I imagined what would happen if my strength gave out and the car started rolling.

"Straining to look over the backseat, I saw a neighbor's car directly in the path of the Oldsmobile. I wondered if I could crank the steering wheel enough to miss that car if my legs gave out. I was all alone and I felt like crying—but I told myself, 'If I die in this car, at least I did the right thing.' Even at that moment, I was thinking about my character.

"Dad came out of the house. I later learned that he was skeptical about what the kids had told him, and even more skeptical when he couldn't see me at first—it looked like there was no one in the car because I was sunk down so low. But when he caught a glimpse of the top of my head, he knew the stories were true. He ran to the car and opened the driver's side door.

"'Move over,' he said. 'I've got it!'

"At first, I couldn't move. I thought that if I stopped pressing against the brake, the car would leap down the driveway at breakneck speed.

"'It's okay, Karen,' Dad assured me tenderly. 'I'll make sure it won't roll down the hill.'

"I let go and Dad slid into the driver's seat, put the transmission into park, and the car jerked to a stop. The crisis was over.

"Dad turned and said, 'You were so brave to do that, Karen! I'm very proud of you!' He hugged me and I felt so good—equal parts relief and pride. The lesson of that experience has stayed with me all my life: you're never too young to build character and demonstrate courage."

It's true. We tend to think of childhood as a carefree time of play, growth, and exploring the world. But sometimes childhood is a time where kids face trials and the reality of death—and some children do so with remarkable character and courage.

John P. Santoro is executive director of leadership communications for Pfizer, Inc., the world's largest research-based pharmaceutical company. John is also cofounder of The Paula Rosina Santoro Foundation, a tax-exempt charitable foundation.

He told me, "After my daughter Paula's death in December 2000, I went through her papers, trying to understand why a beautiful, bright ten-year-old had to leave this life so soon. I came across a card she had made during her religious education. She was thanking the Almighty for all the good things in her life. One line struck me—her prayer of gratitude to her Savior: 'Thank You for making me the way I am.'

"How many adults could have prayed that prayer? Paula suffered from a rare disease, Cushing's syndrome, in which the adrenal glands go haywire. Her body was constantly awash in the stress hormone cortisol. Physically, she was constantly undergoing the level of stress response that basketball players feel when they are a basket behind with seconds left on the clock. That much stress, when prolonged over weeks and weeks without relent, destroys the body in the most insidious ways.

"Paula didn't grow in height, only in weight. From a supple gymnast and soccer player, she got to the point where the common tasks of life wore her out. She had an early puberty, unusual hair growth, and facial features unlike any ten-year-old I knew. Kids

stared at her; some made fun of her. For a parent, it was painfully difficult to watch.

"Yet Paula's life was marked by an amazing grace. She loved her family and friends. She wrote beautifully, and painted with a style far beyond her years. One of the smartest children in the school, she could have accomplished anything she wanted to in life. She was generous to the poor, sensitive to the environment, and spiritual in her outlook on this life—and the life to come.

"Though she had every reason to complain, she remained cheerful. Some might look at her and see only a child who was 'obese' or even 'funny looking.' But Paula rightly saw herself as a creature on God's green earth, happy to be here, and worried about those who didn't have enough.

"She died on December 10, 2000, seven days after coming home from a month-long hospital stay, which we and her doctors had hoped would cure her. Her internal organs just wore out. On Christmas Day 2000, we opened the presents she had lovingly bought and wrapped for us. These are among the most treasured possessions I will ever have.

"But Paula's greatest gift to me was the prayer she wrote: 'Thank You for making me the way I am.' When I am tempted to complain about anything in my life, I think of Paula's beautiful, courageous spirit, and I think, *Thank you, dear Paula, for making me the way I am.*"

How to Instill Courage in Your Kids

How, then, do we train kids to be people of character and courage? Here are some ideas and suggestions:

1. *Give your kids opportunities to stretch their courage.* Encourage them to accept tasks and challenges with an element of risk and the possibility of both success and failure. Get them involved in team and individual sports, or a performance activity like music or drama. Encourage them to start their own business or ministry. Challenge them to accept a task in which the odds

against success are great—but so are the rewards. Let them learn and gain confidence from both success and failure.

2. *Praise the attempt, not just the results.* It's okay for a child to fail as long as he makes a valiant attempt. Young people need to know that you are on their side even when they try and fail. If they know they have your unconditional support, they'll be willing to take on bigger, more daunting risks in return for bigger, more satisfying rewards. So praise courage and character, not just achievements.

3. *Praise your child's courage to be honest.* It's not easy for kids to admit mistakes and wrongdoing. Owning up to sin and failure takes more than integrity. It takes courage. When your kids demonstrate the courage to be honest with you, make sure you affirm them. It doesn't mean you shouldn't correct the mistake or reprimand the wrongdoing—but if your child knows you take courage and character into account, he or she will be much more likely to be courageously honest in the future.

4. *Teach your kids to take a lonely, courageous stand for their values, beliefs, and character.* William Penn, the Quaker founder of the colony of Pennsylvania, said, "Right is right, even if everyone is against it; and wrong is wrong, even if everyone is for it." Let's embolden our young people to stand for what's right—even if they stand alone.

Dave Hart is athletics director at Florida State University. He recalls a time in elementary school when he had to take a lonely stand for what he believed was right. "One time," he said, "I gave an answer in class—and the teacher opened the issue up for debate: was the answer I had given correct or not? Some of my classmates agreed with my answer, some opposed it.

"As the discussion continued, the teacher suggested some arguments against my answer. The more he talked, the more he influenced the class against my answer. When students would speak up in support of me, he subtly suggested that those students might want to think about it some more.

"Gradually, all of my supporters were persuaded to the opposite position. I was standing alone with my belief. The teacher said, 'Mr. Hart, would you like to change your response?' I was tempted to say yes . . . but I didn't. I said, 'No. I'm not going to change my answer.' He said, 'Why not? Everyone in the class says you must be wrong.' I said, 'I still think I'm right.'

"The teacher turned to the class and said, 'Mr. Hart is right. He stood firm when the popular answer was the wrong answer.' He told us that it's more important to be right than to be in the majority. The world needs people who are willing to stand up for what is right, even if the whole world says they're wrong."

Dave Hart never forgot that lesson in courage. He concludes, "I think one of the most important things we can do in training young leaders is to praise them and encourage them when they make tough decisions and demonstrate the courage to not follow the crowd."

5. *Teach young people to manage their fear.* It's normal to be afraid in some situations. In fact, a certain amount of fear is a good thing. Kids should be afraid of destroying their minds with drugs or crossing the street against traffic. But they should never be afraid to tackle a worthwhile goal, never be afraid to stand for truth, never be afraid to defend the defenseless. No one can eliminate all fear, but children can learn to control their fear so that fear doesn't control their lives.

Encourage your children to admit their fears and talk them through. Be honest with your kids about the fears you faced at their age, and (when appropriate) even the fears you face today. Tell your kids you believe in them, and you are confident that they can conquer the thing that scares them. Your affirmation will enable them to face their challenges with confidence and courage.

6. *Build courage by helping young people do the things they fear.* Dr. Larina Kase is president of Performance & Success Coaching, LLC, and author of *The Successful Therapist.* She told me, "In addition to my work as a business coach, I maintain a small private practice in Philadelphia, where I see teenagers and young

adults who struggle with issues of identity, anxiety, self-esteem, and relationships. One of the most rewarding aspects of my work is when I can help young people find their character and courage.

"When I see a child or teenager who worries excessively, has great fears and phobias, or struggles with self-doubt, I know that this young person is out of touch with his or her own courage. We build courage in young people by helping them do the things they fear, so that they can learn they really can handle the situation.

"A thirteen-year-old girl I worked with was deathly afraid of spiders. We created a list of activities to build up her courage. We began by looking at photos of spiders. Then we moved up to looking at spiders from a distance. Then we held a spider in a jar. By the end of our twelve meetings together, she was able to allow three spiders to crawl up and down her arm and was laughing because the spiders tickled!

"With each step, this girl developed more courage and confidence in her ability to handle spiders. At each step, I modeled the actions for her first, so she could see it could be done. She learned that persevering step by step would pay off. She discovered that she could confront her fears and do things she once thought were impossible.

"These lessons don't just apply to spiders. I repeatedly underscored the fact that she could do anything she put her mind to. She tackled an enormous phobia at age thirteen. What did she want to do next? She told me she wanted to become a doctor. Okay, if she wants to enter a competitive field but feels nervous about it, she can remember the lessons she learned in overcoming her fear of spiders. She can conquer her self-doubts, and she can accomplish whatever she sets out to do.

"The method of instilling courage and character in young people is simple and effective: First, establish together an understanding of why the goal is important. Second, model for them the steps they need to do to reach that goal. Third, let them try the steps on their own. Fourth, reinforce their accomplishments with praise,

pointing out how successful and courageous they have been. Fifth, help them generalize from this one example to every other aspect of life. Show them that character and courage can conquer all obstacles and enable them to reach their goals."

7. *Encourage young people to consider military service.* I served in the Army Reserves, and it was a character-building experience. I heartily recommend the service to all young men and women. In fact, we had an understanding in the Williams household which was made plain to all of our children (four birth kids and fourteen by international adoption). "When you graduate from high school," I told them, "one of three things will happen: (1) you'll go to college, including summer school; (2) you'll go to work, which may mean McDonald's or Wal-Mart; or (3) you'll go into the military. There is no fourth option, such as staying home and playing video games while sponging off of Mom and Dad." To reinforce the message, we'd have that old song playing in the background, "The party's over..."

Two of our sons, Peter and David, enlisted in the U.S. Marine Corps. Peter is a marine veteran who will proudly tell you his character has been shaped by the Corps. "If you want a proven leader," he says, "you want a marine." And David, who served seven and a half years in the marines, was part of that courageous first wave of infantry that rolled into Iraq as part of Operation Iraqi Freedom. When I think of courage, I think of young men and women in all branches of the service, willing to go anywhere to defend freedom. There's no better place to learn character and courage than in the U.S. military.

8. *Set an example of character and courage.* Approach life as an adventure—and let your kids see you enjoying the adventure of living. Don't always choose the safest course. Instead, take calculated risks that offer exciting rewards.

Let your kids see you take a risk to reach out and help someone. Let them see you take a courageous stand for a cause, an idea, or a belief. Tell them about your fears and how you overcame

them in order to do something bold and courageous. When your kids see you as a role model of courage, they'll want to follow your example—and they won't want to let you down. Your courage will inspire theirs.

Writing in *The News Journal* of Wilmington, Delaware, my hometown, journalist Kristin Harty tells the story of Bobbie McGowan, an English teacher at Charter School of Wilmington, and her son, Corporal Stephen McGowan. Stephen joined the army shortly after the September 11, 2001, terrorist attacks. He told his mother that war was coming, and he didn't want a younger man going in his place out of a need for college money.

Stephen was sent first to Korea. While stationed there, he volunteered to go to Iraq in place of another soldier, who was married with a three-year-old child. Again, Stephen told his mother, "I'm not married. I don't have children. I feel I should go before these other guys go." Arriving in Iraq, Stephen McGowan turned down promotions that could have placed him in safer rear-echelon posts. He chose dangerous duty in places like the deadly Sunni Triangle, where he served as a medic.

On patrol in Iraq, Stephen felt a great compassion for the Iraqi children he met. With his mother's help, he organized an effort to distribute Beanie Babies to the children in Iraq. These inexpensive stuffed animals had a huge impact on the lives of the poor children of war-torn Iraq. Bobbie McGowan involved her students in the effort to ship box-loads of Beanie Babies to Iraq.

Stephen McGowan was a courageous young man who believed in his mission. He wanted to help the people of Iraq—and especially the children. His mission was to remove the bad guys from the country so the Iraqi people could live in peace. On March 4, 2005, three weeks before his scheduled departure for a ten-day leave in the States, the twenty-six-year-old medic was killed by a roadside bomb.

When Bobbie McGowan heard her son was dead, she wanted to die. But four days after burying her son, another tragedy oc-

curred: two Charter School students were killed and a third injured in a car crash. Though still in the depths of her own grief, Bobbie McGowan knew she needed to return to school and set an example of courage for her students. She needed to show them they could survive their deep losses.

So Bobbie McGowan returned to work and taught her senior English class. Though she wept many times a day, she tried not to let her students see her cry. One day, she read to her class the moving poem "The Death of the Ball Turret Gunner" by Randall Jarrell. It's a brutally frank poem about war, in which a turret gunner in a World War II bomber is killed by enemy gunfire and his remains are unceremoniously hosed out of the turret.

Though Mrs. McGowan taught that poem every spring, her personal loss made it particularly poignant. As the students watched, wondering if she would get through it, she read with a steady voice. She asked the students for their response. After a long, awkward silence, the class began discussing the poem.

After the class, a student named Alex told Bobbie, "For what it's worth, whenever I hit a hard point in my life and think about quitting, I'll remember you and your strength."[1]

Before his death, sports broadcasting legend Ken Coleman admitted: "It's okay to be afraid. It is a part of life. Life is facing your fears and overcoming them. That leads to wisdom, integrity, and, most important of all, character."

Courage is not for the times we feel strong, but for the times we feel weak and afraid. When we demonstrate courage to our kids in our own times of weakness, we hammer the steel rod of courage and confidence into their own souls. They learn and grow by watching our example.

Your example of courage will be the most memorable and inspiring in those times when you are the most afraid. So do the thing you fear, and the death of fear—your fear and your children's fear—is certain.

7

Perseverance: Endure and Outlast

"Perseverance is to the character of man as carbon is to steel."

NAPOLEON HILL
SUCCESS AND MOTIVATIONAL AUTHOR

Most people today remember September 11, 2001, as the day the world changed. For people of a previous generation, the day etched in their memory is December 7, 1941, when Japan attacked the United States at Pearl Harbor, Hawaii.

But for Dr. Clyde Cook, who served as president of Biola University in La Mirada, California, from 1982 to 2007, it is the day *after* the attack on Pearl Harbor he remembers most vividly. He recently shared his story with me. "I was the child of missionary parents, living in Hong Kong," he said. "On December 8, 1941, the Japanese attacked Hong Kong. Our house was located near a couple of antiaircraft batteries, so our neighborhood was heavily bombed.

"I remember hearing the air raid siren, followed quickly by the roar of Japanese dive-bombers, and then the explosions all around us. When we heard the siren, my mother gathered her three children together under the staircase—my sister, the four-month-old baby, and me. Dad was away at sea, and the other three children were in a boarding school in northern China.

"As the bombs fell and the house shuddered, my mother sang

the words of the old hymn 'He Leadeth Me,' with its words of trusting faith in the face of death:

> And when my task on earth is done,
> When by Thy grace the victory's won,
> Even death's cold wave I will not flee,
> Since God through Jordan leadeth me.

"What I experienced in those frightening moments was the steadfast character of my mother. With the bombs exploding all around us, she practiced what she taught us. Her courage and faith revealed the depth of her character and provided an exemplary model for me for the rest of my life.

"The people in my life who set an example and shaped my emotional, intellectual, and moral qualities were my parents. My mother taught me about courage, about not being afraid to be different, about persevering through hardships. My father, who was a sea captain, taught me about integrity and the importance of always telling the truth.

"Their examples of courage and perseverance affected me deeply when the Japanese overran China and the Cook family was imprisoned in a series of concentration camps during World War II. By God's grace, we were all reunited in South Africa, where we lived as refugees. After the war, we came to the United States and settled in Southern California.

"I was eleven years old when we arrived in the States, and I had never seen a basketball in my life. I knew all about rugby and cricket, but they didn't play those games in Southern California. My first day in an American school was extremely painful. In gym class, they chose up sides and because of my height and athletic appearance, I was quickly chosen. However, it wasn't long before the team captain realized he had made a terrible mistake.

"When they threw me the ball, I tucked it under my arm and ran down the court as if I were playing rugby. They blew the whis-

tle and gave the ball to the other team, then they told me I had to bounce the ball every two steps.

"The next time down the court, they threw the ball to me and I bounced it every two steps like they said—but I used two hands and again they blew the whistle. Naturally, they quit throwing me the ball after that. So I just stood there and they blew the whistle again. I said, 'What's wrong now?' They replied, 'You can't stand there more than three seconds.' The next time they chose up sides, nobody chose me.

"My mother had taught me, by word and example, to never give up. I figured if she could persevere when bombs were falling or when we were in a prison camp, I could persevere with basketball. All I had to do was keep working hard and learning the rules. So I persisted, and when I graduated from high school I was voted the California Interscholastic Federation North/South Division Player of the Year. I was offered scholarships to many major universities."

That's the power of perseverance—and the power of a mother and father who exemplified character to their children. Perseverance is a patient commitment to work hard, endure hardship, and overcome every obstacle in the pursuit of a goal. It's the stubborn refusal to quit. It's the determination to accept problems, opposition, and difficulties without complaining. It's the willingness to try again and again for as long as it takes to get the job done.

A marathon is a foot race of 26.2 miles. As of this writing, I've completed forty-five marathons. I usually compete in four a year, and as I get older, the races get harder. It's expensive to compete in a marathon. In addition to the entrance fee, you have to pay your flight and hotel expenses—and for what? For the privilege of enduring torture and exhaustion to earn a medal worth less than a dollar. While I'm running a marathon, my head screams, "This is stupid! Give up! Quit! My body can't take this!" People often ask me why I subject my body to such punishment. My reply: "Four times a year, I want to practice not quitting."

Olympic gold medal swimmer-turned-actor Johnny Weissmuller

was the most famous of all actors who ever played Tarzan in the movies. (He originated the distinctive Tarzan yell.) Weissmuller was once asked what it takes to be Tarzan. His reply: "Don't let go of the vine."

President Franklin D. Roosevelt once said, "When you come to the end of your rope, tie a knot and hang on." Failure is the result of letting go and quitting. As long as you are holding on and trying, you haven't failed. As long as you refuse to accept failure, you are positioned to succeed.

Pressing Toward the Goal, Reaching for the Prize

The Scriptures place a high premium on perseverance. The apostle James writes, "Blessed is the man who perseveres under trial, because when he has stood the test, he will receive the crown of life that God has promised to those who love him" (James 1:12). And in the last book of the Bible, the Lord says to the church in Thyatira, "I know your deeds, your love and faith, your service and perseverance" (Rev. 2:19).

The apostle Paul described his own attitude of relentless perseverance in his letters: "We are hard pressed on every side, but not crushed; perplexed, but not in despair; persecuted, but not abandoned; struck down, but not destroyed" (2 Cor. 4:8–9). And, "But one thing I do: Forgetting what is behind and straining toward what is ahead, I press on toward the goal to win the prize for which God has called me heavenward in Christ Jesus" (Phil. 3:13–14).

Enduring affliction, pushing through obstacles, enduring opposition, striving for a goal, reaching for the prize—that's what the character quality of perseverance is all about. No great goal is ever achieved without problems and setbacks, so we need to learn perseverance.

In October 1974, when I was general manager of the Philadelphia 76ers, I was working on a Halloween promotion for the game

that night against the Knicks. We were planning an apple-bobbing contest, a pumpkin-pie-eating contest, a best costume contest, treats for the kids, and so forth. While I was going crazy trying to manage all the details, my phone rang. It was Barry Abrams, a record promoter who worked part-time at the 76er games.

"Pat," he said, "I'm working with a terrific young recording artist who has a new song. Could you play it at the game tonight?"

"We don't usually do that," I said. "But have him bring me his tape before the game. I'll do what I can." I hung up and forgot about it.

An hour before the game, a lanky, long-haired fellow approached me and said, "Mr. Williams? Barry Abrams said I should see you. I brought my tape." He held out a cassette.

It took me a moment to recall my conversation with Barry Abrams, then I said, "Oh, yeah. I don't know why you want your music played here with these lousy acoustics."

"Mr. Williams," he said, "I've had thousands of these tapes made, and I take them to sporting events, radio stations, school dances, birthday parties—anyplace people get together. I'll do anything to get people to hear my music, because I know if they hear it, they'll buy it."

I told him to give the tape to the sound guys, then went about making preparations for the game and the halftime promotion. The arena filled with fans, the 76ers and Knicks took the court, and the game was under way.

During a time-out, I noticed a song playing on the P.A. It was a smooth, plaintive love ballad. When the song ended, a smattering of applause broke out in the stands. *So,* I thought, *the guy must have brought his mom and his sisters for a rooting section.*

The next time I heard the song was about a month later—on the radio. The song was "Mandy" and it was a huge first hit for a young singer-songwriter named Barry Manilow. That skinny, long-haired young man was well on his way to stardom.

That's the power of perseverance.

You Win with Winners—and Winners Persevere

Derek Waugh is head basketball coach at Stetson University in DeLand, Florida. "As a coach," he told me, "I see perseverance as the ability to play through losses, injuries, and lack of playing time. Many players are unable to persevere through these obstacles, because any adversity sends them into a tailspin from which they can't recover.

"One reason I love sports so much is that it reveals what's inside us as human beings. Athletic competition tests your character, your toughness, and your values at every turn. One of my favorite truths, which I say to my teams on a regular basis, is that adversity doesn't so much build character as it reveals it. Those who have the character trait of perseverance soon get to display it on the court; those who lack it are quickly revealed as well.

"We have had one player at Stetson who really embodied character, toughness, and, most importantly, perseverance. I'll call him 'Rick.' Rick came in as a freshman and had an immediate impact on our program. He set a record for three-pointers made by a freshman and started almost every game that season.

"Going into his sophomore season, we expected big things out of Rick—but then a broken foot required surgery and bone reconstruction. Rick was sidelined for the entire year. While he was on the sidelines, we had one of our most successful seasons. Another freshman came in at his position and had a fantastic year.

"The next year was Rick's redshirt sophomore season, and though his foot was healthy, he was not as quick or agile as before, and he had lost some of his touch as a shooter. So we played the talented newcomer over Rick, who spent a lot of time on the bench.

"In his junior year, Rick continued to have problems with his foot and his shooting. It hurt me to keep him on the bench, because he was a young man of excellent character and a great person off the court, yet I was forced to shelve him because of his lack of production. Rick wanted more playing time, but he understood

that the team came first. His practice habits never slipped, his head was always up, and he led by example.

"We finished that season with a poor record and the program seemed to be in a bit of a slide. I met with each player in the spring and I asked Rick whether he wanted to come back for a fifth year of college. He had already graduated and had spent an entire year on our bench for a team that lost a lot of games. It seemed to me that he might just want to move on and leave basketball behind.

"But Rick said, 'I want to be on the team.' A part of me wanted to free up his scholarship so I could recruit another player—but another part of me respected Rick for wanting to persevere. Even if he no longer performed as he once had, it wouldn't hurt to have Rick on the team as a positive role model. So I kept Rick on, though he got very little playing time. We faced a brutal non-conference schedule, losing almost every game, and started our conference season at 0-4. We had a lot of frustration on the team, with players blaming each other or their coaches. I began to wonder if we'd ever win another game.

"After a disappointing home loss, I sat the team down and vowed that I wouldn't rest until we had turned our team around. I became obsessed about winning, and slept only two or three hours a night while spending every waking moment watching game film and working on team issues. In my heart, I wasn't sure that anything could turn our season around.

"The day after I gave my talk to the team, I went by the gym late at night to pick up some game film. As I entered, I heard a ball bouncing and was taken back. Who would be in the gym? It was nearly midnight!

"I walked to the court and found Rick going through a workout. He was wringing with sweat, so he'd been at it awhile. He had his dog tied to the bleachers and was working on improving his game—and he was doing so even though I'd given him hardly any playing time. Though he had every reason to give up, he was trying harder than anyone else on the team.

"The next game, I gave Rick some playing time. He made two crucial three-pointers from deeper than I had ever seen him shoot—and we won the game in double overtime. While games are won and lost as a team, Rick's play was a key factor in that win. It confirmed what I had been telling the team. From then on, I put Rick in the starting lineup. Even though his skills weren't what they'd once been, he gave the team new energy. His perseverance made him a leader.

"We went on a five-game winning streak and won nine of our next twelve games. We finished the season in the upper middle of our conference and salvaged a season that had once seemed lost. At the end of his career at Stetson, Rick was able to look back with pride, knowing that even though his skills waned after his injury, his character and attitude remained strong—and made him a role model for the entire team. You win with winners. Rick was a winner because winners persevere."

Rob Evans was the head coach of men's basketball at the University of Mississippi ("Ole Miss") from 1992 to 1998, and at Arizona State University from 1998 to 2006. He told me that sometimes we, as parents, coaches, and teachers, often impart values and lessons in young people we need to take to heart ourselves. "I spent twenty-four years as an assistant coach," he told me, "and I got passed over numerous times for head coaching jobs. Once, I got passed over for a job I thought I really deserved. So I complained to my wife and said, 'Once again, I got messed over.'

"My wife said, 'You need to do what you tell your players. You need to look in the mirror. Ask yourself, 'Was there something more I could have done to get that job?'

"I thought it over and I knew she was right. So I spent the next year talking to athletic directors and getting a game plan. Then I interviewed for the head coaching position at Ole Miss and got the job. I had always preached perseverance to my teams, but for a while there I forgot to practice what I preach. When things don't

go your way, you can't just complain about it. You've got to keep pushing toward your goals."

Finish the Drill

Bert Sugar, the great cigar-chomping, fedora-sporting historian of the world of boxing, once asked heavyweight champion Floyd Patterson if he knew he'd been knocked down more times than any other boxer in history. Patterson mildly replied, "Yes—but I also got up more times than anyone."

"Fall seven times, stand up eight," says the ancient proverb. The prize goes to the one who takes one more step past the point of exhaustion. It goes to the one who can take just a little more punishment than the next guy. Perseverance is more crucial to success than intelligence, talent, and luck combined.

Mark Richt, head football coach at the University of Georgia, told me, "We talk a lot about perseverance here at Georgia. The motto we live by is 'Finish the Drill.' That slogan came from our off-season mat drill program where the coaches teach our players to finish the drill as strongly as they started it. Anyone can *start* the drill at full speed, but it takes perseverance and stamina to *finish* the drill at full speed. With each repetition of the drill, you get more and more tired, and you want to fall by the wayside. Only the strong in spirit, the strong in character, can finish the drill.

"I learned the importance of finishing the drill during my days at Florida State with Coach Dave Van Halanger. He was our strength and conditioning coach there before he came to Georgia. I saw the results that come from finishing the drill when Georgia played Tennessee in 2001, my first year at Georgia. We were losing that game, but we came back and beat them with just forty-eight seconds left on the clock. We won because we were the better-conditioned team. We out-endured Tennessee in that game.

"After the game, we celebrated. I talked to the team and tried to articulate what had just happened—but I was at a loss for words. Then one of our players expressed it perfectly. 'We finished

the drill, Coach!' he shouted. I said, 'That's right! You said it! We finished the drill!'

"So that became our slogan: 'Finish the drill!' It stuck. It inspired us. It said to us that you've got to finish as strong as you start. You never, never quit. You don't quit on a mat drill, or a game, or your academics, or your career, or your marriage, or any goal in life. When things get tough, don't quit. Finish the drill."

Another athlete who knows what it means to "finish the drill" is Frank Allocco, head basketball coach at De La Salle High School in Concord, California. "My father was a man of great character," he told me. "He was a volunteer fireman for almost sixty years, gave a lot of his time to the church, and always put others ahead of himself. He raised four competitive sons, all of whom went on to play college athletics.

"My dad raised us to be young men of character and perseverance, and my high school basketball coach, Paul Miller, used to say: 'The All-American gives 100 percent even when no one is watching.'

"But I never quite understood the true meaning of perseverance until I went to Notre Dame. After being a backup quarterback to Tom Clements my entire career, I was penciled in as starting quarterback in the 1975 season. Unfortunately, a separated shoulder in spring practice destroyed my dream. Even so, I learned the importance of character through my injury. I rehabbed each day and the main part of my workout was running the stadium steps at Notre Dame. I did this every day, up and down each gate in the Indiana heat.

"One hot, humid August afternoon, I was running the stadium steps by myself. I hit the thirtieth gate going up and down, and had eight gates remaining. I was exhausted and didn't think I could run one more step. I thought about quitting, then I looked to my right and saw an elderly couple and their young son watching me run. I figured they were parents dropping off their freshman son—and they would know that I was the quarterback because I wore my

practice jersey while working out. Knowing I was being observed gave me a terrific boost of adrenaline and I was able to sprint out those last eight gates.

"Looking back, I realize that the burst of strength I needed to run those last eight gates was within me all the time—but I had been ready to give up short of my goal. We always have more strength within us than we realize. We can find that strength if we are willing to persevere. If we quit, that strength will simply go unused and undiscovered.

"Months later, I received a letter from my best friend's mother. She expressed her sorrow over all the adversity I had experienced in my athletic career. She said, 'Every time your big break came and you were at the threshold of realizing your potential, you suffered an injury. I'm so sorry you never achieved your goal of starting at Notre Dame.'

"I wrote back and told her that even my disappointments had been a good experience in my life. Prior to my injury, I had no perspective on success. I told her the story of running the stadium steps and explained that I would never forget what I discovered that day—that a man on the brink of exhaustion can gather the strength to sprint just because someone is watching. Anyone can run the steps when the stadium is full, but it takes character and perseverance to keep going when the stands are empty.

"For the rest of my life I would truly know what my high school coach was trying to teach me: 'The All-American gives 100 percent even when no one is watching.'"

How to Encourage Young People to Persevere

When the going gets tough, most people quit. Perseverance is a learned response for most of us—not a natural inclination. How, then, do we teach young people to keep going when everything within us wants to quit? Here are some suggestions:

1. Teach your kids that there's no such thing as "impossible." I

once met a young man named David Ring. He was born in 1953 with cerebral palsy, a neurological disorder which causes physical disability. His father died when David was eleven; his mother died four years later, and he spent his adolescence living in foster homes and institutional care. If ever anyone ever had a right to give up on life, it would have been David Ring.

Depressed over his disability and the grief of his losses, David dropped out of school—and he wanted to drop out of life. But thanks to the prayers and encouragement of his sister, David Ring committed his life to Jesus Christ in 1970. He returned to high school and graduated, then earned his bachelor's degree from William Jewell College in Liberty, Missouri.

David Ring learned to accept his physical disability and his sorrows—but he refused to let anything keep him from his goals. Though cerebral palsy distorts his speech, he has become a nationally known motivational speaker, sharing his story in public appearances and media appearances across the country.

Meeting David, you are instantly bowled over by the power of his confidence and enthusiasm for living. When he stands before audiences, he challenges people with these words: "I have cerebral palsy. What's your problem?" We all have problems, limitations, and disadvantages—but we don't have to be stopped by them. The only limits we have are the limits in our thinking. Help your kids to see that nothing is impossible. With faith and perseverance, they can achieve miracles and astonish the world.

2. Teach young people that every worthwhile endeavor faces opposition and attack. Show them that the only way to achieve worthwhile goals is to persevere in spite of the critics and naysayers.

Kelly D. Brownell, Ph.D., is director of the Rudd Center for Food Policy and Obesity at Yale University and an internationally renowned expert on weight control and eating disorders. His research has had an enormous impact on public policy regarding health and nutrition. In 2006 he was named in the *Time* 100,

the magazine's annual list of the most influential people in the world. He attained that honor by persevering against powerful opponents and detractors.

"Competitive sports had a big part in shaping my childhood," Dr. Brownell told me. "As a teenager, I played Babe Ruth baseball during high school and the summer before college. At the end of the season, I received the sportsmanship award. I remember feeling very proud and thinking I would rather have this distinction than the MVP award, because it said something about me as a person, not just my baseball skills.

"My father and my coaches taught me that being a person is at least as important as being an athlete. My father was not a flashy man, but he worked hard and he instilled in me his own quiet decency and a strong desire to do the right thing. He taught my brothers and me that it was important to leave behind a better world than the one we were given.

"Some years ago, I made the point that Americans are exposed to a 'toxic food environment.' I wasn't saying that our food is poisoned, but rather that we as a society have created a 'perfect storm' of conditions leading to unhealthy eating, particularly in children and the poor. Compared to healthy foods, unhealthy foods are more accessible, more convenient, better tasting, more intensively marketed, and less expensive.

"These observations brought me into conflict with the food industry, and with people like Rush Limbaugh and others who defended the industry. There were blistering attacks, hate mail, and even a few veiled threats. For example, someone claimed to have cast a 'pox' on my house.

"The world has changed with time, however, and now people worry about the food environment. The grave concerns I used to talk about are now receiving widespread media attention. The wider public is becoming aware of problems like childhood obesity and type 2 diabetes in young children, and we are seeing action in the public policy arena. Schools are kicking sugary soft drinks

off the campus. Governments are asking whether advertising to children should be curtailed. People are calling for calorie labels on restaurant menus. Political leaders are questioning agriculture subsidies that promote unhealthy eating.

"After being a lonely voice for some time, it was a great honor to be named among the world's hundred most influential people by *Time* magazine. Though it took perseverance and courage to endure the attacks on the credibility of my work, I always felt that the interests of the world, and especially of children, were the most important consideration. Setbacks are often part of the journey that defines progress.

"In nearly every talk I give around the world, I try to inspire people to believe they can make a difference in the world. I relate my own experience and share what has been a great source of inspiration for me—a quote by Gandhi: 'First they ignore you, then they laugh at you, then they fight you, then you win.'"

If you are an achiever, a leader, or a role model, then you are an exposed target—and there will always be people taking shots at you. Don't cave under pressure, don't wilt under adversity, don't shrink from controversy. If you're convinced you are right, keep moving forward. Lead! Act! Speak out! Change the world! And in the process, you'll teach your children that every great achievement comes at a price—and often that price includes criticism and opposition. To win, we must persevere.

3. *Encourage your kids to turn problems and limitations into advantages.* Russ Crosson is the author of *A Life Well Spent* and the president and CEO of Ronald Blue & Co., a nationally recognized financial consulting firm which operates on biblical principles. When I asked him which character quality was the most important in his life, he said, "Perseverance. As a young child I was handicapped due to a rare condition called Legg-Perthes disease. It is usually diagnosed in children between the ages of two and twelve, and most often around age six. It causes the child to be of shorter height than normal because of delayed bone development.

"As a result of this disease, I was on crutches and in braces from age six to ten. It was frustrating for me to be unable to run and play like the other children. But I'll never forget one instance where perseverance paid off and I was able to translate my handicap into a victory.

"I was seven or eight when I participated in a school 'track meet'—more of an organized play day than a sporting event. One of the events they had was the infamous sack race. If you've ever tried to run in a sack, you know you can't really run, because your feet get tangled up and you fall. Since I couldn't run and couldn't put any weight on my left leg, I had to hop everywhere I went without my crutches. Because I did so much hopping, my right leg was very strong—and I was very well practiced at hopping on one leg. This made it easy to 'run' in the sack because I just hopped—and my legs didn't get tangled up.

"Needless to say, I won the sack race by many meters. But the best part of the race was the look on peoples' faces when I dropped the sack and hopped over to my crutches and motored off. Though I had a handicap early in life, I was never content to sit on the sidelines. I naturally developed a desire to persevere in order to overcome my physical limitations.

"This is an important quality to teach to our kids. Don't be stopped by limitations—turn them into advantages! Don't be stopped by obstacles—hop over them or around them! Don't stay in your comfort zone—there are no rewards or achievements there. If you want to accomplish great things, don't let anything stand in your way. Move out and go for the prize."

4. Teach your kids that the problems and obstacles they face are more mental than physical. John Havlicek is one of the best basketball players of all time. He played sixteen seasons with the Boston Celtics, winning eight NBA titles, and was inducted into the Basketball Hall of Fame in 1984. I once asked John about the importance of perseverance to his career. He said, "Perseverance is all-important because the obstacles and opposition you face are

more mental than physical. When two people are playing against each other, the question is who will give up first? It becomes a mental game of one-on-one. The object is to see who is the toughest mentally—not just in the overall game, but on every single move, on every individual shot.

"The guy who wins is the guy who works a little harder, who goes a little longer. I believe you will pass out before you are overworked, but most people don't know that. They *think* they are overworked, so they stop. They could have kept going, but they didn't. They weren't beat physically. They were beat mentally. Those who persevere win."

Dr. Roy E. Yarbrough is director of sport management studies at the California University of Pennsylvania. He told me about a season during his college soccer career when he experienced the principles John Havlicek spoke of—that the obstacles holding us back are more mental than physical. "One person who taught me about character," Roy told me, "was my soccer coach at Greenville College in Illinois, John Strahl. He didn't just teach me how to persevere in the game, but how to persevere in life. He was a Christlike mentor and friend, and he made me feel my life was worth living.

"At one point, I was flunking out, not studying, having girl problems, and running away from God. I went to Coach Strahl and said, 'Coach, you've been in the army. If I leave school, I'll probably end up in the army, and that means Vietnam. What should I do?'

"He said, 'Stay in school, Roy, because if you leave, I'll miss you.' That's all I needed to hear: someone cared about me, and would miss me if I left. So I stayed in school.

"During my junior season, our soccer team played Southern Illinois University, Edwardsville, a nationally ranked team. The score was tied after regulation time, so we went into overtime. During the break before overtime, we surrounded Coach Strahl to get his wisdom. It may well have been the shortest pep talk in history. Coach simply said, 'I have never lost an overtime game yet,' and he walked away. We all thought, *Hey, we don't want to*

be the team Coach remembers as a bunch of losers! So we played our hearts out and, at the end of overtime, we had won.

"Three weeks later, we played the same team again, and the results were nearly identical. We went into overtime, and once again, Coach Strahl gave us that succinct pep talk: 'I have never lost an overtime game yet.' We went out and beat Southern Illinois, Edwardsville, again! Their team was so upset over those two losses that they refused to ever play us again.

"Why did we win those two games? I believe it's because we wanted it more. Physically, our opponent was the superior team—a nationally ranked team. But the game wasn't decided on that basis. It was decided on the basis of mental toughness and perseverance. We didn't beat them physically. We beat them mentally. We out-persevered them."

5. *When your kids want to quit, encourage them to hang tough.* Some years ago, when my daughter Karyn was a high school senior, she was captain of her cheerleading squad. One night she came home completely discouraged. I asked her what was bothering her, and she said, "Dad, I don't want to lead the cheerleading squad anymore. I want to quit."

"Quit? Karyn, why?"

"Because none of those kids recognizes me as the leader. They all want to be the captain, and they all try to impose their ideas on me. I've had it. I'm through."

I said, "Karyn, you're going to have to find a good balance between firmly standing up for your leadership role on the one hand, and listening to their ideas on the other. Try telling them, 'I'm the captain and I will make the final decisions. I'll consider your ideas, but the final decision is mine.' I think if you show them that you're a good listener but you're also in charge, they'll begin to recognize your authority."

She was dubious—and she still wanted to quit. But with some gentle urging from her dad, Karyn stuck it out. It took time, but the situation improved—and Karyn was glad she persevered.

6. *Teach your kids the value of patience.* In this Internet-speed age of fast food, microwave ovens, and email, we no longer have the patience to wait and endure. Patience is the willingness to defer immediate gratification in order to achieve a better future. It's the willingness to be at peace while waiting. Patience is a lost virtue in today's world.

Bill Hilf is the lead program manager for Microsoft's Platform Strategy organization. He leads the company's Linux and Open Source Software technology group. I asked Bill to reflect on the character trait of perseverance. He told me that when he was only seven, his father died of a heart attack. At that moment, Bill's mother and older siblings became his role models and teachers of character. Bill's oldest brother, in fact, taught him a valuable and unforgettable object lesson in perseverance.

"When I was fifteen," Bill said, "my oldest brother told me he was giving me a car for my sixteenth birthday. I was elated! It was what every teenager dreams of—his own car! But my brother didn't tell me what form that car would be in when he gave it to me. What he gave me was the body and parts for building a 1965 Ford Mustang.

"Well, that car was a classic by all measures—or it would be, once it was put together. But it had no engine, there were parts missing from the transmission, and there was certainly no stereo. My brother committed to teach me and help me build that car over the course of a year. He set a goal of completing the car in time for me to drive it when I got my license.

"I worked on it diligently through the year and my brother, an expert mechanic, taught me everything I needed to know about cars—more than I could have imagined. We finished in time for my sixteenth birthday and the Mustang was in cherry condition, fully restored and absolutely beautiful. All the parts were authentic Mustang parts, except for the stereo.

"Then came the ultimate irony: just a few weeks after I completed the car, I was driving it and someone ran into me and totaled

the car. The accident wasn't my fault and no one was seriously hurt, but my beautiful labor of love ended up in the salvage yard.

"Looking back, I realize that what was really important about that experience was not the car, but what I learned through the process of building it. I learned patience, diligence, perseverance—and I learned to laugh even in hard times. The gift my brother gave me was not just a car. It was character. He taught me the value of patience."

The Anvil and the Hammer

In the summer of 1963, I played my final season as a professional baseball player, catching for the Philadelphia Phillies' farm team in Miami. Even before the start of that season, I was pretty well resigned to the fact that I was not going to make it into Major League Baseball. I made plans to leave Miami in late August and drive up to Indiana University in Bloomington to complete my master's in physical education before embarking on a career in sports management.

When I called my mother and told her of my plans to visit her in Wilmington, Delaware, on my way to Indiana, she said, "I have a better idea. Meet me in Washington, D.C."

"Why Washington?" I asked.

"I'm going to the March on Washington," Mom said. "Dr. Martin Luther King Jr. is going to give a speech there on August 28. I'll meet you there and we can hear him speak."

My mother had always been involved in social justice and human rights causes. As for me—well, my focus was on sports, but I still had some inkling of who Dr. King was from the news accounts. He had been involved in the Rosa Parks–Montgomery Bus Boycott in 1955, and had made headlines throughout the late 1950s and early '60s for his nonviolent protests against segregation.

I agreed to meet Mom in Washington. She and my sister made the two-hour drive down from Wilmington, and I drove up from Miami. And that's how I happened to be standing in a vast crowd

on the National Mall in front of the Lincoln Memorial on that hot, humid, historic day when Dr. King gave his "I Have a Dream" speech.

Roughly a quarter of a million people gathered there that day to hear Dr. King give a speech that echoed the great phrases and ideals of the Scriptures, the Declaration of Independence, and the Emancipation Proclamation. I remember the chills down my spine when I heard those words, "I have a dream that my four little children will one day live in a nation where they will not be judged by the color of their skin but by the content of their character."

Though I found Dr. King's speech riveting and powerful, I didn't fully appreciate the importance of that historic event until years later. It took Dr. King nearly eight years to lead the nation from the Montgomery Bus Boycott to the March on Washington. With that speech, Dr. King was able to pressure President Kennedy and Congress to act on civil rights legislation that had been stalled for months.

Martin Luther King Jr. persevered for racial justice until that day in 1968, when an assassin's bullet ended his life. But even death was not the end of Dr. King's persevering spirit. As he once said, "We must accept finite disappointment, but we must never lose infinite hope."

No great thing was ever achieved without perseverance. Never give in to disappointment or opposition or criticism. Let people and circumstances hammer you as much as they like. The anvil always outlasts the hammer.

You are an anvil. Persevere and you will never be broken.

Senator Joseph Biden, from my home state of Delaware, puts it this way: "To me, this is the first principle of life, the foundational principle, and a lesson you can't learn at the feet of any wise man: Get up! The art of life is simply getting up after you've been knocked down. It's a lesson taught by example and learned in the doing."

PART IV

*Character Is
How We Respond
to People*

8

Humility: Putting Others First

"Life is a long lesson in humility."

JAMES BARRIE
SCOTTISH DRAMATIST; CREATOR OF *PETER PAN*

One of the great privileges of my life was the experience of working on a book about one of my true heroes, Coach John Wooden. The book is called *How to Be Like Coach Wooden: Life Lessons from Basketball's Greatest Leader* (Health Communications, 2006). My writing partner, Dave Wimbish, and I spent more than two years looking up everyone we could find who had ever known Coach Wooden, interviewing them by phone, mail, and email, and assembling those recollections and stories into a book. In the more than eight hundred interviews conducted for that book, I noticed that one word kept showing up in interview after interview. That word was *humble*.

For example, former UCLA player Don Saffer told me, "John Wooden is a giant of a man, and yet as humble as humble can be." And Carl Boldt, one of Coach's longtime friends, said, "I have breakfast with John Wooden regularly, and he is always so kind and gracious to everyone. He is such a humble man and being with him is like a religious experience. He's past being a great coach—he's almost saintly."

In interview after interview, people who knew John Wooden

marveled that he never acted self-important, never demanded special treatment, was never impolite or condescending to anyone, and never once said to anyone, "Do you know who I am?" Coach Wooden is one of those truly great human beings who has no awareness of his own greatness. For example, when he calls on the phone and leaves a message for you, he spells out his name in case you don't know who he is.

Coach Wooden not only exemplified humility, he taught humility to his teams. He believed that players had to play selflessly, so they could mesh together and function as one. He understood you can't stay on top with a team made up of supersized egos. To play for Coach, you had to check your ego at the door.

Lucius Allen, who played for Coach Wooden in the late 1960s, was a first-round pick in the 1969 NBA draft and enjoyed a ten-year NBA career. "I used to like to throw the ball behind my back," Allen recalls. "I'd make my behind-the-back pass and the crowd would go crazy and we'd score the layup. I'd be feeling great about the play I'd made. But when the horn sounded and we came off the floor, I'd get an angry look from Coach—and he'd tell me to sit down. The first half would go by and the second half would be halfway through. And finally, Coach would say, 'You ready to play basketball now, Lucius?' 'Yeah, Coach, I'm ready to play.' So that's the way I learned not to throw the behind-the-back pass."

The most important way Coach Wooden taught humility was by example. During his first seventeen years as head coach at UCLA, the only basketball floor on the campus was in the old practice gym. Coach had the university's maintenance department custom-build him a set of six-foot-wide brooms and six-foot-wide mops. Every morning before practice, Coach Wooden and his assistants would sweep off all the dust from the previous day's practice, then they'd damp-mop it shiny-clean.

Throughout those seventeen years, Coach personally wielded a broom and a mop before every practice. He was a humble servant

who refused to send his assistants out to do a job he wouldn't do himself.

Humility Defined

Humility, in its simplest sense, is the ability to put others ahead of self. It has been said that a humble person doesn't think less of himself; he simply thinks of himself less. A genuinely humble person can be confident without being arrogant, and can respect others while maintaining his self-respect. A humble person's self-esteem isn't tied to what other people say about him. As Mother Teresa once said, "If you are humble, nothing can touch you, neither praise nor disgrace, because you know who you are."

Humility is one of the most frequently commended character traits in all of Scripture. The Old Testament prophet Micah wrote, "And what does the LORD require of you? To act justly and to love mercy and to walk humbly with your God" (Micah 6:8). After leading Israel's victorious campaign against the Philistines, King David sang in his hymn to the Lord, "You save the humble, but your eyes are on the haughty to bring them low" (2 Sam. 22:28). And the psalmist wrote, "For the LORD takes delight in his people; he crowns the humble with salvation" (Ps. 149:4).

When Jesus described the essence of His own character, He presented Himself as a man of absolute humility. "Take my yoke upon you and learn from me, for I am gentle and humble in heart, and you will find rest for your souls. . . . For whoever exalts himself will be humbled, and whoever humbles himself will be exalted" (Matt. 11:29; 23:12).

And the apostle Paul wrote to the Christians in Rome, "For by the grace given me I say to every one of you: Do not think of yourself more highly than you ought, but rather think of yourself with sober judgment, in accordance with the measure of faith God has given you" (Rom. 12:3).

So many virtues flow from this character quality called humil-

ity. A humble person is respectful, because he humbly defers to others. A humble person is kind and agreeable, not quarrelsome, because he humbly considers the feelings of others. A humble person is generous, because he humbly thinks of the needs of others.

A humble person can walk tall and hold his head high, secure in the knowledge that he or she has nothing to prove. A humble person has a "team" attitude; he is willing to pass the ball to the player who has an open shot, secure in the knowledge that it's points on the board, not grandstand plays, that win games.

Scott Dawson is president of the Scott Dawson Evangelistic Association, Inc. I asked him to name the role model in his life who taught and exemplified character. The name Scott gave me: Billy Graham. "Though we're not close friends," he said, "Dr. Graham has always been an example of character to me. The first time I met him was in Philadelphia. I was there along with a number of other young preachers. I'll never forget the moment when Dr. Graham entered the room. There's a distinct feeling you get in the presence of greatness, and I felt it.

"Someone in our group went up to Dr. Graham, grabbed his hand, and started telling him, 'I've modeled my ministry after you! Thank you so much for the life you've led!' Dr. Graham stepped back and, with a look of genuine embarrassment on his face, he said politely but firmly, 'Do not model your life after me! I've made so many mistakes. Model your life after Christ.'

"Dr. Graham turned away the compliment because he didn't want it to go to his head. He knew that other men of God had started believing the praise that was showered on them, and they started taking credit that belongs solely to God. Dr. Graham wasn't going to let that happen in his life. He wasn't going to let pride destroy his effectiveness for God.

"On another occasion, I was in Louisville, Kentucky, and had the opportunity to introduce a young man to Billy Graham. After a brief conversation with Dr. Graham, my friend and I walked away—and my friend made an insightful observation: 'He doesn't even know

who he is!' It's true. Dr. Graham had a completely natural and un-feigned humility, as if he wasn't even aware of how famous he was or the kind of admiration and respect that others felt toward him."

As Scott Dawson described to me his impression of Dr. Billy Graham, I was reminded of my interview with Ruth Graham, Billy Graham's youngest daughter, on my weekly radio show in Orlando. I asked her to give me a thumbnail impression of her fa-ther's character. In her wonderful North Carolina accent, she said, "My daddy knows who he is—a flawed human being. In Daddy's mind, he's still just a farm boy from North Carolina."

The apostle Peter says, "Humble yourselves, therefore, under God's mighty hand, that he may lift you up in due time" (1 Pet. 5:6). Without question, Dr. Graham's reputation for character has been exalted in his own lifetime because he has truly humbled himself under God's mighty hand.

The Impact of an Athlete's Humility

Bart Lundy is head men's basketball coach at High Point University in High Point, North Carolina. When I asked him to name some-one who exemplifies character, he told me about a young player he coached at High Point a few years ago named Danny Gathings.

"Danny's from Winston-Salem," Bart told me, "and he played here at High Point after transferring from Virginia Tech. During the time he was at High Point, Danny experienced more growth as a person than any other player I ever coached. When he arrived, he was a kid who was expected to fail. By the time he finished his education at High Point, he was a responsible adult and a role model for other kids growing up in difficult, underprivileged con-ditions. Today, Danny is a professional basketball player in Eu-rope and a caring father. Here's Danny's story:

"On April 14, 2004, I stood with Danny at a convocation ser-vice in the Liberty Vines Center on the campus of Liberty Univer-sity, one of our conference rivals. There, with the Liberty faculty and student body looking on, Danny took the 2004 Big South

Tournament MVP plaque that he'd been awarded and he handed it to Liberty University guard Larry Blair. Why did he give away that award? Because he believed Blair truly earned it.

"The moment Danny handed over that award, he received a standing ovation from the Liberty students—undoubtedly the first, last, and only time I'll ever see the students of a rival school stand and applaud my best player. I have to tell you, I was stunned and moved. It shows how much those students appreciated and valued Danny's act of humility and sportsmanship."

Danny had taken a look at the numbers he put up in the three Big South tournament games. He averaged 11.7 points per game, and shot 16 for 29 (55.2 percent) from the field. Larry Blair averaged 21 points per game and shot 24 for 43 (55.8 percent) from the field. Blair also shot a tournament-record seven three-pointers in the championship game—a game in which Liberty beat High Point 89–44.

Danny Gathings took a realistic look at the numbers and decided he would not think more highly of himself than he ought. "When Danny gave the award to Blair," Coach Lundy recalled, "he said, 'This is something I need to do. Larry deserves this award, and I'm happy to hand it over to him and honor his efforts to help his team win the championship.' Then he grinned and said, 'Hopefully, I'll deserve it next year.'

"I was choked up at that point. I personally know both Danny and Larry, and they are two of the finest young men I've met, whether on or off the court. As a result of this humble gesture on Danny's part, he was awarded the NCAA sportsmanship award that year, and he has also been honored by several other organizations." Though athletes tend to make headlines only for the trouble they get into, it's heartwarming to hear about an athlete who impacts lives with his quiet, humble character.

Chuck Tanner is a former left fielder and major league manager, and at the time of this writing is a scout for the Cleveland Indians. He managed the Pittsburgh Pirates to a World Series championship in 1979. Chuck knows the importance of humility in sports

and in life. "I tell players and young people to always be humble," he said. "All the awards and honors you acquire are fine, but don't let them go to your head. The size of the crowd at your funeral will depend on the weather, so don't get too cocky."

Kindness and Compassion Flow from Humility

The apostle Paul told the Colossian believers, "Therefore, as God's chosen people, holy and dearly loved, clothe yourselves with compassion, kindness, humility, gentleness and patience" (Col. 3:12). I could write an entire book on each of those qualities, but I've chosen to use humility as an umbrella term for all of these qualities. I believe a person who is truly humble will naturally demonstrate all of these other character traits.

If you are humble, you think of others, you empathize with others, you put their welfare and feelings ahead of yours, you care for others and reach out to them when they are hurting or in need—and that's exactly what it means to have compassion. If you are humble, you will naturally show kindness and gentleness to other people. And if you are humble, you will naturally demonstrate patience in your dealings with others. A person of humble character continually puts others first.

Former Major League Baseball pitcher and manager Tommy Lasorda spent more than fifty years in various roles with the Brooklyn and Los Angeles Dodgers organization. He was inducted into the Baseball Hall of Fame in 1997, and managed the gold medal–winning Team U.S.A. at the 2000 Summer Olympics in Sydney, Australia.

Tommy told me, "One day when I was fifteen years old, growing up in Norristown, Pennsylvania, my mom brought home a bag of groceries and set it down on the kitchen counter. I pawed through that bag to see if she'd bought any of the foods I like, and I noticed a can of Carnation evaporated milk. I read the slogan that they had printed on the can in those days: 'Contented cows give better milk.'

"I've remembered that slogan throughout my entire career. I adopted that approach in my managerial career. Every time I managed a group of players—whether it was the Ogden, Utah, Dodgers in 1965 or the Los Angeles Dodgers in 1995—I always believed that contented ballplayers give better performances. That slogan guided the way I managed my teams."

Another legendary manager in Major League Baseball is Sparky Anderson, the fifth-winningest manager in MLB history. He is also the first manager to win World Series championships in both the National League (managing the Cincinnati Reds in 1975 and '76) and the American League (the Detroit Tigers in 1984). Sparky told me, "My father was a man of character who taught me how to act. He didn't tell me. He showed me. He was kind and decent to everyone he met. When I was eleven years old, he told me, 'There's one thing that will make a big difference in your life, and it will never cost you a dime—and that is to be nice to people.'"

Dr. Rick Pribyl is the boys soccer coach at Blue Valley Northwest High School in Overland Park, Kansas. He shared with me a letter he wrote to one of his coaches from more than thirty-five years before, Coach Jack Kersting of St. Louis University in Missouri. Here is the letter, which I've condensed:

Dear Coach,

This letter is thirty-five years overdue. You and I last met in the fall of 1970, after I graduated. I was entering my second year in the air force as a pilot and was on my way to Vietnam.

There you stood with the whistle around your neck, shouting encouragement to your players. When I walked up, you came over and gave me a firm handshake and a hug. We talked for about ten minutes and you closed by saying, "The air force has no idea what a great athlete they have in their cockpit. I want you to come home safe."

The air force never found out I was an athlete, but I did come home safe. More important, ten years after the air force I found myself teaching, coaching, and giving my players the same kind of positive reinforcement you always gave me.

I thank you for letting me start for you for two years—the first year as split end and the second year as outside linebacker; for letting me do some of my soccer kicking in our on-side plays; and for nominating me for All-American. But the highest compliment ever given to me by a coach was in the college newspaper where you commented on all the players. You called me "one of the most coachable players on the team." I've always tried to live up to that compliment.

As a coach, I've learned that there are two ways to light a fire in a player and motivate him. One is to light a fire *under* him—to push him, yell at him, and goad him into working hard. That way may get results at first, but the coach soon finds that the fire is constantly going out, and has to be relit again and again. The second way is to ignite the passion in his heart. That fire burns eternally. That's the kind of fire you lit in our team. I have never lost that fire.

Thanks, Coach, for being such a friend and mentor when I was at the threshold of my adulthood. You somehow knew that the young men you coached were afraid and innocent in the ways of the real world. Through football, you offered a boy a secret way to sneak up on the mystery that is manhood.

Sincerely,

Dr. Rick Pribyl

Proudly No. 82 of the 1968 and

1969 team coached by Jack Kersting

Both Rick Pribyl and Jack Kersting understand that coaching is about more than winning games. It's about shaping souls—and they both go about their business with kindness and humility.

The Character Test

Lawrence W. Reed is president of the Mackinac Center for Public Policy. He shared with me a story that could be filed under a number of character headings, such as kindness or integrity. But I chose to place this story here because it is really a story about a man—a total stranger—who humbly placed others ahead of himself.

"In 1989," Mr. Reed told me, "I visited Cambodia with my friend Dr. Haing S. Ngor, the Cambodian physician and actor who won an Academy Award for his role in *The Killing Fields*. Dr. Ngor was himself a survivor of the Cambodian holocaust depicted in the film.

"Our preparations for the trip received considerable press attention because I was taking donated medical supplies from the U.S. to a hospital in Phnom Penh. A Michigan woman, Sharon Hartlein, asked me to do a favor for three Cambodian families who had escaped and resettled in the States. The families asked me to take letters containing cash to their relatives in Cambodia. I agreed.

"When I arrived in Cambodia, I found that two of the families were in Phnom Penh, the capital. I had no trouble finding them. The third family, however, was quite a distance away in Battambang. Getting there would involve train travel and personal risk, plus the trip would take more time than I had. I was told that if I couldn't locate the family, I should give the cash to any needy Cambodian I could find.

"The day before my departure, I realized I simply would not make it to Battambang. So I approached a man I had seen several times in the hotel lobby. He was always friendly, and he spoke enough English that we were able to converse. I knew he was desperately poor. I told him I had a letter containing two hundred dollars in cash, intended for a family in Battambang. I said he could keep fifty dollars if he would take the rest to the family in

that city. He consented and we said good-bye. I was sure I'd never hear what became of him or the money.

"Several months after I returned to the States, I received a call from Sharon Hartlein. She was very excited and told me she had received a letter from the family whose relatives were in Battambang. She read the letter to me over the phone. One sentence in the letter stunned me and brought tears to my eyes. It read, 'Thank you for sending the two hundred dollars.'

"I was dumbfounded. The needy man I had entrusted the money to had taken it to Battambang, had located the family, and had given them the entire amount, all two hundred dollars. He had not even kept the fifty dollars I had offered him. He had sacrificed his own time and safety, and had delivered that money without thinking of himself at all!"

If that needy Cambodian man had delivered all but the fifty dollars he was offered, it would be a story about integrity. But since he didn't even take the money he had earned, it is a story of amazing selflessness and humility. If you and I were in the same position as that poor Cambodian man, would we have passed the character test?

How to Raise Young People of Humility

Humility is one of the rarest of all the character traits—and the most desperately needed. Here are some ways we can encourage this character trait in our kids:

1. Teach your kids to be servants. Jesus repeatedly taught this lesson to His disciples: "Sitting down, Jesus called the Twelve and said, 'If anyone wants to be first, he must be the very last, and the servant of all'" (Mark 9:35). There's no such thing as an arrogant servant; a servant is humble by definition. If kids learn to see themselves as servants of God and others, they will naturally develop an attitude of humility.

After the publication of my book *Coaching Your Kids to Be Leaders* (FaithWords, 2005), I received an email from Tom Walsh,

a reader teaching his kids character and humility at an early age. He told me, "Thanks for writing this book! As a father of two boys, ages two and four (with a third child on the way), I found a lot of ideas in your book about how to raise emotionally and spiritually healthy kids. Your book inspired me to action."

He went on to say that, one Saturday, he took his two boys out to a bagel store for breakfast, then they went to a local nursing home to visit some of the residents. He had never done this before and wasn't sure of the procedure, so he walked up to the desk and told the receptionist that he and the boys would like to visit someone.

"Who have you come to visit?" the receptionist asked.

"Anyone," Tom replied. "We just want to visit someone who could use a little company."

The surprised receptionist informed a staff member, and the staff was very accommodating. They let Tom and his boys wander around and talk to people wherever they went. Finally, they came to a lounge where a number of residents were gathered, eating doughnuts and sipping coffee.

George, Tom's four-year-old, walked right up to people, put out his hand, and said, "Hi! My name is George! It's nice to meet you!" The boy gave each person a hearty handshake. The people at the home were charmed by Tom's two boys—and it was an uplifting experience for Tom. For his sons, it was the beginning of their training in becoming servants to others—an invaluable field trip in the school of humility.

Tom Walsh concluded with these words: "I don't think you can ever start too early training kids to consider other people and serve them. At the same time, you are teaching them to sharpen their social skills, overcome shyness, and build their confidence. Thanks again for providing that spark of inspiration in your book!"

I'm pleased my book inspired Tom to take action—but I feel his story has inspired and touched me even more! He showed me it's never too early to start teaching humble servanthood to our kids.

2. Encourage kids to admit mistakes. You can't be a person of humility if you can't admit being wrong. Our kids need to see that people think more of them, not less, when they admit mistakes. When our kids face criticism, they need to learn to consider the merits of that criticism instead of instantly defending themselves.

One way to encourage kids to admit mistakes is by showing mercy when they confess their sins and errors. Tell them over and over again that, when they fail or sin, they can always be forgiven and accepted. A confession will always make life easier for them than a cover-up or a lie will. Kids who feel they can safely go to their parents with the awful truth are much less likely to be dishonest and defensive.

Another way to encourage kids to admit mistakes is to set an example by admitting our own errors. Some parents feel they need to keep up a false front of perfection in front of their kids. They feel that admitting mistakes would diminish them in their children's eyes. In reality, when we as parents say to our kids, "I was wrong, please forgive me," we are actually magnified in their eyes.

3. Teach kids to demonstrate empathy toward others. Because humility is essentially a matter of considering the needs and feelings of others, children need to learn sensitivity to the feelings of others.

Debbie Fahmie is the music specialist at Cypress Elementary School in Osceola County, Florida, and president of the Florida Elementary Music Educators Association. She uses music education to build character—and especially to encourage empathy in young people. She has a heart for students with problems and needs.

"The neediest of students," she told me, "are the ones who made me really dig deep into my soul. It's the students who are life's 'throwaways,' the 'unlovable kids,' who inspire me and bring out my empathy for others. I don't believe a person can have true character without empathy for all of humankind. The person of true character will do good to others—not to be recognized, but simply because it's the right thing to do.

"I use cooperative learning to bring out my students' empathy for each other. I teach my students how to help the child who is struggling, how to befriend the unlovable child, how to bring out the best in others around them. Again and again, my students discover it feels good to do good to others. Instead of bribing kids with candy and tokens, we should motivate kids to seek that inner incentive and warm feeling of doing good to others. That intrinsic reward is so much more valuable than a material incentive.

"Music is the perfect medium for allowing students to experience the harmony of working together and the pitfalls of focusing purely on self. Empathy and humility work together in the lives of these students to produce character and compassion. If we can influence young people to become caring and compassionate, we will give a wonderful gift to the world."

4. *Teach young people to take satisfaction rather than pride in their accomplishments.* When children perform well or achieve a goal, it's good for them to feel that warm glow of joy that comes from a job well done. But let them know that arrogant or disrespectful behavior is not permitted.

When kids excel in academics, sports, music, or some other endeavor, monitor their attitude and behavior. Be alert to signals that they feel superior or look down upon their peers. Encourage good sportsmanship. Help them understand that people of great character acknowledge the achievements of others; only small-minded people engage in smack talk and put-downs.

Encourage your kids to use their abilities to serve God and help others. Teach them to enjoy the feeling of a job well done and to thank God for His gifts of talent, strength, and health which make it possible for us to achieve our goals. Everything we have is a gift. We can't take credit for a gift; we can only be grateful to the Giver.

5. *Set a zero-tolerance policy toward disrespectful attitudes and talk.* Children should never be permitted to behave rudely or use profane language. Train them to speak and behave respectfully from an early age. Make it clear you will listen to your kids and

consider any complaint or objection they may have—as long as it is stated respectfully.

Peter Roby, director of sport in society at Northeastern University, told me a story from his boyhood. "My father will always be my hero and role model," he said. "He demanded that I show respect on the field or court toward the officials, opponents, and fans. When I was about ten and playing Little League baseball, I got visibly upset with an umpire's call on some of my pitches. When I came in after the inning, my father said, 'If you ever act disrespectfully to an umpire again, I'll come out on the field and drag you off the mound.' He expected me to respect everyone. I did from then on."

Here are some suggestions for dealing with kids who show disrespect:

- If a child becomes disrespectful during an argument or disagreement, stop the conversation and remind the child that you will only listen to his or her opinions if they are stated courteously. You might interrupt and say, "Would you like to restate that in a respectful tone?"
- When children correct their tone and show they can discuss disagreements in a respectful way, affirm their maturity and character. Let them know that you notice their character growth, and you are proud of the way they conducted themselves, despite the disagreement.
- If your children persist in being disrespectful, impose consequences that are age-appropriate and consistent. Don't discipline out of anger, simply because your kids pushed your buttons. Discipline out of love, because you want to shape their character.

Thomas M. Doran, a partner with Hubbell, Roth & Clark, Inc., recalls, "In my youth, I was prone to biting and indiscriminate criticism. My dad's best friend was my godfather, and one time he was visiting from Chicago. He was a big-hearted, cheerful man and an ex-marine like my dad. The three of us got into a political discussion and I made a disparaging remark about my dad, but he ignored it. Later, after my dad left the room, my godfather

took me aside and said, 'Your dad is my friend, and I won't tolerate my friend being insulted—not even by his own son.'

"That was the first time my godfather ever spoke to me man to man. It wasn't pleasant being talked to that way, but even then, I realized that this man wasn't threatening me. He was doing what a godparent is supposed to do. He was instilling moral character in me. I had shown disrespect, and he was letting me know that disrespect for parents is a blot on my character.

"My godfather never mentioned that incident again, and we had a great relationship until the day he died. He was a man of character, and he cared enough about me to take me aside and strengthen my character."

6. *Encourage kids to be teachable and coachable.* Our kids need to be willing learners. No matter how much they think they know, they can always grow and improve.

Since 1968, I have worked alongside some of the legendary coaches of the NBA—Jack Ramsay, Dick Motta, Cotton Fitzsimmons, Gene Shue, Billy Cunningham, Matt Guokas, Chuck Daly, Doc Rivers, Brian Hill, and more. When it's time for the NBA draft in the summer, when all the information has been gathered about the top college players, there is always one question every one of these coaches has asked: "Can I coach this kid? Will he listen to me?"

If being coachable is so important in pro basketball, how much more important is it that our own young people be teachable and coachable? Here are some suggestions for raising coachable kids:

- First, when you teach or coach your kids, be positive. Kids respond to positive coaching, but they resent yelling, shaming, and belittling. If they come to know you as a positive and encouraging parent-coach, they will be more likely to listen and follow your instruction. We sometimes forget how children view the world. If we expect too much of them or treat them harshly, we'll shame them and undermine their confidence.

- Second, be a good role model. Your kids are watching every move you make. If they detect hypocrisy in your life, they'll use it as an excuse to disregard what you say. As someone has said, our children will become what we are—so we'd better start becoming what we want them to be.
- Third, praise effort, not results. If a child is only affirmed when he succeeds, he'll become fearful of failure. When a child feels affirmed even when he tries and fails, he has more confidence to take risks and go out on a limb for you. So when your child fails, don't let your disappointment show. Always say, "Great effort! Way to hustle! I'm proud of you!"
- Fourth, treat your child as a unique personality. Every child is an individual, and the kind of coaching that works with one child may not work with another. Train each child according to his or her unique needs.

7. Be a role model of humility. Let your kids see you serving others. Let them see you asking for directions and not having all the answers. Let them see you reading, listening, and seeking knowledge and wisdom. When you get cut off on the freeway, let them see you responding gently—no honking or obscene gestures. Let your kids see how teachable and coachable you are. Ask them to teach you something they know and you don't.

Cal Ripken Jr. is a former shortstop and third baseman who played his entire career for the Baltimore Orioles from 1981 to 2001, and is famed for his 2,632-game "Iron Man" streak. A few years ago, he wanted to take a laptop computer on the road with him to keep in touch with his family via email—but he had a problem.

"I'm a little intimidated by the technology," he said, "but my daughter Rachel is at the age where she can teach me. She's seven years old." Ever coachable and teachable, Cal Ripken was not ashamed to seek technical advice from his little daughter. Humility is an attractive trait. When your kids see humility in you, they will want to be humble too.

It Doesn't Take Much

Dr. Charles T. Menghini, president of VanderCook College of Music, told me a story from his experience that illustrates the profound importance of being a person of kindness and compassion, a person who humbly puts others first. "Several years ago," he said, "I received an email from a former high school student of mine. He refreshed my memory about a situation that took place many years ago.

"I was the band director at a suburban Kansas City high school, and our jazz band was playing for a church social. That evening, the first-chair trumpet player couldn't make it to the performance, so the second-chair student (the fellow who wrote the email) got to play the solo that evening.

"His email recounted how he hit the last note of the solo—a difficult high note—and he hit it perfectly. He said he would never forget the smile I flashed him at that moment. He also said that of all the experiences of his high school career, that was the moment he remembered most vividly.

"I read that with amazement. Our high school band that year had a national reputation. We had won national-level competitions. We had toured the country and traveled to Europe. That was a memorable time, filled with exciting experiences. And what did this young musician remember? One smile of approval for a single note played in the basement of a church!

"That email stopped me dead in my tracks and choked me up. No, it wasn't that I was pleased with myself for giving that kid a smile of approval. The reason I felt like crying was that I instantly wondered, *How many kids did I not show some approval to when they needed it most? How many negative comments did I give? How many opportunities did I pass up to show some much-needed kindness in a student's life?* It's amazing how little it sometimes takes to make a huge difference in someone's life."

There's a big lesson in that story for you and me: it doesn't take much to impact the lives of others with humility, kindness, and

compassion. Who is the person in your life, in my life, who needs a smile and a nod of approval? How many chances to impact and influence lives have we allowed to slip through our fingers?

While completing work on this book, I had a conversation with Jamaal Wilkes, who played for Coach John Wooden at UCLA. Jamaal went on to play twelve seasons in the NBA, averaging almost 18 points per game over his career. He is now a successful businessman. I asked Jamaal, "How would you summarize Coach Wooden as a human being? What quality set him apart?"

Jamaal replied, "It's interesting you ask, because I was talking to Coach about that very thing a short while ago—and the answer to your question would have to be Coach Wooden's incredible humility. Here he is, at age ninety-six, an absolute legend of the game of basketball—and he has absolutely no awareness of his own greatness. I asked him, 'Coach, what made you so successful?' And you know what he did? He *argued* with me for fifteen minutes, telling me that he was *not* successful!"

I said, "Jamaal, you can't be serious."

"I'm serious," he replied. "For fifteen minutes, he tried to convince me he was not successful. I listed his accomplishments, and he just waved it off like he was embarrassed that anyone would make a big deal about it. Finally he said, 'Jamaal, if I had any success at all, there were two reasons: One, I always tried to be organized and prepared for every practice. And two, I truly cared for you young men and I wanted each of you to do well in life, long after your basketball careers were over.' Well, that was Coach—totally humble and never focused on his own success, only on the success of his players."

That's a great example for you and me. Let's commit ourselves to becoming humble servants, people of compassion and character who care about others above all, changing the world one life at a time.

9

Love: An Unconditional Choice

"I believe that unarmed truth and unconditional love will have the final word in reality. This is why righteousness, temporarily defeated, is stronger than evil triumphant."

MARTIN LUTHER KING JR.
CIVIL RIGHTS LEADER AND MARTYR

Gerald R. Ford, the thirty-eighth president of the United States (1974–1977), died the day after Christmas 2006. When I heard the news of his passing, I remembered a phone conversation I had with Mr. Ford in July 2002. I was writing a book about my friend Rich DeVos, who was a friend of the former president. I wrote to Mr. Ford, seeking an interview, and one day my office phone rang and a voice on the other end of the line asked, "Are you available to take a call from President Ford?"

Was I? I was! Moments later, I heard a familiar voice come on the line and say, "Pat Williams, it's Gerry Ford." He was calling from his vacation home in Vail, Colorado.

With my pen poised over my yellow legal pad, I proceeded to interview the former president regarding his friendship with Rich DeVos. We talked for about fifteen minutes and he gave me some good reminiscences.

Then the conversation turned to basketball. Mr. Ford was a Denver Nuggets fan—but he was also very interested in Orlando's

prospects for the coming season. "Who did you guys draft?" he asked.

"Ryan Humphrey," I said.

"Oh, yeah, the forward from Notre Dame. How does he look?"

"Very good," I replied. (As it turned out, Humphrey gave us three lackluster seasons and now plays basketball in Italy.)

"How about the two guys our Nuggets drafted? Do you think they're any good or are they overhyped?" He was talking about Nikoloz Tskitishvili, a power forward from Tbilisi, in the nation of Georgia, and Nenê, a big forward-center who played for Team Brazil in the 2001 Goodwill Games.

I said, "We had good scouting reports on them both."

"That's good to hear," Mr. Ford said. "The Nuggets could use a lift."

As we ended the call, I thought to myself, *Wow! Here's the man who was at the center of so much history! Vietnam, Watergate, the Nixon pardon, the energy crisis, and more—and he sounded like he felt honored to talk to me! And what's more, the man really knows his basketball!*

That was July 2002. Fast-forward to December 2006. President Ford is dead and the nation mourns. The pundits all agree his historical legacy can be summed up in one word: forgiveness.

The Ford presidency is remembered primarily for a single decision Mr. Ford announced in September 1974—the decision to pardon his disgraced predecessor, Richard Nixon, for any and all crimes he might have committed as president. Mr. Ford said he pardoned Nixon because the humiliation of resigning from office was punishment enough—and Mr. Ford felt the pardon would finally move the nation past the Watergate scandal.

At the time, Mr. Ford's decision was not merely controversial—it was widely reviled. The new president was accused of arranging the pardon in a secret deal (which Mr. Ford has steadfastly denied). The nation was hardly in a forgiving mood. The pardon

ended Mr. Ford's chances of being reelected in 1976. Defeated by Jimmy Carter, Ford left the White House and passed into history, living out the rest of his life in relative obscurity.

Time passed. Tempers cooled. With the perspective of hindsight, people came to see that Gerald Ford's instincts were right all along. The nation needed to forgive and move on.

In time, people who had suspected Mr. Ford's motives began to see things differently. After all, Gerald Ford, the man who pardoned Nixon, was also the man who offered pardon to young men who had deserted or dodged the draft during the Vietnam War. People began to see that forgiveness wasn't a political act for Mr. Ford; it was an act of unconditional love that flowed from the depths of his soul.

As they laid Gerald Ford to rest, most of the eulogies, obituaries, commentaries, and editorials were filled with discussions of love and forgiveness. What greater legacy could anyone leave than that?

Love Is a Decision

What is love? There is no one definition everyone agrees on. Some see love as an emotional fondness, a tender affection, or even an attraction between two people. Others see love as a sense of connection between people. I believe if we want an authoritative definition of love in its truest sense, we need to go to the Scriptures.

Paul, writing to the Christians in Corinth, Greece, defined love this way: "Love is patient, love is kind. It does not envy, it does not boast, it is not proud. It is not rude, it is not self-seeking, it is not easily angered, it keeps no record of wrongs. Love does not delight in evil but rejoices with the truth. It always protects, always trusts, always hopes, always perseveres. Love never fails" (1 Cor. 13:4–8).

What is love, according to this definition? The kind of love Paul describes is not an emotion or an affection or an attraction or a connection. This kind of love is a *decision*. It is, in fact, a *character trait* a person can *choose* to build into his or her life.

. .Paul says that patience and kindness are found in authentic love. These attributes do not come naturally; they are *choices* we make. Negative emotions and attitudes, such as envy, boastfulness, pride, rudeness, selfishness, anger, and grudge-bearing, are completely natural and easy for us to do—but we have to make a deliberate and difficult *choice* to be humble, selfless, and forgiving. We have to *choose* to love people when it's not easy to love. We have to *choose* to rejoice with the truth, to protect the weak, to trust and hope, to persevere and not let go.

The writers of the New Testament had to use a special word for this kind of love. In the original Greek language of the New Testament, the word they used—the word Paul uses in 1 Corinthians 13—is *agape*. This kind of love is *unconditional*. It makes the tough decision to love people who are unlovely, unlovable, and unloving.

This unconditional love is the kind of love God shows to the human race. It's a love that does not favor one person above another. It is even a love that enables us to do good to those who hate us and hurt us, to those who are our enemies. Jesus described this decision-based love when He said, "You have heard that it was said, 'Love your neighbor and hate your enemy.' But I tell you: Love your enemies and pray for those who persecute you, that you may be sons of your Father in heaven" (Matt. 5:43–45).

God's love is unconditional, and our love should be like His. Unconditional *agape* love is expressed in many ways. It's expressed as a willingness to forgive those who hurt us, even before they ask to be forgiven. It's expressed in acts of kindness, compassion, charity, and generosity for people in need. It's expressed in a tolerant love for all of humanity, regardless of race, ethnicity, national origin, or religion. We don't have to approve of the things people do, but we can unconditionally accept all people as our brothers and sisters in the human race.

Unconditional Love in Action

As we look around us, we see that this kind of all-accepting, all-inclusive, all-forgiving love is rare in this world. We see racial intolerance, ethnic cleansing, religious strife, and political divisiveness. There is all too little forgiveness, and far too much hatred and revenge. But sometimes, we hear a refreshing and inspiring story of unconditional love and forgiveness.

One such story was told to me by Andy Benoit, author of the annual *Andy Benoit's Touchdown* series of NFL books. Andy told me about a man whose life is an inspirational example because he chooses every day to live a lifestyle of unconditional love. "To me," Andy said, "my grandfather is a role model of character. In 1966, he was loading a Christmas tree onto a car when a drunk driver ran over him. The accident cost him both legs. He was in the hospital for three months, then underwent ten months of rehabilitation.

"At the time of the accident, my grandfather's three daughters were in high school and junior high. He was expected to spend the rest of his life in a wheelchair, and was predicted to live no more than ten years after the accident. Forty years later, however, he is alive and healthy, getting around just fine on two artificial legs. He was able to resume farming less than a year after the accident, and to this day he's still very active.

"Because of nerve damage, his legs sometimes flare up with terrible pain. He suffers infections and sometimes falls. So he has had to live with the painful consequences of another man's negligence for all of these years—yet he never complains. Never.

"One time, my grandfather and I were driving and discussing the pain he was suffering that day. I asked if he ever found out who the drunk driver was. He said, 'Oh, yes. He was a man in his twenties.' I said, 'Well, if you knew who hit you, why didn't you go after him in court?' He said, 'Oh, he didn't have much. He was a young fellow with his whole life ahead of him.'

"I was floored by this. At the time of the accident, Grandpa

was a relatively young man with three daughters. His entire family suffered because of the accident, and his own physical pain never completely went away. How could he put the needs of that man ahead of his own?

"That was an amazing display of character. The reason I think Grandpa exhibits such character is because he chose forgiveness forty years ago, and he still chooses forgiveness today. He has never given in to blaming or complaining. He's consistent in his commitment to forgive."

Andy Benoit's grandfather is living proof: love is a choice.

Love for the Marginalized People

Columnist Abigail Van Buren, author of the "Dear Abby" syndicated column, once said, "The best index to a person's character is how he treats people who can't do him any good and how he treats people who can't fight back." By this measure, a person of character is one who shows unconditional love for all people, including the least, the last, and the lost.

Dave Hart, athletics director at Florida State University, told me his parents taught him to reach out to help the marginalized people in the world. "My mother and father instilled in me core values of respect for others, regardless of their circumstances," he said. "My dad always told me that the true mark of a person of character is that he helps people who are in no position to help him back. In other words, don't just help those who can return the favor. Help everyone—simply because it's the right thing to do.

"I remember when I was a young man, traveling through a crowded airport, hurrying to make my connection. I spotted a mentally challenged young man at the top of the escalator. He was crying and asking for someone to please stop and help him. No one was paying any attention to him.

"Though worried about making my own plane, I heard my dad's voice in my mind. So I stopped and offered to help. He showed me his ticket, and I figured out where he was going and

accompanied him on the tram to his gate. Once I knew he was all right, I hurried off to make my own plane.

"Then I heard a shout behind me—'Stop!' I turned around, and this fellow ran to me and gave me a big hug. He said, 'You helped me! Thank you!' I don't know that I ever had a better feeling in my life than I felt right then. I also made my connection."

Darrell Scott is a father who has taught his children, by word and example, to reach out to the marginalized kids around them. His children attended Columbine High School in Littleton, Colorado. On April 20, 1999, Darrell's daughter Rachel sat on the school lawn near the cafeteria, eating lunch, when two boys in trenchcoats walked up to her. One boy pulled a gun from his coat, pointed it at Rachel, and shot her in the leg. When she tried to get up and run, he shot her again in the chest. She fell, wounded but alive.

The boys turned their guns on the boy next to Rachel, shooting him several times. They left him on the bloody grass, paralyzed but alive. The two boys strode into the cafeteria, guns drawn, where more than four hundred students were gathered for lunch. Earlier, the boys had hidden butane tanks in the cafeteria and planned to set them off as firebombs, hoping to kill every student in the building. By God's grace, the bombs failed to explode.

Frustrated, the boys went outside. One knelt beside Rachel. Just a few days earlier, she had tried to reach out to the boy, telling him about the love of Jesus. He had sneered at her then. Now, as she lay dying from her wounds, he lifted her head and asked, "Do you still believe in God?"

She answered, "Yes, I do."

"Then go be with Him," the boy said. He placed the gun against her head and fired.

Rachel Scott was only the first Columbine student to die that day. Before the two murderers were done, they took the lives of twelve students, a teacher, and themselves. They left many other students wounded.

Weeks later, Rachel's grieving father, Darrell Scott, was visited by one of Rachel's classmates, a boy with a congenital deformity that left him with a disfigured face and a speech impediment. Because of his appearance, his cruel classmates called him "Alien."

The boy said to Darrell Scott, "I want you to know that Rachel was always nice to me. Every day at school, she put her arm around me and said, 'How are you doing today?' I saw her just an hour before they killed her. She gave me a hug and said, 'Someday soon, we'll get some coffee and go to a movie, and we'll have a good time.' Every night since she died, I cry and cry for Rachel, because she was the only person at school who was nice to me."

We need more young people of character like Rachel Scott—young people who will reach out to those who are marginalized and mistreated. We need to show our kids how to love the least and the last and the lost.

Unconditional Love Is the Great Motivator

Lauded by *Ebony* magazine as one of the "Thirty Leaders of the Future, Thirty and Under," Lamell McMorris is the founding principal and CEO of Perennial Strategy Group, a lobbying and consulting firm. As spokesperson for the National Basketball Referees Association, Lamell McMorris helped negotiate a historic collective bargaining agreement with the NBA. He was selected by Martin Luther King III to serve as executive director of the Southern Christian Leadership Conference (SCLC), a position once held by Dr. Martin Luther King Jr. himself.

I asked Lamell McMorris about the role models who had influenced him. He said, "One of my good friends is Martin Luther King III. I've had the occasion to work in his office, intern with him, and travel with him. I'm always amazed that he can go from city to city, school to school, and see his dad's story and image plastered everywhere—a constant reminder that when he was just ten years old, he lost his father to an assassin's bullet.

"I asked Martin how he was able to cope with his loss. He

said that what sustained him and his family was an overriding commitment to principles of love and faith. That was how he got through not only the assassination of his father but the murder of his grandmother, Alberta King, who was killed while playing the organ in church in June 1974. He told me that the teachings of his father were instilled in him and his siblings from the time they were very young.

"Their dad taught them that there are different levels of love, but the highest of all was unconditional love—a love that reaches out to people regardless of race, color, or status in life. It's a love that says, 'No matter what you have done to me and my family, I'm still going to seek the best for you.' That kind of all-inclusive love affects every aspect of one's character.

"Authentic love is unconditional. Martin could have given up and turned bitter after having lost his father and grandmother to violence. Instead, he's continued his father's legacy of unconditional love."

When people of character exemplify love, it's expressed in acts of service to God and other people. Scott Harding is executive director of National Relief Network, an organization which coordinates volunteer relief efforts in declared disaster areas. He told me, "As the executive director of National Relief Network, I work with hundreds of teenage volunteers from all across our nation. I've found that young people can be inspired to express their character and love for humanity. Let me share an example.

"Some years ago, we had a group of volunteers from Kansas City who had gathered to help a man named Harry in South River, North Carolina. Harry was eighty years old and lived in a house built by his father when Harry was a young boy. The house, built of solid oak, had stood strong for all those years. Then came Hurricane Floyd, and the house was flooded by the storm surge and rains. The house was condemned and had to be taken down in order for Harry to have a new home built on the same spot.

"A home that was originally constructed of moist oak and iron

nails does not come down easily, but fifty-five hardworking high school students from Kansas City worked on the project through four hot and humid days. Their donated efforts saved Harry the cost of demolition—more than thirteen thousand dollars.

"After about three and a half days of intensive work, I noticed that a lot of our students and chaperone volunteers were exhausted and were sitting around under the shade trees in Harry's yard. I knew from past experience that, if everyone helped, we could finish Harry's home in the next three hours—but it wouldn't happen unless everybody pitched in.

"Everyone had gotten to know Harry over the past few days. We'd heard him talk about helping his dad build the house, how he'd joined the Coast Guard at sixteen by lying about his age, and so forth. Everyone had come to love this wonderful old man and wanted to finish the job—but the hot, sweaty work had sapped everyone's strength. I had to find a way to motivate the crew to finish the job.

"So I said, 'Let's break!' and we gathered under a large oak tree. I said, 'Did everyone get a chance to meet Harry?' I knew they had, but I wanted everyone to reflect on their love for this man.

"'I know everyone's hot and tired and ready to drop,' I continued. 'You've all done an incredible job, but I'm looking at the clock and I see that we have only three more hours out of our entire lives to give to Harry—then we'll probably never see him again. That's three short hours to finish giving him the gift we came halfway across the country to give—our time and caring. Three short hours to show Harry who we are. I want him to remember me as someone who gave everything I had—and I, for one, am going to work like I've never worked before. Who wants to join me?'

"With that, I headed back to work. Right behind me came fifty-five newly energized volunteers. We finished the job that day. Before we left, Harry hugged each one of us."

Unconditional love compels us to go the extra mile and give the extra measure. We all have more to give than we realize, and sometimes we just need to reach inside and find that extra measure of love for our fellow man in order to motivate ourselves to finish strong.

Team Love

Love is the key to teamwork and winning, as Chuck Priefer, special teams coordinator for the Detroit Lions, told me. "Years back, when I was appointed head football coach at a high school in Parma, Ohio," he told me, "the school had gone through four head coaches in nine years and never had a winning season. We played in the toughest conference in Ohio at that time, and were used to losing fifty to nothing every week.

"When I took over, we started what we called 'victory camp.' Coaches and players went away for three days and worked with two professionals on team building. We did not touch a football or diagram a play during those three days. We focused on one thing: forging a team out of young men of great character. We taught them to care for one another, to sacrifice their egos for the sake of the team, and to replace personal goals with team goals.

"The season after our first victory camp, we won seven games. Two years later, we were the number one team in Cleveland. They played for the love of the game and the love of the team—and they became champions."

Rob Yowell, vice president of sponsorship sales for The Bonham Group, a sports marketing firm, told me, "My first year of prep school at Woodberry Forest School in Orange, Virginia, I was invited for early football practice in August. As a fifteen-year-old at boarding school, I learned that my teammates were going to be the people I counted on most.

"The team went undefeated the previous year, but the All-State quarterback was dismissed for violating the honor code during summer school. Lacking our star quarterback, we went 3-6 that

season. Adversity makes young men grow up fast, especially when they're away from home. The special bond that began on the practice fields in those hot and steamy August days produced friendships that I maintain to this day. We made a commitment to return the program to its rightful place as Prep League champs. We went 7-2 as juniors, and we won the championship as seniors.

"During that final season, one of our top players lost his father to a heart attack just hours before a game. He insisted on playing the game because that's what his dad wanted him to do. As a team, we all attended the funeral, and we presented our teammate's mother with a game ball from our victory the day before. Because of the team love that bonded us, we hurt and grieved almost as much as our teammate.

"As captain of that 1983 championship team, I thought back to those first few days when I arrived, the new kid, away from home for the first time in my life. I thought about all the lessons I had learned during my three years at boarding school. It hit me that I had grown more in my character than I ever could have imagined. I had learned that a team is more than just a bunch of guys in matching uniforms. A team is a fellowship of people who truly love each other and who work as a unit to achieve a common goal."

That's the power of team love—an unconditional caring for your teammates that lifts you over grief, setbacks, and adversity. Team love makes you more than teammates, more than friends. It makes you champions.

Unconditional Brotherly Love

My dad, Jim Williams, was a coach at the Tower Hill School in Wilmington, Delaware. In 1956, he and Bob Carpenter, the owner of the Philadelphia Phillies, spearheaded the first Delaware High School Football All-Star Game to benefit mentally retarded children (the game became an annual tradition, and still benefits the same cause today). It was a North-versus-South game, and it hap-

pened that two top players in the North—Joe Peters and Alvin Hall—were African American athletes from Wilmington's predominantly Black school, Howard High.

For two weeks prior to the game, players from high schools in the North worked out at Sanford Prep School in Hockessin, near Wilmington. Unfortunately, the Sanford headmaster was nervous because he assumed his students from the Deep South would be prejudiced against Blacks. He laid down a condition: Joe and Alvin could only use the practice facilities during the day but had to spend the night off campus.

My dad was incensed! He said it was stupid and insulting to impose separate conditions on two young athletes because of their skin color. When the Sanford headmaster refused to relent, Dad said, "Okay, they'll stay at our house." I had just gotten my driver's license, so during the two weeks of practice, I got up early every morning and drove Joe and Alvin to the prep school. I picked them up at the end of each day.

That experience in 1956 deeply affected my thinking. Here were two guys who were just like everybody else except the color of their skin, and they were being treated in a humiliating way. I said to myself, "This is crazy! How could anyone think that segregation is acceptable?"

Coach John Wooden had a similar experience in 1947 while coaching basketball at Indiana State. One of his players was an African American named Clarence Walker from East Chicago, Indiana. Walker was not a starter, but he was a solid contributor from the bench—and he helped Indiana State win a slot in the National Association of Intercollegiate Athletics (NAIA) National Tournament in Kansas City.

As Coach was preparing to take the Indiana State Sycamores to the tournament, the NAIA officials called him and told him that Clarence Walker was not welcome. In their conversation, they used an ugly racial epithet. At that time, John Wooden was at the start of his career. He had a lot to lose if he upset the "powers that

be." But the discrimination against one of his players had fired up his righteous indignation.

"Listen," he said, "if I can't bring Clarence, we're not coming."

The NAIA didn't budge—and Indiana State stayed home. But the story didn't end there.

The story hit the national newswires and the NAIA was pressured into ending its policy of racial discrimination. The following year, Indiana State again won its conference and Coach Wooden took his team, including Clarence Walker, to the tournament. Walker became the first Black athlete to play in a post-season intercollegiate basketball tournament. During his two seasons at Indiana State, Coach Wooden's Sycamores went 47-14. He was offered the position at UCLA the following year.

R. L. "Bobby" Vaughan, the highly regarded African American basketball coach at Elizabeth City State University in North Carolina, told me about a 1962 coaches' convention he attended in Louisville, Kentucky. "Those were the days before full integration," he said, "and the Brown Hotel refused to let Black coaches stay or eat there. Coach Wooden stepped up and said that if we couldn't eat there, neither would he. He skipped the banquet and ate with us at a 'colored' restaurant. It was a true act of character."

That's the character of a man who has an unconditional love for all of humankind. We need more people of character like Coach Wooden—people who are willing to unconditionally love all of humanity, regardless of race, ethnicity, and skin color.

Stephanie Benavidez is the supervising naturalist at the Rotary Nature Center and Lake Merritt Wildlife Center in Oakland, California. She oversees the oldest urban wildlife refuge in the United States (established in 1870). I asked who her role models were and what they did to teach her about character.

"The key people in my life were my parents," she told me, "both of whom were from culturally diverse backgrounds. My mother's culture was African and Italian. My father's was Mes-

calero Apache and Spanish. His father was hanged by vigilantes just for being an Apache. The obstacles my parents encountered due to their heritage motivated them to fight hard against racism. They taught me that it's not the color of a person's skin that matters, but their character and the way they treat other people.

"When my father passed away, my mother was left to provide for a family of five, including a son who had cerebral palsy and later died at age seven. Determined to hold the family together, my mother went back to school, made the dean's list several times while holding a full-time job, put her children through parochial school, graduated with a double major from Mills College, got her master's, and became a professional woman.

"My mother exemplified and instilled in me all of the values that combine to make a person of good character. She taught me and my siblings the importance of treating others as you wish to be treated. She filled me with a love for the human race, and especially for young people who lack many of the advantages that help people get ahead in life. That's why I work hard to help young people find their inner strength.

"The key to changing young lives is to love them unconditionally, regardless of differences, because it's their differences that make them unique. We are all connected to each other."

My dad, Coach Wooden, and Stephanie Benavidez are all saying one thing: it's time we learn to unconditionally love our 6.5 billion brothers and sisters in this vast human family.

Love Demonstrated Through Charity

Born in 1918, Bob Feller enjoyed an eighteen-year career as a pitcher for the Cleveland Indians. He retired in 1956 with 266 victories and 2,581 strikeouts to his credit, as well as three no-hitters and a major league record of twelve one-hitters. He was MLB Player of the Year in 1940 and was inducted into the Hall of Fame in 1962.

The darkest day of Bob Feller's baseball career was Mother's

Day 1939. The Indians were playing the White Sox in Chicago. White Sox third baseman Marv Owen was at the plate when Feller unleashed his fastball. Owen lined the ball into the stands behind first base—right into the surprised face of Bob Feller's mom! Happy Mother's Day! Poor Mrs. Feller was laid up for two weeks in a Chicago hospital with two black eyes.

Bob's pro baseball career was interrupted by World War II; during his hitch in the navy, he was an anti-aircraft gunner aboard the U.S.S. *Alabama*, earning five campaign ribbons and eight battle stars.

He learned to play baseball from his father, an Iowa farmer. In fact, when Bob was only twelve, his dad built a *Field of Dreams* ballpark right on the farm, complete with fences, bleachers, scoreboard, lights for night games, and an electric generator. The Feller family hosted games between local and traveling teams, charging a small admission to cover expenses. As a teenager, Bob pitched for the local team.

"My father taught me that your character is like your shadow," Bob told me. "It's always with you. No matter how far or fast you travel, it follows you all your life. Your character determines your reputation. Once you lose your reputation, it can never be regained."

During his playing years, Feller was an outspoken opponent of racism in baseball. He's impressed by people of character, and he enjoys telling a story about a letter he received in 1949 from a fellow named Ronald Reagan. This was during Reagan's acting career, three decades before he was elected president of the United States. Reagan wrote the letter from a hospital bed in Southern California after breaking his leg in a charity baseball game. (He bunted off a pitch by comedian Bob Hope, then injured himself in a collision with the first baseman.)

In the hospital, Reagan befriended a ten-year-old boy receiving psychiatric care. The boy was orphaned when his father killed his mother and then shot himself. The boy was a Bob Feller fan, and

when Reagan mentioned he knew Bob Feller, the boy's eyes lit up for the first time. (The two men met years earlier when Feller was a high school ball player in Iowa and Reagan worked for radio WHO in Des Moines.)

So Ronald Reagan wrote Bob Feller a two-page handwritten letter, asking the Cleveland baseball legend for an autographed ball as a birthday gift for the boy. "You'd contribute a lot," Reagan wrote, "toward pulling this little guy out of a dark world. I know this is an imposition, Bob, and I would hesitate to bother you if I didn't believe it could do a lot to really help a little kid who can very easily end up going haywire." Feller had the ball autographed by the entire team and sent it to Reagan.

Feller saved the letter, not because it was from a Hollywood actor, but because it said so much about the brotherly love of a fellow named Reagan.

Another way we show love for humanity is by sacrificing a part of ourselves to save the life of another person—including people we don't even know. Dr. Thomas J. Graham is a renowned hand surgeon who serves as the chief of the Curtis National Hand Center in Baltimore and director of MedStar SportsHealth. He told me, "Mark Heppenstall has been my closest confidant for nearly thirty years, ever since he was the first person I met at boarding school in 1977. We greet each other as 'my blood brother.' He's been there for all the major milestones in my life. For nearly thirty years, we've shared every triumph and tragedy.

"One day, Mark casually mentioned that he was going to donate his bone marrow to a stranger with whom he was matched by the National Marrow Donor Program. Mark was tested years earlier and his tissue type was registered in a national database that presently contains information on six hundred thousand potential volunteer donors.

"Mark got the call out of the blue, and without thinking twice, he immediately agreed to donate. Even after he was informed that this would require additional blood testing, general anesthesia,

and having bone marrow surgically harvested from the pelvis, he didn't hesitate.

"The procedure takes about an hour and is typically performed on an outpatient basis. Each year, the number of marrow transplants increases and now exceeds ten thousand per year. Even so, about two-thirds of people in need of marrow transplants go without because a matching donor can't be found. The chances of a non-related donor match are about one in a million, while related donors match about a quarter of the time.

"The best way to improve the odds is to recruit more donors. This is also true of organ donation. We need more people willing to sign the back of their driver's license to make hearts, eyes, kidneys, and so forth available in the event of unexpected death. About fifty thousand Americans await organ transplants right now, and each year about five thousand will die before a transplant becomes available. One organ donor can improve or save the life of more than fifty people—but less than 20 percent of healthy individuals who die unexpectedly are organ donors.

"Three days after the procedure, Mark played paddle tennis. Within a week, he resumed training for the Pittsburgh Marathon, which he finished in a time that qualified him for the Boston Marathon.

"Mark doesn't know the name of the man whose life he saved, but he does know that the patient is healthy and thriving. The success rate for the transplantation procedure is about 80 percent.

"We all like to think that we care about our fellow human beings, but Mark set an example by literally giving of himself to help someone he'd never met. We all talk a good game when the risks are theoretical, but are we willing to actually put our money, our time, or our own bodies on the line? Our heroes in the military are prepared to sacrifice everything for us. What sacrifices are we willing to make?"

Dr. Thomas Graham has issued a challenge to you and me. Are we willing to follow the example of love for humankind set by his

friend, Mark Heppenstall? To learn more about bone marrow donation, call the National Marrow Donors Program at (800) MAR-
ROW2, or you may visit www.marrow.org.

"Service Is the Rent We Pay for Living"

Marian Wright Edelman grew up under segregation in Bennettsville, South Carolina. As a child, she was not allowed to play in
the park or buy a soda at the drugstore. Her father, the Reverend
Arthur Wright, was a Baptist preacher who taught Marian and her
four siblings to serve God and others. He exemplified love for others by creating parks and soft-drink stands Black children could
use, and he founded a retirement home for African Americans. He
died when Marian was fourteen, and his last words to her were,
"Don't let anything get in the way of your education."

She earned her degree at Spelman College in Atlanta, then studied law at Yale, graduating in 1963. She worked for the NAACP
Legal and Defense Fund in New York and Mississippi, becoming
the first African American woman to practice law in Mississippi.
There she worked hard to fight poverty, malnutrition, and insti-
tutionalized illiteracy. After marrying civil rights attorney Peter
Edelman in 1968, she moved to Washington and served with several organizations, including the Poor People's Campaign.

In 1973, Ms. Edelman founded the Children's Defense Fund, a
powerful advocate for poor children in America. She is the author
of numerous books, including *The Measure of Our Success: A
Letter to My Children and Yours*. When I asked Ms. Edelman to
reflect on the examples of character in her life, she offered these
thoughts:

"I learned about character," she said, "from my parents and
the other adults and community elders in Bennettsville. The lega-
cies that parents, teachers, and church left to my generation of
Black children were priceless but not material: faith reflected in
daily service, the discipline of hard work and stick-to-it-ness, and
a capacity to struggle in the face of adversity.

"Giving up and 'burnout' were not part of the language of my elders. You got up every morning and you did what you had to do. You got up every time you fell down and tried as many times as needed to get it done right. My elders had grit. They valued family life, family rituals, and tried to be good role models and expose us to examples of character.

"Role models were of two kinds: First, there were those who achieved in the outside world, like Marian Anderson, my name-sake—the contralto who broke the color barrier in the music world and received the UN Peace Prize. Second, there were those who didn't have a lot of education or worldly status, but who taught us by the special grace of their lives the message of Christ and Gandhi and Dr. King: the kingdom of God is within you—in what you are, not in what you have.

"I still hope I can be half as good as church and community elders like Miz Lucy McQueen, Miz Tee Kelly, and Miz Kate Winston, who possessed enormous mother wit, integrity, love, strength of will, and a spirit that no degree could confer. They cared for me as if I were their own child, and when I went away to Spelman College, sent me shoeboxes with chicken and biscuits and grease-stained dollar bills.

"The adults in our churches and our community made children feel valued and important. They took time and paid attention to us. And while life was often hard and resources scarce, we always knew who we were and that the measure of our worth was inside our heads and hearts, and not in our possessions.

"We were told that the world had a lot of problems; that Black people had an extra lot of problems, but that we were able and obligated to struggle and change them; that being poor was no excuse for not achieving; and that extra intellectual and material gifts brought with them the privilege and responsibility of sharing with others less fortunate. In sum, we learned that service is the rent we pay for living. It's the very purpose of life and not something you do in your spare time."

Marian Wright Edelman is right. We've been given life and the privilege of occupying our little corner of this planet—and we pay the rent for living here through acts of unconditional love and service to other human beings. We must become the kind of people who daily lift up others.

It's time to pay the rent.

How to Raise Young People of Unconditional Love

Here are some suggested ways to instill love and encourage acts of service and charity in our kids:

1. *Let your kids witness and participate in acts of love and service to the human race.* Young people will learn the character trait of unconditional love for others if they see it modeled in your life. They will experience the character trait of unconditional love for others if you engage them in activities and projects that teach them about other people and other cultures. Involve them in clothing drives, food drives, short-term mission trips, volunteering at the downtown rescue mission, and other forms of service.

John C. Dean is the fire marshal for the state of Maine. He has spent thirty-five years in the field of public safety and also served two tours of duty as a medic in Vietnam. He told me, "I've noticed over the years that when someone needs to be rescued from a burning building or the wreckage of a vehicle, they don't care about the color of your skin. All they want to know is that you are going to rescue them from their circumstances.

"Skin color and race are superficial. What counts is who we are inside. I want my children to understand that we are all brothers and sisters in the human race, and when we have been blessed, we need to help those who are less fortunate. So our family has sponsored a child through the Christian Children's Fund. The first child we sponsored was from Thailand; when she outgrew the program, we sponsored a boy from Mexico.

"In the process, our children have become more knowledge-

able about the rest of the world and more interested in people of other cultures. They have learned to appreciate all the blessings of living in America, and they're not so quick to complain about anything that goes wrong or that they lack. They've also learned that we are all responsible to help each other."

2. *Teach your kids what the Scriptures say about love.* Children should learn from an early age to live a lifestyle of unconditional love. Teach them Jesus' parable of the Good Samaritan, found in Luke 10. Discuss it with them and help them see how the Samaritan traveler showed selfless love to the man who was robbed and hurt. Read to them Jesus' teachings about loving our enemies (see Matthew 5:43–48). Show them how God's unconditional love is revealed in John 3:16, then examine Jesus' command that we love one another (see John 13:34–35; 15:9–17).

Discuss verse by verse Paul's hymn of unconditional love in 1 Corinthians 13. Read Galatians 5:13–15 to them, and discuss how the true nature of love requires self-sacrifice. Examine Romans 14:15 and ask your kids what it means to "act in love."

John's first epistle is all about unconditional love—God's love and ours. In 1 John 3:18, John says that love is demonstrated by deeds. In 4:20, he shows that our relationship with God hinges on our love for our brothers and sisters. And 4:8 teaches that God is love, so if we do not love, we do not know God.

God's unconditional love is the model for our own unconditional love. Teach these scriptural principles to your children and they will have a lasting foundation for living as people of character and love.

3. *Be a role model of unconditional love.* When your kids disappoint you, exemplify the patient, forgiving love of God. Yes, kids must learn that sin has consequences—but you can administer those consequences lovingly. You can say, "Even though we still have to ground you and take away these privileges, I forgive you and nothing will ever change my love for you." Love should always loom larger in the child's mind than discipline.

Having raised four birth kids and fourteen adopted kids, I have found that consequences are much more effective when surrounded by love than when imposed in anger. Kids regret having failed a parent who loves them, but they resent being punished by a parent who shames and berates them. A child who feels unconditionally loved usually needs less discipline.

If you want to see what parental love should look like, just look at the unconditional love of God as portrayed in the parable of the lost son (see Luke 15:11–32). It's the story about a father whose son is demanding, rebellious, and insulting. The son goes away, squanders his inheritance, then returns in disgrace. Yet the father's love for the lost son is unconditional. He receives the wayward son, forgives him, and restores him.

That is how we should express our love to our children—freely and unconditionally. Never give up on your kids, never stop loving them, never stop accepting and forgiving them, no matter how far they stray. To raise kids of character and love, we must be role models of character and love.

4. *Teach kids to identify with others.* Help them empathize with people less fortunate than they. Kathy Megyeri has taught high school English for more than three decades and serves as a volunteer coordinator, helping make sure students complete their service hours. Now retired, she lives in the Washington, D.C., area. She told me about a project she once assigned to her students.

"We had just completed Harper Lee's *To Kill a Mockingbird*," she said, "which is a powerful study of character. The students remembered the words of the protagonist, Atticus Finch, when he tells his daughter Scout, 'You never really know a man until you stand in his shoes and walk around in them.' That's what empathy means—treating others as if you could stand in their shoes and feel what they feel.

"So our students launched a 'Walk in My Shoes' project. They collected shoes that were still wearable, refurbished and sized them, then wrote stories about the person who might have worn

them. Students imagined a possible name and life story for the shoe's donor. The students presented their stories orally while wearing the shoes.

"One year, over a thousand shoes were collected from our high school to be donated to earthquake victims. A student whose uncle had died in Vietnam brought in the combat boots his uncle had worn on the day of his death in 1968. A pair of sandals provided the material for a composition about 'the world's greatest surfer.' High-top sneakers prompted an essay about Michael Jordan.

"One year, the compositions were tucked into the refurbished shoes and displayed at a local shoe store. People stood in line to read the papers and examine the shoes. The money from shoe purchases was donated to charity. Leftover pairs went to Goodwill. The project was a natural way to blend character-building, community service, family involvement, and imaginative writing."

5. *Help kids define their own rules for living as people of character and love.* Assign children the task of writing down a set of rules to define their own character and way of life. Kathy Megyeri gave her classes this assignment and was surprised at the maturity and wisdom expressed by many of her students. We're not talking here about such rules as "Keep your room clean" or "Thou shalt not steal." Rather, Kathy Megyeri encouraged students to think of rules to guide their character. One student, Kate Tessier, offered a list of rules later printed as a poster. Some of her rules:

"Knowing many people is far better than knowing only yourself." "Unanswered prayers can be one of God's greatest gifts." "Never lose a friendship because true friendship is a rarity." "When someone asks, 'Do I have food on my face?' don't lie. Tell them. You wouldn't want anything on your face." "Spend time to get to know your parents." "Let people help you." "When saying 'I love you,' mean it; that is the most important phrase in your life and defines your true character."

There were many other rules on that list, all of them wonderful—and I have to tell you that Kate Tessier is one of my fa-

vorite philosophers! Encourage your kids to define their rules for living and see if they don't surprise you with their wisdom and character.

"We Must Not Think Evil of This Man"

On Monday morning, October 2, 2006, a thirty-two-year-old milk truck driver approached the West Nickel Mines School, a one-room Amish schoolhouse in Lancaster County, Pennsylvania. He carried guns, wires, boards, nails, and flexible plastic ties. Entering the small building, the gunman (who was himself a father of three) ordered the students and adults to line up against the chalkboard. Then he divided up the hostages, sending a pregnant woman, three parents with infants, and all the boys out of the classroom. He ordered the girl students to remain with him.

The schoolteacher, who was released by the gunman, called the police. Law enforcement arrived within ten minutes. The standoff lasted about an hour. The man with the gun ordered the police to pull back. When the police didn't comply, he began shooting hostages.

The police stormed the building and broke in through the windows. When they got inside, they found the room bullet-riddled and splashed with blood. Girls were on the floor, some dead, some dying, some wounded. Also on the floor was the body of the gunman, who had killed himself.

The story of what happened in the schoolroom during the standoff is a story of horror—and unconditional love. The oldest girl in the room, thirteen-year-old Marian Fisher, volunteered to be the first victim. She pleaded with the man, "Shoot me first." Her plan was that by convincing the man to shoot her first, her sisters would have a chance to live. It worked. Though Marian died, her sisters were wounded but survived. Marian's sister Barbie also volunteered to be martyred, and she survived being wounded in the hand, leg, and shoulder.

Naomi Rose Ebersol (age seven) and Anna Mae Stoltzfus (age

twelve) were shot and killed. Lena Zook Miller (age seven) and Mary Liz Miller (age eight) were mortally wounded. In all, the gunman killed five girls and injured five others. Most of the victims were shot in the back of the head, execution style. They ranged in age from six to thirteen. One of the murdered girls, shortly before she died, was reported by a survivor to have told the other girls, "We must not think evil of this man."

The martyr's words were soon echoed in the response from parents and other members of the tight-knit Amish Christian community. The world was stunned to hear grieving parents respond with unconditional love. One Amish man told a CNN reporter, "Nobody here wants to do anything but forgive. We want to reach out not only to those who have suffered this loss, but to the family of the man who committed these acts."

Within hours after the tragedy, an Amish neighbor went to the house of the gunman's family to offer comfort and express forgiveness toward their husband and father. A few days later, the Amish community set up a college fund for the killer's three children.

Author Kasey S. Pipes writes with great insight about Dr. Martin Luther King, Jr.: "King marveled at how Gandhi used good to overcome evil and preached nonviolence as a weapon against violence. 'He was probably the first person, in history, to lift the love ethic of Jesus above mere interaction between individuals to a powerful, effective social force on a large scale.' Never again would King see preaching as something to be done only in the pulpit, on Sundays. As he graduated from Crozer in the early 1950s and headed to Boston for his doctorate, King was a changed man . . . he believed that sermons were to be lived, not preached. He was convinced that the cancer of hate could be overcome with the radiation of love."

"Love your enemies," Jesus said, "and pray for those who persecute you, that you may be sons of your Father in heaven" (Matt. 5:44–45). That's what it means to be people of great character, people of unconditional love.

10

Responsibility: The Rule of the River

"The price of greatness is responsibility."

SIR WINSTON CHURCHILL
BRITISH STATESMAN

In 1989, doctors cut into Mike Westhoff's thigh and removed a tumor the size of an egg from his left femur. Westhoff, the special teams coach of Don Shula's Miami Dolphins, was forty years old.

"When you're diagnosed with a life-threatening disease," Mike told me, "you find out a great deal about yourself. Fighting bone cancer changed my life. It took eight major surgeries to help me beat the cancer, including a surgery that saved my leg from being amputated by removing the femur."

It required two metal plates, twenty-five screws, and a seven-inch bone from a cadaver to patch his bone back together. Coach Westhoff had no intention of sitting and feeling sorry for himself.

"I had a serious illness," he said, "but I didn't want to sit around and think about how sick I was. Sure, you feel like putting yourself in a box and shutting out the world, but life doesn't work that way. Even though you have cancer and you're fighting for your life, you still have day-to-day troubles. Everything is still there—your job, family and friends, stress and bills. How do you handle all of these issues along with cancer? I had to dig deep and find new strengths within myself in order to beat the cancer."

Westhoff told Dolphins head coach Don Shula he wanted to stay on the job despite the weeks of chemotherapy he had ahead of him. "Okay," Shula said, "but let's get back to work."

"Coach Shula wasn't going to tuck me in and go easy on me, just because I was sick," Mike told me. "He's an intense coach and he has high demands for his staff and players. While I was battling cancer, Don Shula was supportive, but he didn't treat me any differently than he had before.

"At first that was hard on me—but then I realized that he was treating me the way I could be, not the way I was. He never looked at me as if I was handicapped. That helped me to see myself as Shula saw me—not a guy on his back in a hospital bed, but as a coach who was going to get the job done. That, as much as anything, helped me get past the cancer."

Mike Westhoff arrived at Dolphins training camp looking exactly like a guy who had been through cancer and chemo. He was pale, thin, bald, and walking on crutches. Shula treated him like any other coach, and he made sure that Westhoff did his homework.

"It's all about responsibility," Westhoff told me. "I was responsible to do my job—and I was responsible for my own recovery from cancer. Going through that experience has made me a better coach. I preach and teach personal responsibility to my players. They're accountable to learn the system and do it right. As a result, my teams have traditionally been among the least penalized teams in the NFL."

After beating the cancer, Mike took on some physical challenges. "I took up white water rafting," he told me. "I went rafting on the Snake River in Wyoming. Each raft had about six or eight people on it. The guide explained that if someone got thrown from the raft, all attention must be directed toward rescuing that person.

"But the guide also explained that there is something known as 'The Rule of the River,' which states that if you fall into the water,

you must be active in your own rescue. You can't just sit there in the water waiting for someone to pull you out. Do that and you may end up floating all the way to Mexico. You have to take responsibility and work with your fellow rafters to get yourself back to safety.

"Responsibility in the NFL is a lot like 'The Rule of the River.' You can't coast along and let your teammates pick up your slack. Every player has to know and execute his assignment. If one player fails to shoulder his share of the load, even for one down, the whole effort collapses.

"In the NFL, responsibility easily gets skewed. When Tiger Woods misses a put, you know the miss was his responsibility, because golf is a solo sport. But in a team sport like football, you might have a player think, *I played pretty well today*, even though the team lost 35–0. So in the NFL, you have to look at responsibility from a team perspective."

At the time of this writing, Mike Westhoff is assistant head coach and special teams coach for the New York Jets. He demands personal responsibility from his players—and gets it. Over his first six seasons with the Jets, Westhoff's special teams unit has averaged a phenomenal 31.3 yards per kick return.

What's true on the river is true on the football field, in the cancer ward, and in every other aspect of life. The people who overcome the odds and the obstacles are those who possess the character trait of responsibility. They never wait passively for someone else to rescue them. They shoulder their share of the load. They get the job done.

A Straight Shot to Responsibility

Responsible people act without having to be told, without having to be monitored, without having to be guided or goaded into action. Responsibility is the capacity to admit and correct one's own mistakes without making excuses or shifting blame. You can always depend on responsible people because they do what they say. They keep their word.

Dan Wood is executive director of the National Christian College Athletic Association (NCCAA), an association of roughly a hundred Christian institutions of higher education in the United States. Dan told me about a lesson he learned in personal responsibility.

"I was six years old," he said, "and I had become quite proficient with the slingshot I had received as a Christmas present. I climbed to the top of an old oak tree, which was my hideout in those days. A car pulled into the driveway, and a man from our church got out.

"My dad, who was the pastor, came out and said hello. The man was angry about something and he went into a tirade about how another farmer in our community had treated him. He ranted on, and my dad tried to reason with him, but to no avail. Finally, the man cursed at my father and climbed back into his old Rambler station wagon.

"At that point, I decided to strike a blow for my dad's honor. As the man started to pull out of our driveway, I loaded my slingshot and took aim. My shot was straight and true. The glass in the back of the Rambler shattered. The car stopped abruptly and the man jumped out of the car, looking in all directions.

"My dad came out of the house and the man asked if he had done it. Clearly, he couldn't have, since he was in the house. Coming to no conclusion, the man left and Dad returned to the house.

"I sat in the tree, watching all of this. On the one hand, I was proud of my aim. On the other hand, I knew I had *really* messed up. I had damaged a man's car. If I got caught, this was *big* trouble.

"I climbed down from the tree, turned, and was startled to see my dad sitting on our porch, looking at me. He motioned for me to come over and sit down. Once I was seated, he asked if I'd had anything to do with the broken glass. I acknowledged that I had—but I immediately defended myself: 'After the way he yelled at you, I had to do something!'

"My dad didn't say anything. He just got up, went inside, and made a phone call. When he returned, we sat in silence and waited. About ten minutes later, the man in the Rambler drove up, angrier than before.

"Dad laid out the facts and had me apologize—and he had me promise to pay for the broken glass. The man left, somewhat appeased.

"My dad taught me a lesson that has stuck with me for life: I'm responsible for my actions. Even when others are unfair, I'm responsible to do the right thing.

"Over the years, I saw my dad respond to many situations where he was treated unfairly, yet he always responded in a godly manner. Dad often said, 'Life was unfair to Jesus Christ too.'"

Learning Responsibility Through Sports

Steve Nicol is head coach of the New England Revolution (nicknamed "The Revs"), a Major League Soccer team owned by New England Patriots owner Robert Kraft. Steve told me, "I was raised in Troon, on the west coast of Scotland, and my father, James Caldwell Nicol, exemplified what it means to be responsible and truthful. There were no gray areas in his life and he taught me that the decisions you make in life are either right or wrong. I've always tried to live up to the example he set.

"With my players, I like to give them responsibility and set high expectations for them. When you expect things from people, they usually want to be productive. They rise to those expectations. When they fall short, I expect them to take responsibility for that, and to correct their mistakes. I've learned that if you're honest with yourself and willing to take responsibility, all the other character qualities will fall into place."

Dan Wood told me about an experience he had while coaching soccer at the college level. "As a coach," he said, "I had certain team rules and goals that centered around my philosophy and Christian faith. I wanted to instill these values in my players,

and I wanted our program to become known for these traits, particularly by our opponents. I wanted our players to be known as people of character, integrity, and responsibility.

"I had a junior captain who made a poor decision in our final match of the regular season. The penalty I imposed was a one-game suspension, to be applied in our next match—a crucial play-off game. That set the stage for a confrontation. The captain agreed that he deserved the penalty, but argued that it shouldn't be imposed during such an important game. He got a number of teammates on his side, arguing against my decision. I refused to budge. The penalty stood.

"The day of the match, we played poorly and lost in the first round of the postseason. Many on the team blamed me for the loss. What had originally been *our* team rules were now viewed as *my* rules—and many felt my strict adherence to the rules had cost us a chance of advancement.

"After the off-season, we came together for spring practice. Many players came in with a different perception than they'd had at the end of the previous season. Apparently, with time to reconsider, they saw that the players are responsible to live up to the team rules. The rules shouldn't be bent just for the sake of winning. Character counts, and our players reaffirmed their desire for our team to be a character team.

"The players selected a captain—and I was surprised to see that they selected a different player than the previous season's captain. They chose a player who had supported my decision to enforce the suspension the previous season. In fact, the previous year's captain, whose election had been unanimous before, didn't receive even one vote.

"This confirmed to me that we, as teachers, coaches, parents, and leaders, need to take a stand for what is right—even if that stand is costly and unpopular. When we demonstrate character in tough situations, it becomes a powerful teaching moment for everyone involved.

"About six years later, I received a letter from the young man I had suspended. He told me he was coaching a high school team in Indiana, and had run into a situation almost identical to the one I had faced with him. He had learned from our experience how to deal with such situations, and he wanted me to know he appreciated the example I had set.

"The field of athletic competition is a great training ground for character and responsibility. When we, as coaches and leaders, set a firm example, we teach lessons that young people can draw upon in every aspect of their lives."

Frank Allocco is head basketball coach at De La Salle High School in Concord, California. He shared with me one of his favorite quotations: "Bart Starr, the Hall of Fame quarterback of the Green Bay Packers, once said, 'A person who possesses a strong character realizes that his destiny ultimately is his own.' In other words, great people and great teams take responsibility for their actions."

He went on to tell me a story. "We don't allow our players to argue with an official's call," he said. "In fact, we never allow our players to make an excuse for a loss or even for an error. We encourage players to take full responsibility for their mistakes, learn from them, and never repeat them.

"Before coaching at De La Salle, I coached at Northgate High School. In 1996, we were coming off of a 34-2 record and a state championship at the Division III level. We had graduated four starters and moved up to Division II. Our team overcame all odds and achieved a 31-4 record and got to the Division II state championship game.

"At the conclusion of our loss to the second-ranked team in the nation, a television crew came out on the floor and interviewed our point guard—who was also my son, Frank. The reporter asked Frank how it felt to lose in such a big game. As disappointed as he was, my son looked into the camera and told the reporter he felt badly that he had let his teammates down. He had always come

through for them in the past, and he was sorry he couldn't do it for them one last time.

"Now, here's a young man who was a first-team All-State Player two years in a row and had led his team to an incredible record of ninety wins, eleven losses in three years. And he was taking responsibility for his team's loss in a game where the deck was stacked against them. That's character!

"These days, it's all too common for people to shift blame to others. When our children do poorly in school, it's the teacher's fault. When a player doesn't get enough playing time, it's the coach's fault. When we don't get the promotion we want, it's the boss' fault. We can't grow and succeed until we learn to accept responsibility for our own failures, analyze why we failed, then make the changes that lead to success."

Steve Nicol, Dan Wood, and Frank Allocco offer coaching perspectives from the pro, collegiate, and high school levels, and all three coaches agree: sports is the great training ground for personal responsibility. If we want to raise people of responsible character, there's no better training ground than a hardwood court, a grassy field, or a dirt track.

Humbled to Lead

F. Christopher Goins of James B. Dudley High School in Greensboro, North Carolina, was honored as Guilford County's "High School Teacher of the Year" for 2005–2006. When I asked him to reflect on character and responsibility, he shared with me a profound quotation by that wise Marvel Comics philosopher, Spiderman: "With much power comes much responsibility." Then he told me a story about a tough lesson he learned about responsibility.

"In the spring of 1999," he said, "I was in my junior year at North Carolina Agricultural and Technical State University and was a member of a fraternity. I had just been elected president of my fraternity's chapter and was head drum major of the nationally known marching band.

"All of us in our fraternity had gone through a time of hazing, and we saw nothing wrong with hazing the new incoming pledges. All of the fraternity brothers enjoyed the pledging time, but the pledges did not. Just as we had endured a pounding when we pledged, we were administering a pounding to our new pledges.

"Apparently we took it too far, because some of our pledges reported the treatment to university authorities. As a result, I, as president of the fraternity, was called upon to assume responsibility for the episode. This was the only way to keep the entire chapter from being banned from school. I lost my position as drum major, was almost kicked out of school, and felt humiliated and unfairly treated. I begged the band director to let me keep my position, but he insisted that I learn a hard lesson.

"I was furious! I hated my band director for punishing me and making an example of me! Sure, I had broken the rules—and yes, I had known the rules regarding hazing. But the entire chapter was involved. Why did I have to take all the punishment myself? I was the best drum major he ever had! I had worked hard to win that position! This was unfair!

"One day, Brian Millsapp, my band director from my high school days, called and asked me to come by his office. He had heard about the hazing incident and the punishment, and he invited me to talk it over. I went and we talked, and throughout our conversation I kept pointing fingers at the band director and my fraternity.

"After listening to me rant for a while, Brian explained that I was a leader on campus, and as a leader, I had no business participating in hazing. He told me that a leader has to have impeccable character. I was never going to be a leader until I accepted responsibility for my actions. I tried to argue with him—but I knew he was right. It was a 'tough love' moment. Brian helped me realize that the punishment I had received was fair. Leaders *must* be held to a high standard, because their example affects everyone."

Passing the Responsibility Test

Sometimes we find ourselves at an ethical crossroads—and only the character trait of responsibility can tell us which way to go. That's the intersection where Dr. Stephanie A. Parson once found herself.

Dr. Parson is the president and CEO of Crowned Grace, Inc., and a gifted and inspiring public speaker. She has also served as a vice president of Walt Disney World's information technology group, a dean of Disney University, and a commissioned officer in the United States Air Force. "I grew up in a military family," she told me, "and my parents were the key people in my life, shaping my values, character, and sense of responsibility.

"Once, when I was an air force officer stationed in Alaska, we were in the middle of a training exercise. I walked into the command center and was instantly peppered with accusations that my troops had disobeyed a direct order to check the surrounding area for unexploded bombs. The senior ranking officer told me to discipline my troops for their failure.

"I met with my troops and they told me they were following air force policy. According to that policy, they were not permitted to check for unexploded bombs until an all-clear had been given by the official. They were waiting for the all-clear, which hadn't come.

"At that point, I had two options. I could go back to the senior ranking officer and share the air force policy with him—which would mean saying, in effect, 'You're wrong.' Or I could wrongly discipline my troops in order to remain in favor with the ranking officer—even though my troops did exactly what they were supposed to do.

"I knew I had a responsibility to my troops and to my own character, even if it cost me. So I backed the decision made by my troops. While my choice didn't sit well with the officer, it was the right decision. Later, I found that my organization became one of the top-rated organizations on that base—and I attribute it to the

fact that I earned the respect and trust of my troops by going to bat for them. Later, one of my leaders told me I was the best officer he had ever worked for in eighteen years of service. That was a satisfying tribute."

It's not easy to do the right thing in every circumstance. Most of us know the right thing to do, but we don't want to pay the price. When you are tested and you pass the test—as Stephanie Parson did—you *know* you have character.

Hank McKinnell is the former CEO and current chairman of the board of Pfizer, Inc., the world's largest pharmaceutical company. He's also the author of *A Call to Action: Taking Back Healthcare for Future Generations*. Mr. McKinnell told me, "You can delegate responsibilities, but not responsibility. The person who taught me the most about character and responsibility was my father, my namesake, Henry McKinnell.

"My father was a sea captain. He owned a number of small ships that hauled freight along the coast from Oregon to Alaska. I learned from him that even though a leader delegates responsibilities, a leader must always accept responsibility for events, and prepare accordingly. My father worked hard to gain a measure of success, and eventually managed a string of boats. Even late in his life, he always took the helm of one of the boats himself.

"He approached his work with the professionalism one would expect from a leader who took responsibility for the lives and welfare of his crew. My father had a strict policy—no alcohol on board, none. Even so, crews wanted to sign on to work with my father because they knew he was a responsible man who would always look out for them. In his half century of piloting cargo-laden ships, he never had an accident.

"The attributes of loyalty, professionalism, and responsibility defined my father's character. As I navigate the shoals of business, I try to remember that, at Pfizer, a hundred thousand colleagues have put their trust in me. It's my job to come ready to do my job to standards that reinforce their trust."

People of responsibility make the best employers—and the best employees. You know you can depend on them, trust them, and even bet your life on them.

How to Raise Responsible Young Souls

Here are some suggested ways in which we, as parents and teachers, coaches and mentors, can instill the character trait of responsibility in the children we seek to influence:

1. Assign appropriate goals and tasks. Allow your kids to either rise to the challenge or incur the consequences of failure. Set performance expectations and let them take responsibility for meeting those expectations. No reminding, no nagging, no standing over your kids with a ruler.

Sometimes a child will seem intimidated by a project or goal that is too large or complex. She may not know where to begin or how to go about it. Help your child break the task down into smaller, more manageable "bite-size" tasks. Once the child gets started, back off and let her do the job without interference.

If the job isn't done right the first time, don't take over. Patiently and gently point out what isn't right and say, "Do it again. You'll get it right this time. You'll feel good when you know you did it well."

2. Praise responsible behavior and affirm responsible character. Young people thrive on praise. In fact, we all do! Reinforce and praise good decisions. Let them know you noticed that they performed a task on their own, without being told to do it. Make sure the young people you are raising, teaching, mentoring, or coaching know that you recognize character growth and responsible behavior. When you reinforce positive behavior, you'll see more of it in the future.

Dick Vermeil has coached the UCLA Bruins to a Rose Bowl victory and the St. Louis Rams to an NFL championship in Super Bowl XXXIV. He began his NFL coaching career in 1976 with the Philadelphia Eagles. That first year was a tough year, and Coach

Vermeil had a number of players with significant personal issues that affected their performance on the field. After that first difficult year, he reflected, "I spent almost all my time with my problem guys and I neglected the character people. I'm never going to let that happen again."

When you have "character people" on your "team," make sure you don't neglect them. Affirm them and let them know how much their character means to you.

3. *Accept no excuses.* Don't let young people shift the blame. Don't let them wriggle out of their responsibility. When they fail to act responsibly, turn that failure into a life lesson.

"Once, when I was six years old," Charles Colson told me, "I threw a rock through a neighbor lady's window. I went home and told my dad, 'I broke the window, but nobody caught me.' I thought that if I didn't get caught, everything was okay.

"My dad sat me down and said, 'The most important thing in life is telling the truth and owning up to the things you do wrong. Son, I forgive you for throwing the stone through the window. I don't hold it against you and I'm not going to punish you. But you have to go tell the woman that you broke her window. And then you'll help fix the window.' My dad handled the situation very wisely, and the lesson has stuck with me all my life."

4. *Teach kids to take responsibility for their academic success.* School is preparation for life. Young people need to take responsibility for their schoolwork now—or they may never take responsibility for their adult lives later. Some suggestions:

- Encourage kids to write down their assignments in a notebook or planner. Show them the advantages of having a well-planned, organized approach to home and projects.
- Let kids live with (and learn from) the consequences of mistakes and failure. Avoid running to school to bring them the assignments they left at home. Don't throw the whole family's schedule out of whack to compensate for a child who leaves an assignment till the last minute.

- Put up signs or sayings about responsibility. Post them in the child's room, on the family bulletin board, or on the fridge. For example: "The willingness to accept responsibility for one's own life is the source from which self-respect springs" (Joan Didion).
- Explain to your kids why academic responsibility is important, and talk to them about school as preparation for life. Tell them they are building character and habits now that will prepare them for a lifetime of satisfaction and success.

Patsy Summers recently retired from the Delaware Elementary School in Springfield, Missouri, after thirty-seven years as a teacher in the Springfield school district. She told me, "Character education is a valuable life asset, and it must be taught at home and at school. I explain to my students that we have only one class rule: 'Be Responsible!' Most students are quick to realize that responsibility is the key to success. Once you develop this character trait, you're ready to meet the challenges of life."

5. *Teach kids to be responsible with money.* Give kids an allowance so they can learn to budget, save, and plan their purchases. Avoid "paying" kids to do chores; young people should not get into a mind-set of feeling entitled to be paid every time they do some dishes or clean their room or take out the trash. They should understand that chores are a normal part of their lives.

The amount of allowance you give your kids should be limited to a point where they are forced to make purchasing decisions. Kids should have to forego or delay some purchases in order to buy what they want most. If kids never have to discipline their spending, they'll never learn the value of a dollar—and they'll never learn responsibility.

Children should be taught to give a portion of their weekly allowance to God, and they should be encouraged to save a bit (say, 10 percent) in a piggy bank or a savings account.

As your kids reach their teen years, encourage them to find ways to make outside money—a paper route, yard work, and so

forth. When they are old enough, encourage them to seek part-time employment (Christmas rush or summer employment or after-school jobs) where they can start making "real money." Working to please an employer is a different experience from working to please Mom and Dad—and a good way for young people to learn yet another facet of personal responsibility.

6. *Teach teens to be responsible with the car.* Nothing strikes fear to a dad's heart like the question, "Dad, can I have the car keys?" Very few sixteen-year-olds really appreciate the responsibility of driving a two-ton killing machine down a city thoroughfare. *They* think they're "responsible adults." *You* remember how responsible you were at that age—and you quake in your boots.

When your teen gets his or her learner's permit, make a commitment to spend a lot of time in the car with your student driver. Correct problem behavior and bad habits. If your teen has a bad attitude about being corrected, suspend driving privileges until the attitude improves. A teachable attitude is part of being responsible.

Establish rules and limits with the car. Insist that all laws be rigorously obeyed, including laws regarding the number and ages of passengers when your teen is driving. Encourage a sense of responsibility in your teens by having them wash the car, keep it clean inside, and share the expenses for fuel, insurance, and mechanical maintenance.

After your teen gets a license, be willing to impose rules of your own, based on your own preferences and your teen's driving habits. You may want to have a "no passengers" rule for a while, since teens are statistically more likely to have an accident when friends are in the car.

Don't believe your teens' boasts about how "safe" they are as drivers. Teens are more likely than any other age group to be involved in a single-car crash. While teens make up 7 percent of all licensed drivers, they are involved in 20 percent of all accidents and suffer 14 percent of all fatalities. Teens are also statistically more likely to be the cause of their accidents than older drivers.

7. *As young people grow toward adulthood, let them take increasing responsibility for fighting their own battles.* When children are little, they are vulnerable. You naturally want to shield them from dangerous situations, people, and influences. That's your responsibility as a parent. As your children grow older, you gradually expose them to more and more situations where they must learn to solve their own problems. By the time they reach young adulthood, your kids should be shouldering their own load, solving their own problems, and fighting their own battles.

Keith Jones is the head athletic trainer for the Houston Rockets. He told me how his father let him know it was time to fight his own battles. "In my junior year in college," Keith said, "I purchased my first vehicle. I had nothing but problems with that car. I called my dad and asked him to talk to the guy who sold me the car. My dad had always stuck up for me in the past, and I figured he would speak for me if someone was cheating me. I knew my dad would just light this guy up for me.

"Well, my dad flipped the script on me. He told me it was my car and my responsibility. If I felt that strongly about it, I needed to confront the guy. He said it was my time to handle my business—and I knew he was right. So I talked to the man myself, got the car fixed, and felt about ten feet tall because I had taken responsibility and handled it myself."

8. *PERSEVERE!* As you raise, teach, or mentor young people, you may find your spirit and strength waning. Don't lose heart! This is a battle worth fighting—and it's a battle you can win if you persevere.

Stephanie Benavidez, supervising naturalist at the Rotary Nature Center in Oakland, California, told me about a teen employee who needed to learn responsibility. She recalled, "I first met Malcolm when he was fourteen. He had brought his six-year-old brother to the Rotary Nature Center to show him the live animals we had on display. I'm a pretty good judge of character, and I felt that this soft-spoken young man was someone I wanted in my pro-

grams—not only because I thought he could help us, but because I wanted to save him from the streets.

"In 1999, I took Malcolm on as a volunteer. I had him learn the ropes around the Nature Center and told him it was okay to bring his little brother with him. Like Malcolm, I had been the oldest sibling in my family, so I understood the responsibilities Malcolm felt. He began working at the Center on a seasonal, volunteer basis.

"When he was sixteen, I offered him a job as a recreation aide. He was very responsible in working with the animals. In time, however, his work ethic and attendance slipped. I got calls from his mother about his behavior at home. She reached a point where she felt she needed to lock him out and let the streets have him because she had two other children to care for.

"One day Malcolm failed to show up for work, so I phoned his house and asked to speak to him. His mother answered and told me he was disrespectful, he was sleeping late, and he wouldn't come to the phone. I said, 'Put the phone by his ear.' She did.

"I said, 'Malcolm, I know you can hear me, so listen carefully. I'm not your mother. I'm your supervisor. You work for me. No matter what problems you have at home, you're responsible to come in to work or call me if you can't. Someday, you'll want me to give you a reference so you can get another job. If you want a positive reference, then you need to be responsible. If you don't want to work here anymore, write me a letter of resignation and I'll give your job to someone who wants it. Now, hand the phone back to your mother.'

"I asked Malcolm's mother to call me after Malcolm left the house. A short time later, she did. I told her, 'I empathize with what you're going through and I want you to know, I'm not giving up on Malcolm.' We talked for a few minutes, and I closed by encouraging her to persevere. 'No matter how hard it is,' I said, 'it's better to leave a door open for Malcolm to come back home than to have to close the lid on his casket. I know you're going through

a crisis with him now, but I'm sure the qualities I saw in Malcolm when I first hired him are founded on your love for him.'

"Malcolm showed up for work, and he continued working throughout the summer. I placed him with an older staff member named Brian who mentored Malcolm and talked to him about his problems.

"The following summer, Malcolm showed up at my office, hoping to be rehired for another season. I could see a big change in Malcolm—a greater sense of peace and maturity. He told me his mother had allowed him to take a trip to Africa with his stepfather. We talked about what he saw there, and he told me that seeing another part of the world, where people lacked even running water, had made him appreciate where he came from.

"Malcolm also talked about needing to be a role model to his brother and sister. In short, he had begun to look at life in terms of responsibility. Today, Malcolm leads his own beginner's class. He's helped instruct more than five hundred young people, and he's touched the lives of many more. He's becoming a young man of responsibility."

Never give up on kids. Persevere! Keep challenging, encouraging, and reaching out to your kids. They will challenge you, disappoint you, and give you gray hair—but never let go.

The Statue of Responsibility

Dr. Viktor Frankl (1905–1997) was an Austrian-Jewish psychiatrist who survived the Holocaust. In 1943, he was sent to a Nazi concentration camp, along with his wife and parents. His family died in prison, but Dr. Frankl was liberated by American forces on April 27, 1945. Out of those experiences came his classic book *Man's Search for Meaning.*

In 1970, Dr. Frankl proposed that the United States construct a three-hundred-foot-tall Statue of Responsibility. "The Statue of Liberty on the East Coast," he said, "should be complemented by a Statue of Responsibility on the West Coast." These "book-

end monuments," he believed, would remind the American people that our freedom depends not only on liberty but on responsibility as well.

As noble as Dr. Frankl's idea may be, I believe you and I are engaged in something far more important than building a three-hundred-foot-tall steel monument. We are building character into ourselves and our children. We are building souls of steel. May these be our gifts to the world, our living Statues of Responsibility.

PART V

Character Is How We Respond to God

11

Faith: The Engine
of Character

"Faith is not belief. Belief is passive. Faith is active."

EDITH HAMILTON
AMERICAN SCHOLAR AND EDUCATOR

On Sunday, August 12, 1973, Charles W. Colson went to see an old friend, Tom Philips, the president of the Raytheon electronics firm. Colson knew Philips had recently become a Christian, and everything about Tom Philips seemed different. Colson wanted to know what happened in his friend's life.

Colson was facing a crisis. He was implicated in Watergate, the biggest political scandal of the twentieth century. He had resigned as counsel to the president of the United States and fresh accusations against him (most of them false) appeared in the news almost daily. He expected to be called before the Senate Watergate panel, and he knew he faced indictment.

Tom Philips seemed to have found the answers to the riddles of life—and Colson was looking for answers. So Chuck Colson asked his friend why he seemed so changed. "I've committed my life to Jesus Christ," Tom explained. "It's been the most marvelous experience of my life. Everything in my life has changed—my attitudes, my values, everything."

Tom picked up a copy of C. S. Lewis's *Mere Christianity* and read a passage to him. "Pride," Lewis writes, "has been the chief

cause of misery in every nation and every family since the world began. . . . As long as you are proud you cannot know God. A proud man is always looking down on things and people: and, of course, as long as you are looking down, you cannot see something that is above you."[1]

Those words forced Colson to see himself from a new perspective—the perspective of a once-powerful man who had been stripped of his pride by scandal and adversity.

"How about it?" Tom asked. "Are you ready to make a decision?"

Colson shook his head. "I don't want a foxhole religion," the marine veteran said. "I don't want to believe in something just because I'm in a crisis."

"I understand," Tom said. "Here." He handed the book to Colson. "Read it. And read the Gospel of John. And the Psalms. I think it will all make sense to you very soon." Then Tom prayed with Colson . . .

And Colson seemed to feel that God Himself was present in the room.

After Tom prayed with him, Colson said good-bye and walked out of the house. He got into his car, still determined not to surrender himself to a "foxhole religion." But his determination melted away before he had driven to the end of the block. There in his car, Colson offered himself to God. When he arrived back at his own home, he was a changed man.

Charles Colson only told a few close friends about his conversion experience, but someone leaked the story to the press. When the story came out, Colson—the man the media had dubbed "Nixon's hatchet man"—became the subject of widespread scorn and skepticism. Editorial cartoons in newspapers ridiculed Colson's conversion as a publicity stunt.

Today, more than thirty years after his conversion, no one sneers at Charles Colson's faith. His consistent lifestyle of compassion and integrity has proven his transformation was real and

his character is genuine. I asked Chuck Colson who he looked to as role models of character. He named two people: "My dad," he said, "and Al Quie."

Who is Al Quie? He's the man who stood by Chuck Colson through the darkest days of his life. "Al Quie," Chuck told me, "was a member of Congress for twenty-six years and later served as governor of Minnesota. After my conversion to Christ, we were both in a small prayer group together. Al continued to be with me throughout my ordeal in Watergate. He was at my sentencing and my trial."

In 1974, after he was indicted by a grand jury, Charles Colson pleaded guilty to charges in a non-Watergate matter involving the famed Pentagon Papers leaker, Daniel Ellsberg. Colson was sent to Maxwell Federal Prison in Alabama, where he served seven months.

"Al Quie visited me in prison," Chuck recalled. "That was a risky thing for a politician to do, but Al is a very bold and committed man. While I was in prison, I learned that my son had been arrested for marijuana possession. My dad died while I was in prison. My mother was having a tough time. My wife was having a tough time. And I learned I was disbarred in one state—all in a period of one week. My world had collapsed.

"But while all this was happening, Al Quie called to tell me my prayer group was praying for me. He told me he was asking for an appointment with the president to see if he could come serve my prison sentence for me. When I went to my bunk that night, I actually thanked God that I was in prison. Why? Because it was there, in that prison, that I learned what it really means to lay down one's life for another. That's what Al Quie was willing to do for me."

After his release from prison, Colson told the story of his spiritual transformation in his book *Born Again*. He used the royalties from the book to start Prison Fellowship Ministries, which has grown to become the world's largest outreach to prisoners, their families, and crime victims.

I asked Chuck Colson where character comes from. "True character," he said, "is built through a Christian conversion. Before I was a believer, I knew what was right but I often didn't do it. As a believer, you not only know what is right, but God gives you the will and the ability to do it."

The engine that drives character is a thing called *faith*.

What Is Faith?

The character quality of faith involves a willingness to live and act in accordance with the nature and promises of God. Authentic faith must be distinguished from the "easy believism" that characterizes so many churchgoers today. True faith is not demonstrated in what we *say* we believe, but in authentically living it out on a daily basis. If we say we have faith, but we are not living lives of integrity, honesty, diligence, humility, responsibility, courage, and perseverance, what kind of faith do we have? We should not mistake a set of religious doctrines and dogmas for a genuine faith in God; they are not the same thing.

A person of genuine faith is absolutely committed to truth and integrity. Before going to the cross, Jesus prayed that all who followed Him would be committed to the truth. "Sanctify them by the truth; your word is truth" (John 17:17). And when He was on trial before Pontius Pilate, Jesus said, "For this reason I was born, and for this I came into the world, to testify to the truth. Everyone on the side of truth listens to me" (John 18:37). People of authentic faith, said Jesus, must be on the side of truth. Believers must take a stand for absolute integrity and absolute truth.

Unfortunately, this word *faith* is widely misunderstood by many, if not most, people. Many people think faith is "choosing to believe in something for which there is no proof." In other words, they think of faith as a leap into the dark—what is sometimes called "blind faith." This kind of so-called "faith" is really nothing but wishful thinking.

The Bible never encourages "blind faith," belief without evi-

dence. In fact, when the Bible speaks of faith, it speaks of substance and evidence: "Now faith is the substance of things hoped for, the evidence of things not seen" (Heb. 11:1 KJV). God intended that we approach our worldview with a dose of healthy skepticism. He doesn't want us to be "blown here and there by every wind of teaching and by the cunning and craftiness of men in their deceitful scheming" (Eph. 4:14). The Christian faith is based on reliable evidence, not wishful thinking.

The psalmist said the evidence for faith in God can be found in the heavens. He writes, "The heavens declare the glory of God; the skies proclaim the work of his hands. Day after day they pour forth speech; night after night they display knowledge" (Ps. 19:1–2). What was true then is even more true today, as astronomers and cosmologists find increasing evidence the universe is an intelligently designed artifact created by a vast cosmic Intellect.

Physicist Tony Rothman puts it this way: "When confronted with the order and beauty of the universe and the strange coincidences of nature, it's very tempting to take the leap of faith from science into religion. I am sure many physicists want to. I only wish they would admit it." Astronomer Alan Sandage observed, "I find it quite improbable that such order came out of chaos. There has to be some organizing principle. God to me is a mystery but is the explanation for the miracle of existence, why there is something instead of nothing." And astrophysicist Paul Davies concludes, "The impression of design is overwhelming." Today more than ever, the heavens declare the glory and reality of God.

I'm not saying faith is simply a matter of looking at facts and drawing intellectual conclusions. Faith demands action. Jesus calls us to *follow Him*—but He doesn't call us to follow blindly. The Christian faith is a reasonable faith, supported by evidence, not wishful thinking. You don't have to turn off your brain when you give Him your heart.

If you want to read further about the evidence for faith, I suggest the following books: *The Creator and the Cosmos* by Hugh

Ross; *Answers to Satisfy the Soul* by Jim Denney (my writing partner); *Mere Christianity* by C. S. Lewis; *Scaling the Secular City* by J. P. Moreland; *The Case for a Creator, The Case for Faith,* and *The Case for Christ* by Lee Strobel; and *How to Be Like Jesus* by Pat Williams with Jim Denney.

Faith for the Journey

One of the most profound expressions of what it means to live the life of faith is found in the Old Testament book of Proverbs: "Trust in the LORD with all your heart and lean not on your own understanding; in all your ways acknowledge him, and he will make your paths straight" (Prov. 3:5–6).

Bobby Bowden, head football coach at Florida State University, told me that his entire coaching career has been a journey of faith and trust. "I graduated from Howard College in 1952," he said. "The athletics director there told me to go get my master's degree and he would hire me as an assistant football coach. I did as he said, and he did as he promised. In 1955, South Georgia College offered me the head football coaching job. I accepted. In 1959, South Georgia dropped its football program. Samford University in Homewood, Alabama, gave me the head job there.

"In 1963, Bill Peterson at Florida State University offered me an assistant coaching position there. I accepted. Three years later I was hired at West Virginia University as offensive coordinator, even though I didn't seek the job. In 1970, after Jim Carlen left, WVU offered me the head coaching job. Six years later Florida State called and offered me the head job there. I accepted. In more than fifty years of college coaching, I have held many jobs, but I never sought or applied for one of them. All of my coaching jobs were handed to me as Christ, my Lord and Savior, led me through my career. All I did was trust in Him and have faith. He did the rest."

Faith in God enables us to make sense of this journey of life we are taking. When you know God has a plan for your life, you have

confidence God is in control, even when you encounter pot holes and speed bumps along the way.

Dominic Carola is the president and creative producer of Project Firefly Animation Studios in Orlando. He began working for Walt Disney Feature Animation in 1993, animating such popular films as *The Lion King*, *Pocahontas*, *The Hunchback of Notre Dame*, and *Mulan*. He was a lead animator on *Lilo & Stitch* and director of animation for the Animation Pavilion at Walt Disney's California Adventure, which received the THEA Award as the best themed attraction of 2001.

In the spring of 2004, the Disney Company announced it was shutting down Walt Disney Feature Animation Florida—and Dominic Carola was out of a job. Now, Dominic wasn't worried about his future. Almost instantly, he received attractive job offers from major animation houses—but he turned them all down. He and three other former Disney animators decided to put everything on the line for a dream.

Dominic and his friends mortgaged their homes, pooled their resources, and bought up the used studio equipment and office furniture from their former bosses at Disney. They set up a brand-new animation studio in the Universal Florida backlot. Calling their new enterprise Project Firefly, their mission was to create family-friendly animated films using both two-dimensional cartoons and three-dimensional computerized animation.

When I asked Dominic for his thoughts on character, he said, "Years ago, my dream was to get a job at Disney. I studied my craft, I prepared my portfolio, and I applied at several studios, hoping that Disney would offer me a job. With the help of God and an intense focus on my dreams, I reached that goal. I worked at Disney Feature Animation for eleven years, and they were great years.

"A time came when I realized you can't stop dreaming new dreams. Reach one goal, and it's time to dream a new dream. Everything we are doing now is preparing us for the next chapter in

our lives. God has a purpose for every situation we go through. We're learning and gaining knowledge and building character to take on the next big challenge.

"I'm a man of faith. It wasn't until I put my faith in God that I truly began to understand the qualities that make up character. I'm still learning those qualities on a daily basis. But I see now that character is not an abstract issue—it's a very practical matter that affects our lives and the decisions we make on a daily basis. One of the most important aspects of character is faith—the willingness to trust God and rely on Him for the direction of our lives.

"Over the years, I've gone through valleys of doubt, and I've received encouragement from my wife and my friends, which got me through it. I've tried to pass that same encouragement on to others. I want people to know that they should trust God, step out in faith, and pursue their dream, whatever it may be. Faith, prayer, hard work, commitment, focus, perseverance—put all of these things together and your dedication will eventually pay off. Even if you are on a path less traveled and the odds are against you, your dreams will pay off if you have faith and persistence."

And while we trust God for our own future, let's trust Him to guide the lives of our children. Frank Lucchesi is a former Major League Baseball manager (Phillies, Rangers, and Cubs). He told me, "When I was a minor league manager, struggling to get to the big leagues, my mother would go to church every day and pray for me. Though the odds were against me, her prayers were answered. There's no doubt in my mind—I made it to the big leagues because my mother prayed for me every single day."

Faith Generates Character

Of all the character traits, the character quality of faith is the one which can actually generate other character qualities in our lives. A person of faith in Christ is motivated to follow the example of Christ. As a result, he becomes more Christlike—more humble, compassionate, truthful, bold, persistent, and on and on.

Robert C. Andringa, Ph.D., served as president of the Council for Christian Colleges and Universities from 1994 to 2006. In 2001, he was appointed by the U.S. secretary of education to chair the National Advisory Committee on Institutional Quality and Integrity. He was the GOP staff director for the Education and Labor Committee, U.S. House of Representatives, from 1969 to 1977. Dr. Andringa told me, "I had many role models of character throughout my life—my parents, teachers, and coaches. I also saw character exemplified again and again when I worked for the House of Representatives."

I thought that was an interesting observation. Thanks to bribery scandals, sex scandals, and charges of influence peddling and money laundering, politicians as a class are widely viewed with cynicism and distrust. But Dr. Angringa offers a different perspective.

"I watched members of Congress in their day-to-day activities," he told me, "and I saw them working hard, doing their homework, keeping their word, sharing credit with others for their accomplishments, and accepting blame and responsibility for mistakes.

"One of the most impressive examples I saw again and again was that these lawmakers would often express strong political differences on the floor of the House, yet they would never let their ideological differences ruin a personal relationship. It's very important to keep political divisions from becoming personal when you are doing the people's business. One day you might oppose someone on a piece of legislation and the next day you might need to work together with that same person on a matter of mutual interest.

"I've found that faith is a big factor in motivating people to treat their political enemies with respect. On one occasion, I remember working in the wee hours of the morning. My congressman had won a vote on a major issue that we had worked on for two years. I was tired but elated that we had beaten the opposition leader with a bipartisan vote.

"The congressman was happy about the victory too, but rather than gloat about his victory, the congressman said, 'Come in here. We need to pray for the opposition leader. She's been defeated, and she feels hurt and distraught right now.'

"My first thought was, *Pray?! We've won! We should celebrate!* But then I realized the congressman was right. As a follower of Jesus Christ, I knew that He would have us extend love even to those with whom we disagree. That's what it means to live a life of character, 24-7."

The moral to Dr. Andringa's story: our faith in God determines the shape of our character. It guides our thinking. It drives our behavior—especially our behavior toward opponents.

Gene Pemberton is the Houston Astros chaplain and the only full-time chaplain in Major League Baseball. He travels with the players six months out of the year, providing counseling and prayer support to the twenty-five-man team throughout the 162-game season. Gene's duties range from praying with players who are dealing with injuries or personal problems to distributing boxes of player-donated toys to kids at the children's hospital. He joined the Astros in 1994 at the urging of his friend Drayton McLane Jr. the team's owner.

"As chaplain," Gene told me, "I'm fortunate to work for an owner like Drayton. He emphasizes Christian principles in every company he owns, including the Astros. During the season, I come in at 6 a.m. and Drayton often joins me and we pray together.

"He has entrusted to me the responsibility of challenging our players to become champion competitors and champions of character. We have mid-week Bible studies and Sunday morning chapels (which draw fifteen to twenty players plus a few coaches). We also have a voluntary pre-game prayer that draws about ten to fifteen players. We never pray for victory—I don't think God cares who wins a baseball game.

"People ask me why I minister to a lot of 'spoiled millionaires,' as ballplayers are sometimes called. But I don't see them that way.

Whatever the size of their paychecks, these players are someone's kids, and they need the Lord the same as anyone else. It can be a heavy responsibility, and I don't claim to be up to the task—not in my own human strength. I have to rely completely on God. I get up in the morning and say, 'Lord, You know I'm nothing, but if You can use nothing, then here I am, use me.'"

I asked Gene who his role models of faith and character were. "I grew up in a Christian home," he told me, "so my parents raised me to know God and serve Him. My parents exhibited character every day of their lives. So did my uncle, who is in his late eighties now and has been in the ministry for over sixty-five years. These three people have had a big influence in my life, showing me what character and faith are all about. They never compromised their Christian character for the things of this world, and as a result, they have brought many souls into a relationship with Christ.

"Biblical principles were the foundation I grew up on. I accepted Jesus Christ as my Savior at an early age and He's always been my strength and my salvation. Without Him, I can do nothing, but 'I can do all things through Christ who strengthens me' (Phil. 4:13 [NKJV]).

"Another passage of Scripture that has become very meaningful to me is John 3:30, where John the Baptist said of Jesus, 'He must increase, but I must decrease' [NKJV]. I had read those words many times over the years, but one day I saw that passage in a new way. The Spirit of God spoke to my spirit and said, 'Gene, *must* is not a request but a command.' That realization changed my life because character comes through Jesus Christ and is developed because of Him."

In a quiet and unassuming way, Gene Pemberton lives out his faith and his character as the "spiritual coach" of the Houston Astros. As former Astros pitcher Andy Pettitte once said, "Just by his presence and the way he lives, Gene earns everyone's respect." Truly, Gene's faith is the generator that energizes all of the other

traits in his character—and he in turn sparks the faith and character of everyone around him.

Faith to Face Life—and Death

Dan Wood, executive director of the National Christian College Athletic Association, told me about the example of faith set by his mother at the end of her life. "Mom was diagnosed with multiple sclerosis just months after my birth," he told me. "I never really understood the pain and discomfort everyday chores caused her until I left home after college. Walking was a struggle, but she walked. Cleaning was a struggle, but she cleaned. Playing the piano at church was painful, but she played as an act of worship to her Lord.

"In the last days of her life, the doctors sent her home to die after the cancer had spread. She lay in the bed at my brother's house after having had a great Sunday with the family. We worshiped at church, then had a great lunch, and we reflected together on our heritage as a Christian family.

"As Mom prepared to go to sleep, we sang hymns and prayed with her. According to the doctors, we had every reason to believe we had six to eight more weeks with her. But after prayer and hugs, someone asked Mom if she needed anything. She said, 'No, I think I'm ready.'

"You could see the same question on every face in the room. My sister asked, 'Ready, Mom? Ready for what?'

"And Mom said, 'To be with Jesus.'

"That kind of trusting faith was Mom's legacy to us all. Less than an hour after she said those words, without any struggle at all, she went to be with the Lord she loved."

Faith enables us to face life with confidence and death without fear. The New Testament book of Hebrews tells us that God's Son immersed Himself in our humanity "so that by his death he might destroy him who holds the power of death—that is, the devil—and free those who all their lives were held in slavery by their fear of death" (2:14–15).

Stu Inman was my friend for almost forty years. A strong Christian, he served as a basketball executive and interim coach in the NBA for many years. In 1969, he helped build the Portland Trail Blazers expansion franchise and served as the team's first scout. Stu drafted the legendary Bill Walton and was the architect of the Trail Blazers' 1976–77 NBA championship team—the team, incidentally, that knocked our Philadelphia 76ers out of the NBA Finals.

While this book was being written, I picked up the newspaper and read that Stu Inman had died of a heart attack. He was eighty years old and passed away in his Lake Oswego, Oregon, home on January 30, 2007. I immediately called Stu's widow, Eleanor, and she told me, "Stu was in his closet, getting dressed to start the day, when he simply collapsed. I rushed to his side where he lay on the floor, and his last words were, 'Lord, I'm ready.' He was gone before the paramedics could get here."

Stu Inman was a man of faith, and his faith carried him safely into eternity with his Lord. Don't you want to have that kind of strong confidence in the last moments of your life on earth? I certainly do! Faith enables us to trust God in all circumstances, to have confidence in Him no matter what may come. It's the assurance that, whether in life or in death, we are safe in the arms of our heavenly Father.

How to Raise Young Souls of Faith

In our postmodern, post-Christian era, faith in God seems to be on the wane and under attack. As Chuck Colson warned in a commentary in the Prison Fellowship Ministries *Jubilee* newsletter (Summer 1996):

> Truly, America has forgotten God. And it is reaping the consequences. I spoke before a board of newspaper editors recently, where one of them—striking a pose of enlightened urbanity—boasted that he had led a cam-

paign in his city to remove the Ten Commandments from classroom walls. Yet not fifteen minutes later, the same editor was bemoaning the crime infecting our nation's schools—rampant violence and stealing. "Hmm," I said, "maybe you should put a sign on the wall: 'You shall not steal.'" The man looked embarrassed as he slowly made the connection.

When faith in God is under assault in our culture, how do we help our kids build the character trait of faith into their lives? Here are some profound and practical suggestions:

1. *Encourage true inner godliness, not mere "religious behavior."* All too many people view the faith aspect of their lives as a "religion," a matter of attending church, engaging in "religious" rituals, donating to "religious" causes, and so forth. True faith is not a religion but a transforming relationship with Jesus Christ. It must affect not only our outward behavior but our innermost being.

"Be imitators of God," Paul says in Ephesians 5:1. In other words, we are to be God-like people, living in a world that is un-God-like, and which does not like God. Although there is only one God, and there is no one else like Him in His power and purity, we are to pattern ourselves after the character of God, as demonstrated in the life of His Son, Jesus. We are to be God-like men and women, raising and mentoring God-like children.

One way to know whether your faith is producing truly God-like character is to ask yourself this question: "Whenever my thoughts roam freely, whenever my mind goes wherever it pleases, what does my mind dwell on?"

For example, do your thoughts turn to anger and bitterness toward someone who mistreated you? Do you think about ways to get even? Do you think about lust, pornography, or sexual conquests? Do you think about ways to attain more wealth so you can buy that fast car or that high definition plasma time-waster you've

got your eye on? Do you focus your thoughts on your outer self, your image, your looks? Do you dwell on thoughts of worthlessness and inferiority? Or thoughts of egotism and an inflated view of your own greatness? Do you worry about the future?

None of these is a God-like thought. These are the thoughts of a mind that is focused on the world, not on the things of God. Our Father searches our hearts and tests our minds; He knows what we are thinking and where our thoughts are focused (see Jer. 17:10; 20:12; Rev. 2:23).

Paul, in the New Testament, tells us that we should have the same mental focus Jesus has—a focus on serving God and others with every ounce of His energy (see Phil. 2:5). Paul said we should set our minds on things above, not the things on earth (see Col. 3:2).

How do we encourage God-like thinking in ourselves and our kids? Paul, in Romans 12:2, tells us to be transformed by the renewing of our minds (see also 2 Cor. 4:16; Eph. 4:23). And in Philippians 4:8, he writes, "Finally, brothers, whatever is true, whatever is noble, whatever is right, whatever is pure, whatever is lovely, whatever is admirable—if anything is excellent or praiseworthy—think about such things."

My friend, speaker and entertainer Ken Hussar, told me, "I've come to the realization that my character can only be maintained by committing myself daily to complete inner integrity. That means I have to commit my thoughts to God on a continual basis, constantly reminding myself to focus on things that are true, noble, righteous, pure, and so forth. Paul said we're to present ourselves to God as 'living sacrifices,' but sacrificing ourselves is not a one-time thing. It requires a daily recommitment. As someone once said, 'The problem with a living sacrifice is that it keeps crawling off the altar.'"

As a parent or mentor, encourage kids to memorize Scripture and meditate daily in God's Word. The psalmist said, "How can a young man keep his way pure? By living according to your word. I seek you with all my heart; do not let me stray from your com-

mands. I have hidden your word in my heart that I might not sin against you" (Ps. 119:9–11). Memorizing and meditating in God's Word will enable our kids to focus on true inner God-likeness so they can grow in their faith and character.

2. *Talk to your kids at every opportunity, applying faith and biblical principles to everyday life.* Show your kids that a relationship with God is not something we only focus on during church on Sunday mornings. Our faith relationship must affect every aspect of our daily lives. As parents, teachers, mentors, and youth leaders, we should seek to turn every encounter with our kids into a teaching opportunity.

As the Scriptures tell us, "These commandments that I give you today are to be upon your hearts. Impress them on your children. Talk about them when you sit at home and when you walk along the road, when you lie down and when you get up" (Deut. 6:6–7).

Kirk Weaver, founder and executive director of Family Time Training, shared with me some stories from his adventures as a father to his daughter, Madison, and his son, McKinley. Once, when Madison was seven years old, she and her dad were talking on the way to swimming practice. The subject of the conversation turned to friends—and boyfriends. "I don't have many friends right now who are boys," Madison said. "When I get older, I'll have friends who are boys and someday I'll have boyfriends. Boyfriends are ones that you love and might marry."

Kirk asked Madison what qualities she would look for in a boyfriend. The primary quality she identified was the character quality of faith: "First," she said, "I would see if he loved Jesus. If he didn't, then I would tell him about Jesus. If he still didn't love Jesus, then he could still be my friend—but not my boyfriend." If only more Christians in their teens and twenties showed that much wisdom in their dating choices!

There's a game Kirk described to me which provides a powerful object lesson about listening to God's leading. He told me,

"We'd have Mom stand at one end of the room, and the children took turns being blindfolded, two rooms away. The goal of the game was to find Mom by following her voice. But there was a catch that we didn't tell the kids about before we blindfolded them: Mom wouldn't be the only one calling to them.

"We had Grammy stationed by another wall, calling, 'Come here! I'll give you a cookie!' And I would be over by another wall, saying, 'Look out! You're going to run into that chair! Stop! Take your blindfold off!' Despite all of our temptations, Madison went directly to Mom. Three-year-old McKinley also made his way to Mom—though he did take a detour for one of Grammy's cookies.

"The important thing is that our kids learned a lesson: with all the voices trying to tempt them away from God, they need to keep listening for that still, small voice of God's Holy Spirit, directing them through life."

3. *Build and strengthen your children's faith through acts of service and ministry.* There are many ways children and adolescents can actively serve God and others. As they see God use them to minister to others, their faith will grow. Kids can adopt a missions project, then pray for that project, collect donations, and write letters of encouragement. They can visit retirement centers, greeting people or performing music. They can visit a Habitat for Humanity house-building worksite and serve snacks and drinks to volunteers. There are so many needs, the possibilities are limitless.

Todd Shaw, president of On-Track Ministry, recommends sending kids on short-term mission projects. "One of the best ways to build character, and especially the character quality of faith," he told me, "is by sending kids out on short-term mission trips. I have never seen young people go out on a mission trip for a week or ten days who did not come back completely changed and fired up to serve God.

"Living here in America, a paradise of material wealth and opportunity, can be a mixed blessing. Kids grow up surrounded by

iPods, cell phones, and every form of entertainment imaginable. When everything is provided for you and you can put on a set of headphones and zone out, you forget to be grateful for God's hand of provision in your life.

"A mission trip to Latin America can really open a kid's eyes and clear his thinking about his own relationship to God. Kids who already have a faith return with their faith strengthened and re-energized. And kids who have never made a commitment to Christ come back as changed people."

Todd shared a story with me how he involved his young son Jason in his work with On-Track Ministry, an outreach through the motorsport of karting. "Jason was five at the time," Todd said, "and we were at a race, standing near the starting grid, talking with the drivers and crews. The drivers in this event were seven- and eight-year-olds, and they were waiting their turn to take the track for a race.

"Jason asked, 'Can I go talk to the drivers?'

"I didn't know what he had in mind, but I said, 'Sure.'

"He went over and shook the hand of each driver, then he stepped back, grinned, and gave them all a big thumbs-up. I was proud of him and of the way he reached out to be an encourager to the young drivers—and yes, I was a bit choked up.

"'Jason,' I said when he returned, 'you did a great job.'

"He said, 'Daddy, I want to be just like you.'

"'How's that, Jason?'

"'You know how you're always helping the big people and telling them about Jesus? I want to do that for the kids my size.'

"What can you say to that? At age five, my son Jason had a very mature understanding of what it means to live out his faith."

4. *Take responsibility for raising your young people in the faith.* Your church can help and support you as you raise your children in the faith, but no one can replace you, the parent. It's your job to teach them and show them, by word and example,

what it means to live out their faith in God. Here are some key actions every believing parent should take:

- Pray for yourself. Ask God to mold and shape your character so you can set a good example for your children to follow. Pray for grace to model Christlike character, even in tough situations. Ask for the wisdom to say nothing when your kids need your listening ear, and for the boldness to speak up when your kids need your instruction.
- Pray for your children. Pray they will experience a personal faith-relationship with Jesus Christ. If your children have already professed a faith in Christ, ask God to deepen and strengthen their faith. Ask Him to give your kids a sense of mission in life and a desire to serve God and others. Pray that He would refine the character of your children.

As you pray for your children, meditate in Scripture passages that guide us in how to pray for others. Some excellent examples: Ephesians 1:15–19; 3:14–19; 4:12–15; 6:19–20; Philippians 1:9–11; Philemon 1:6; Colossians 1:9–12; 3:12–17.

Ask God to protect your kids from the mind-set of this world, so they develop a moral Christian worldview. Ask Him to guard your kids from the dangers all around them: drugs, alcohol, violence, sexual immorality, peer pressure, cults, the occult, and other forces out to destroy their souls.

Keep a journal of your prayer times. Write down prayer requests, pray over them daily, then record the date and the manner in which your prayers were answered. You'll be amazed to see the power of prayer at work.

- Pray with your children. God calls us, as Christian parents, to teach His truth to our children, to pray with them, and to lead them in a daily worship experience with God. Worship is not just something we do in church. God intends worship to be the mainstay of family life.

This means we have to switch off the TV, hold all calls, and stop the homework while everyone gathers for a family devotional time. In some families, this is a nightly ritual; in others, family devotions take place at the breakfast table. Begin by reading Scripture together. Choose a Bible translation that's easy to understand.

Take a few minutes to talk about the passage. As the parent-leader, ask questions and facilitate discussion. Let others share their ideas before you sum up. Never make a child feel he or she has given a "wrong" answer. Affirm all ideas, then build on what your kids say in order to unwrap the truths embedded in God's Word.

Share prayer requests, and pray together for those requests. Take all requests seriously and pray for each one. Pray around the circle—and short, sentence prayers are okay.

Avoid boredom and empty ritual. Show you are enthusiastic and excited about spending time with God and your family. Let your kids know it's a joy to be in the presence of the Lord.

5. *Lead your children to the Lord.* This is your number one responsibility as a believing parent. Invite your kids to pray with you to receive Jesus Christ as Lord and Savior. There is no joy like the experience of watching your children respond in faith to the simple plan of salvation. You can lead your children through a prayer like this one:

> Heavenly Father,
> I thank You for loving me. I'm sorry for my sins, and right now I want to turn away from my sins and live for You. I invite Jesus into my life as Lord and Savior. Thank You for hearing and answering my prayer. Please help me to live the rest of my life for You!
> In Jesus' name, Amen.

My Discovery of Faith

When I was a minor league baseball manager, just twenty-seven years old, I worked for Mr. R. E. Littlejohn, owner of the Spartanburg Phillies. He was a man of faith and character, and he exemplified what it means to be like Jesus. In fact, I once told him, "I'll bet Jesus was a lot like you."

I meant it as a compliment—but he looked at me as if I had uttered blasphemy! "Pat," he said gently but firmly, "no human being can compare with the Lord Jesus." His humility made me admire him all the more.

Around that time I attended a concert and someone handed me a little booklet with the title "Have You Heard of the Four Spiritual Laws?" Intrigued, I flipped the booklet open and read:

> Law One: God loves you and has a wonderful plan for your life.
>
> Law Two: Man is sinful and separated from God. Therefore, he cannot know and experience God's love and plan for his life.
>
> Law Three: Jesus Christ is God's only provision for man's sin. Through Him you can know and experience God's love and plan for your life.
>
> Law Four: We must individually receive Jesus Christ as Savior and Lord, then we can know and experience God's love and plan for our lives.

From the moment I read that booklet, my mind whirled with questions. I couldn't concentrate on my work. I thought, *This must be why my life has felt so empty!* Finally, I decided to talk to Mr. Littlejohn. He would have the answers! So I jumped into my car and drove over to his office. I told him what I had been going through ever since reading about The Four Spiritual Laws—and

his response made my jaw drop: "Pat," he said, "this is wonderful! This is what I've been praying for!"

I said, "What's 'wonderful' about it? I'm miserable!"

"But don't you see? God's been tugging at your heart. You're ready to make a decision to follow Jesus. Pat, now's the time."

Well, he was right. It was time—and God had been leading me to that very moment. I was ready to follow Jesus for the rest of my life. I knew I was lost in my sins—but Jesus has taken all the punishment for my sin so I could live forever with Him. All I had to do was say yes.

So, at 3:45 p.m. on February 22, 1968, I surrendered to Him. From that day forward, I understood why Mr. R. E. Littlejohn reminded me so much of Jesus. He patterned his life after the life of his Lord.

The character quality of faith is the most important of all. All the other character traits will carry you successfully through this life. Faith in Christ will carry you safely into eternity.

PART VI

The Power of Character

12

Character Wins

"My strength is as the strength of ten, because my heart is pure."

ALFRED, LORD TENNYSON
NINTEENTH-CENTURY ENGLISH POET

When I was general manager of the Philadelphia 76ers in the 1970s and '80s, I was fanatically devoted to the Philadelphia Phillies. Founded in 1883, the Phillies have only won a single World Series championship—and I was blessed to be living there when it happened. It was the magical 1980 season, and I attended many home games, watching such players as Mike Schmidt, Tug McGraw, Pete Rose, Bob Boone, Larry Bowa, Garry Maddox, Greg Luzinski, and Steve Carlton.

The ballclub was managed by the intense, emotional six-foot-five Dallas Green. He was always out there yelling and firing up his players. Dallas had a voice like Gabriel's trumpet, and even now I can hear him bellowing, "*WE NEED SOME CHARACTER PEOPLE ON THIS TEAM!*" Well, Dallas Green's Philadelphia Phillies definitely had some character people on its roster.

The 1980 World Series pitted the Phillies against the Kansas City Royals. The Phillies won the first two games, lost the next two, then won game five. Game six was a nail-biter for the fans who filled Vet Stadium in Philadelphia. Though the Phillies maintained a big lead throughout the game, the Royals loaded the bases in the eighth inning—and then again in the ninth.

As Phillies pitcher Tug McGraw faced Royals outfielder Willie

Wilson, the score was 4–1, Phillies leading, two away, top of the ninth. The bases were loaded and Wilson was a dangerous hitter (230 hits in the regular season). The crowd held its breath as McGraw hurled a pair of strikes. More than six hundred Philadelphia policemen ringed the field. If the Phillies won, the police had the responsibility of controlling 65,838 delirious fans.

Up in the booth, NBC Sports announcer Joe Garagiola told the television audience, "The crowd will tell you what happens."

McGraw threw the pitch. Wilson swung—and missed it, strike three!

As promised, Garagiola offered no commentary. The roar of the crowd said it all. At 11:29 p.m. on October 21, 1980, Dallas Green's Phillies captured the only World Series title in franchise history.

As I witnessed that historic moment, I could hear Dallas Green's voice ringing in my mind: "*WE NEED SOME CHARACTER PEOPLE ON THIS TEAM!*"

Dallas Green got exactly what he asked for. He had a roster full of character people, and they got the job done. Character wins.

Character Is Essential to Teamwork

The year before Marvin Lewis took over as head coach of the Cincinnati Bengals in 2003, the team had a 2-14 record and had not had a winning season in thirteen years. Two years later, Lewis's Bengels won the AFC North Division with a record of 11-5. Marvin attributes the turnaround to character.

Marvin Lewis learned the importance of recruiting players of character early in his college coaching career. Once, during the recruiting season, Marvin heard about a talented junior college player who was being courted by a number of major schools. Lewis's team needed the very skills this young man demonstrated, but none of Marvin's assistants and scouts had suggested his name. Marvin asked why. His assistants said, "The guy's a bad apple. Yes, he's got talent and ability—but he's also got huge character flaws. Steer clear of this guy."

"I didn't listen," Marvin told me. "I recruited him and signed him for his talents alone. Once he was on our team, he was nothing but trouble. Even worse, his character flaws infected at least two other promising players, including a talented freshman. I learned then and there that, while talent is important, character is essential."

We are all, at some level in our lives, involved in a team endeavor. If we do not have good character, we let the whole team down. This is true whether the team is a sports team, a real estate office, a retail store, a city council, a Scout troop, a church board, a White House administration, a platoon of marines, or a family.

Michael Lombardi, former Oakland Raiders personnel executive, told me, "It takes many ingredients working together to make a successful team. Obviously, you must have talent, leadership, preparation, and chemistry. But one of the most overlooked and underrated factors in a winning team is character."

I asked Michael when he first became aware of the importance of character in a team setting. He said, "I attended Valley Forge Military Academy in Wayne, Pennsylvania. A military setting is a constant reminder of character. My coach at Valley Forge, Roger Sicoli, was a Vietnam vet who had been exposed to the chemical defoliant Agent Orange. He battled cancer, yet he had the courage to come out and fight each day and try to shape the character of all of us on the team. He was a role model. He understood what Churchill meant when he said, 'We make a living by what we get, but we make a life by what we give.' Roger Sicoli gave plenty."

Michael went on to give me his philosophy of what makes a great coach and a great team. His philosophy centers around character. "Adversity tests character," he said, "and anything that *tests* your character *builds* your character. When you're on a winning team, there are few demands made on your character. But when you hit some bumpy roads, you find out what you're really made of—inside, where it counts.

"We need to teach young people the skills they need to compete and win. But we also need to teach them the character to hold

their heads up when they lose. They need to learn how to fight through the adversity, pain, and sorrow of losing. That's where the lessons of victory are learned. If you never learn the lessons of defeat, you'll never learn what it takes to be victorious."

The pros know: good character is essential to teamwork and success in every endeavor, from running a sports team to running a business to running a family. Talent alone may win a few games in the short term, but you can't stay on top for long without some character people on your team.

Character: The Key to Winning

Nobody ever accused Leo Durocher of being a nice guy. After his retirement from Major League Baseball, he was ranked the fifth-winningest manager in MLB history with 2,008 career wins. Bombastic and controversial, "Leo the Lip" continually clashed with umpires and was the most frequently ejected manager in the history of baseball. He coined the most famous phrase in all of sports: "Nice guys finish last!"

Was Durocher right? Is it true you have to be mean in order to win? I disagree with Durocher. I believe nice guys—people of genuine character—not only *can* win but are *favored* to win. What do I base that belief on? The testimony of proven winners who are also people of character.

Sean Callahan is the head football coach at Armwood High School in Seffner, Florida. "We are currently one of the most successful football programs in the state of Florida," Coach Callahan told me. "Three state championship appearances in a row, winner of two. At the state semifinals in 2000, we lost to Belle Glades Central, and I knew it was a game we should have won. Why did we lose? Lack of character. We had good athletes but we were a selfish team, lacking in humility, teamwork, and discipline.

"So, in 2001, I selected only kids with character. If they were athletes, that was a bonus—but character came first. We not only recruited character but we preached it. One of the biggest char-

acter traits we seek is humility. We are a *team*, not a collection of egos. We will intimidate our opponents by our speed and strength, but we will not taunt, boast, or trash talk. I figure, why give your opponent reason to be mad at you? That could raise your opponent's energy level, which would work against you.

"Our 2001 team—our first all-character team—had a rough season, ending up with a 4-6 record. It was the first time since 1994 that we had missed the play-offs. But I loved that team. Everyone who suited up was a young man of character.

"In 2002, we improved to 9-3, and we made the play-offs— and again, it was an all-character team. In 2003, we went 15-0, and were the state champs. Character won. In 2004, 14-0, and again were state champs. Character again. In 2005, we went 13-2 and were state finalists. Once again, the number one reason for all of that success: character. When your players work together unselfishly as a team, good things happen."

Cleo Hill Jr. is head men's basketball coach at Cheyney University of Pennsylvania. Coach Hill played professionally in Australia for two years (1990–91), averaging 41 points and 8.3 assists per game in his final season. During his first year as a collegiate coach, he guided the Cheyney Wolves to the NCAA Division II Tournament.

I asked Cleo to name his first role model of character, and his answer was his father, Cleo Hill Sr. The senior Mr. Hill was a phenomenal basketball player who averaged 23.2 points per game during his four seasons at Winston Salem Teachers College (now Winston Salem State University). Those who saw him play say he was nothing less than "Jordanesque." His energy and creativity on the court took his game to a very high level. In 1961, he was the first-round draft pick of the St. Louis Hawks.

"My dad talked to me a lot about character," the younger Cleo Hill recalls, "especially when I was entering my teens and getting serious about basketball. He shared stories of his career and the many challenges he had to overcome while playing basketball in St. Louis

in the early 1960s. Dad always expressed the importance of being humble, and he said that character would always pay off."

Cleo Hill Jr.'s first coaching job was with a girls' team in Australia in 1991. He recalls, "All the players were under fourteen. My star player's father was a noted motivational speaker. He gave the girls a talk about character just before our championship game. What a speech! In the fourth quarter, we were up by two with a minute left to play when our star player got punched in the face. It was clearly no accident—the opponent, though smaller than our star player, was a tough and physically aggressive girl.

"Our star came over with blood streaming from her nose. One of our other players said, 'You should have punched her back!' But the girl with the bloodied nose replied, 'My dad always told me to win with class, especially against inferior players.' That was a classic line I'll remember all my life! That was a statement of character."

Dave Hammer is head men's basketball coach at Aquinas College in Grand Rapids, Michigan. Before coaching at Aquinas, he served as an assistant coach at the University of Michigan and Southern Methodist University.

"When I was coaching girls' basketball in 1980," Dave told me, "we had a game against the first-place team. We started the game with eight players. By the fourth quarter, because of injury and three girls fouling out, we were down to four players. In the final quarter, at every timeout, we talked—but we didn't talk about strategy. We talked entirely about character qualities—the character those girls would have to display in order to win that game.

"By the four-minute mark, we were down to three players. With a minute and a half left we had just two girls on the floor. If we had lost one more player, we would forfeit the game. We played the final minute and a half with two players—and we won!

"I attribute that win to sheer character and nothing else. Perseverance, hard work, and individual and collective responsibility are the building blocks of good character—and the key to success in any endeavor."

Jim Israel, my former baseball teammate at Wake Forest, is a retired airline pilot living in North Carolina. He told me, "When I was a junior in high school in Hampton, New Hampshire, I was a first-team all-state quarterback. Starting my senior year, our coach—Coach G—told us we could win the state championship. To help achieve that goal, he said we would start having Sunday afternoon practices beginning the next Sunday.

"My younger brother, Kenneth Ray, was a sophomore and starting tight end on the team. Our dad was a Southern Baptist minister who had been chief of chaplains for the Military Air Lift Command. He had taught us to respect the Lord's Day as a day of rest. So, after much prayer and discussion with my brother, Ray and I went to Coach G's home the Saturday night before the first Sunday practice. We told Coach G that if he was going to practice on Sundays, Ray and I couldn't play for him. We said it respectfully, but firmly—and Coach G was speechless—he really didn't know how to respond.

"The next day at practice, we weren't there. Lacking his starting quarterback and tight end, Coach G canceled the practice and the team didn't practice on Sunday again. I went on to make first-team all-state quarterback again, was named to the Shrine Bowl, and had numerous scholarship offers to play football.

"I never told Dad about our meeting with Coach G. Dad only found out about the stand we took several weeks later when Coach G came by for a visit and told Dad what had happened. The coach also told Dad that Ray and I had taught him a lesson about character. Coach G made me captain of the football team and for years he told the story about how the Israel brothers had taken a stand and made a statement about character.

"The final postscript to the story: we won the state championship that year."

Kevin Towers is executive vice president and general manager of the San Diego Padres. He told me, "One of the first trades I ever made was in 1995, two weeks after I was named general manager. There were questions about the chemistry in our clubhouse, and

I suspected it was actually a character problem. So I traded away a speedy, talented second baseman who had questionable character, and I brought in a great character player, Wally Joyner, who I teamed with at Brigham Young University. Wally's positive influence completely changed our clubhouse chemistry—and led us to two divisional championships over the next three years."

Tracey Bloodworth-Fisk is head women's basketball coach at Ferris State University. As I write these words, Tracey's career record after eight seasons as coach of the Ferris State Bulldogs is an impressive 135-88 (.605). She told me that one of the examples of good character on the court of competitive athletics is Czech-American tennis star Ivan Lendl.

"I remember watching him in a televised tennis match," Tracey said. "Ivan's opponent served and there was a borderline call. The umpire called the ball out. The opponent went to the umpire and argued that the ball was in. The umpire was not persuaded, said the ball was definitely out, and awarded the point to Lendl. Well, Ivan agreed with his opponent and knew that the umpire had made a bad call. He refused to take the point, and instead conceded the next point to his opponent. Ivan Lendl showed how to win with character. When talking to my players, I often use Ivan Lendl as a role model of genuine competitive character."

The Power to Triumph over Tragedy

Super Bowl XLI will go down in history as the first NFL championship game won by an African American head coach. That coach was Tony Dungy of the Indianapolis Colts (formerly of the Tampa Bay Buccaneers). That Super Bowl victory was the capstone of a phenomenal 123-70-0 career coaching record for Tony Dungy.

In his playing days, Dungy was a Steelers safety and part of the vaunted Steel Curtain defense of the 1970s. He played a pivotal role in Super Bowl XIII, forcing a Dallas Cowboys fumble that resulted in a Steelers touchdown. The Steelers prevailed over the Cowboys, 35–31.

Tony Dungy also holds the distinction of being the only NFL player since the NFL-AFL merger to throw an interception and intercept a pass in the same game. It happened in a Pittsburgh Steelers–Baltimore Colts game on October 20, 1977. After QBs Terry Bradshaw and Mike Kruczek were felled by injuries, Dungy—who had started the game at safety—was tapped as an emergency quarterback. The Steelers lost—but Dungy's strong performance kept the game from being a blowout.

I first met Coach Dungy in the 1980s, when I spoke at a Christian outreach breakfast in Pittsburgh. He was a defensive coordinator with the Steelers while I was with the 76ers. A few years later, I moved to Orlando, and then Tony Dungy took the head coaching job with the nearby Tampa Bay Buccaneers a few years after that. I don't know Tony well, but our paths have crossed a number of times. He has always impressed me as an outspoken Christian and an unusually even-tempered man in a sport known for hot-tempered coaches.

After his Super Bowl XLI victory at Miami's Dolphin Stadium on February 4, 2007, the whole world discovered what so many Buccaneers and Colts fans already knew: Tony Dungy is a man of extraordinary character. Sports writers marveled that a coach with Dungy's coaching style could win the Big Game. After all, he never uses profanity, screaming, or intimidation to motivate his players—*never*. He encourages his players and assistants to put faith and family ahead of football—*always*. Dungy never even raises his voice to his players, remaining calm and serene even when a game goes badly. His players don't fear him; they love him.

The opposing coach in Super Bowl XLI was Lovie Smith of the Chicago Bears—a man who, as linebackers coach of the Buccaneers from 1996 to 2000, was mentored by Tony Dungy. Both Dungy and Smith are committed Christians, and Smith once observed that while most people expect NFL coaches to scream and cuss at their players, "Tony Dungy showed me you don't have to act that way."

Away from the sidelines, Tony Dungy is committed to serving Christ and the community. He's actively involved with Athletes in Action, Fellowship of Christian Athletes, Big Brothers/Big Sisters, Boys and Girls Club, Prison Crusade Ministry, Family First, foster parenting organizations, and youth mentoring organizations. In Indianapolis, he helped launch Basket of Hope which provides help for children being cared for at the city's Riley Hospital for Children.

Tony Dungy's faith and character were put to the ultimate test three days before Christmas 2005 when his eighteen-year-old son James was found dead in his Lutz, Florida, apartment. The coroner's report concluded that James had committed suicide. At the funeral in Tampa, which was attended by the entire Colts organization and many members of the Buccaneers, plus others from around the NFL, Tony stood before fifteen hundred mourners and urged them never to take family for granted.

He recalled the last time he had seen his son, which was at Thanksgiving, as James was leaving for the airport. "I said, 'I'll see you later,'" Dungy recalled. "I didn't get to hug him. I knew I'd see him again pretty soon, so it didn't really bother me very much. We talked on the phone a lot the last few days. . . . He was saying—as the guys on the team know he would—he was saying: 'Dad, we're going to the Super Bowl, and when we do, will I be on the field?'"

At that point, he choked—then finished his thought. "I said, 'Yeah, man. You know the hard part is getting there, but if we do, you know you're going to be on the field.' But I never got to hug him again. That's one thing I'll always think about and always remind people to do: Hug them every chance you get. Tell them you love them every chance you get because you don't know when it's going to be the last time."

After the funeral, David Thornton, then a Colts linebacker, said, "The things he reminded us of—character, being a role model—well, we were there to support him, but, in the end, he supported us."

As a result of Tony Dungy's strong Christian testimony at his son's funeral, many people committed their lives to Jesus Christ as Lord and Savior. The *Baptist Press* reported that Tony Dungy said, "If God had talked to me before James's death and said his death would have helped all these people, it would have saved them and healed their sins, but I would have to take your son, I would have said, 'No, I can't do that.' But God had the same choice two thousand years ago with His Son, Jesus Christ, and it paved the way for you and me to have eternal life. That's the benefit I got, that's the benefit James got, and that's the benefit you can get if you accept Jesus into your heart today as your Savior."

That's a powerful statement of the faith and character of Tony Dungy—and so was the statement he made on the victor's podium after Super Bowl XLI. During the presentation of the Lombardi Trophy, Jim Nantz of CBS Sports asked Tony Dungy for his thoughts on becoming the first African American head coach to win the Super Bowl.

"I'm proud to be representing African American coaches, to be the first African American to win this," Dungy replied. "That means an awful lot to our country. But again, more than anything, I've said it before, Lovie Smith and I, not only the first two African Americans, but Christian coaches, showing that you can win doing it the Lord's way. We're more proud of that."

To put it another way, Leo Durocher was wrong. Sometimes nice guys, character guys, finish first. Legendary sportswriter Grantland Rice probably had this in mind when he wrote that Lou Gehrig had "a quality of character that certainly no one I ever knew has topped . . . a mixture of strength and gentleness, of courage and complete cleanness in everything he did."

Character is the necessary ingredient for teamwork and success; it's the catalyst for winning; and it's the key to overcoming tragedy and adversity. That's why character matters. That's why character wins.

13

Heroes: People of Impact and Influence

"You don't have to be a 'person of influence' to be influential. In fact, the most influential people in my life are probably not even aware of the things they've taught me."

SCOTT ADAMS
AMERICAN CARTOONIST; CREATOR OF "DILBERT"

On March 30, 1981, a little over two months into his first term, President Ronald Reagan was shot and wounded by a lone gunman outside the Washington Hilton Hotel. The young would-be assassin, John Hinckley Jr., also wounded three other men. Hinckley was wrestled to the ground by the Secret Service as the president was whisked away in his limousine.

Most people are aware of Hinckley's bizarre motivation: He watched the movie *Taxi Driver* at least fifteen times, and he was obsessed with the young actress in the film, Jodie Foster. Hinckley identified with the film's lead character Travis Bickle (played by Robert De Niro), and he worshiped Bickle as a hero. To impress Jodie Foster, Hinckley decided to assume the Travis Bickle role and shoot the president. Any president would do; he had also stalked Reagan's predecessor, Jimmy Carter.

But here's a little-known twist to the story: There was another man present that day—a man who played a decisive role in the drama. He was on the scene because he, too, had become fasci-

nated with a character in a movie. That man was Jerry Parr, the agent in charge of the Secret Service Presidential Protective Division in Washington, D.C. When the shots rang out, Jerry Parr shoved President Reagan into the limousine, then flung himself over the president's body as the car sped from the scene.

At the time, President Reagan didn't know he'd been shot. He thought the pain in his chest was the result of being thrown into the car. However, a bullet had entered under his left arm, nicked his seventh rib, and was deflected into his lung where it was lodged less than an inch from his heart.

When the president began coughing up bright red blood, Parr knew that Reagan's lung had been punctured. He immediately ordered the driver to take the president to the hospital instead of the White House. If not for Jerry Parr's quick action, President Reagan would have died that day and the history of the world would have turned out very differently.

How did Jerry Parr happen to be there that day, crucially positioned to save President Reagan's life? In a *National Geographic* special, "Inside the U.S. Secret Service," Parr told an interviewer he knew he wanted to be a Secret Service agent in 1939 when he saw an action-adventure movie, *The Code of the Secret Service*. "I made my dad take me to that movie quite a few times," he said. The hero of the film was Agent Brass Bancroft—and Bancroft became Jerry Parr's hero. The role of Brass Bancroft was played by a rising young actor named Ronald Reagan.

The boy Jerry Parr grew to become a young man. In 1962, after graduating from college, Parr interviewed for a position with the Secret Service in New York City. He got the job, and he worked his way up the ranks until he achieved his dream job of protecting the president.

After Reagan recovered from the assassination attempt, President Reagan and Jerry Parr had a conversation at Reagan's "Western White House" ranch near Santa Barbara, California. Jerry Parr told the president his early film, *The Code of the Secret Service*,

inspired him to join the Secret Service. President Reagan laughed and said, "That was the worst picture I ever made!"

"Well, Mr. President," Parr replied, "for a kid like me, that movie made the life of an agent seem exciting and worthwhile. You know, when you made that movie, you determined your own destiny."

The president considered that—and realized it was true. Ronald Reagan the actor played Brass Bancroft, a fictional character. Bancroft inspired Jerry Parr to become the real-life Secret Service agent who, some forty-two years later, saved the life of Ronald Reagan the president.

And consider this irony: John Hinckley Jr. wanted to *kill* the president because of a character in a movie he saw many times. Jerry Parr was inspired to *save* the president by a character in a movie he saw many times.

The moral of this story? Actually, there are three: First, we need to be careful who we choose as our heroes. For better or worse, we will become what they are. Second, we need to give our kids positive, inspiring role models to emulate. We need to give them heroes who will bring out the best in them, not summon the worst. Third, and most important of all, we need to *be* their heroes.

It's All about Impact and Influence

My friend Rich DeVos is the cofounder of Alticor, Inc., and, with his four children, co-owner of the Orlando Magic. In 1997, after suffering two strokes, undergoing sextuple bypass surgery, and waiting five months in London for a donor heart, Rich received a heart transplant under circumstances that were nothing less than miraculous. Here's what happened:

While Rich was waiting for his new heart, a thirty-seven-year-old woman with diseased lungs also awaited a donor for a transplant operation. When a European man was killed in a car crash, his healthy heart and lungs were sent to London and transplanted in the woman. Though her lungs were diseased, her heart was healthy—so Rich received her heart. A few days after the opera-

tion, Rich was walking in the hospital hallway as part of his post-op therapy. He met a woman in the hallway who had also had an operation. The woman realized who Rich was and said, "You have my heart!" Rich thanked her and they hugged.

How many heart transplant patients get a chance to thank the heart donor? As far as I know, Rich is the only one. He later wrote about his miraculous experience in his book *Hope from My Heart.*

But there's more to the story, as Rich recently shared with me. "The other day," he said, "a Vietnam veteran told me he had a pistol in one hand and my book *Hope from My Heart* in the other. He had lost all hope and his reason for living. He was ready to shoot himself but something in the book made him realize that God loves him and he should not take his own life. That man gave me credit for saving his life—but Pat, you and I both know I didn't do that. God touched him that day."

It's true. God spoke to that veteran and stayed his hand—but God used the story of Rich's life in that book to have an impact and an influence on the man. We never know how God may use our lives to touch others. That's why we need to live every day as positive role models of faith and character.

Jeff Hartung is the sports products manager of Impact Innovative Products, a company which produces body protection gear for sports and industry. I recently talked to Jeff about his life and the powerful lessons he has learned about influence and character. "Throughout my boyhood and adolescence," he told me, "I dreamed of playing baseball in the major leagues. In 1980, I finally got my chance. I tried out with the Pirates, and eventually signed a contract with the Padres. I was eighteen and I thought I was sitting on top of the world.

"In 1982, the dream ended. I was released by the Padres, and my pro baseball career ended just like that. I failed to perform at a big league level and I had no one to blame but myself. It was all a matter of character. I had a poor work ethic, and I lacked self-control with regard to peer pressure, drugs, and alcohol. I went

along with the poor choices other people made instead of making good decisions for myself. My playing suffered—and after only two years, it was over.

"After I was cut by the Padres, I continued to take my life in the wrong direction. I felt I had lost my way in life, and I relied on drugs and alcohol to numb my pain. I was married at this time, with two kids whom I dearly loved, and my marriage ended in divorce. Because of the divorce, I was separated from my kids. My life had gone from a dream to a nightmare, and soon I started not even caring about life at all.

"Realizing I had hit rock bottom, I knew I had a choice to make. I could continue destroying myself with drugs, and maybe end up dead on the street—or I could find some way out of the situation. I got on my knees and said to God, 'I need to get my life straight. Please lead me out of the mess I've made of my life.'

"Soon after that, my friend Dave called me. He worked with an organization called Christian Sports International. He said, 'Jeff, why don't you go with me to New York? You can help me work with underprivileged kids there.' So I went with him to one of the roughest neighborhoods in the country. At first, I thought, *What am I doing here?* But, at Dave's urging, I talked to those kids about some of my experiences in baseball and in life, and the kids ate it up. It hit me that, by giving back to others, doors were opening in my thinking and in my life.

"After that trip, I finally kicked the drug and alcohol habit. With the help of friends and family, and by the grace of God, I've been able to turn my life around. Since then, I've never looked back. I just keep looking forward, staying open to the people—especially kids and young people—God wants to bring into my life, so that I can have a positive influence.

"Life is all about choices. We all seem to want the acknowledgement and accolades for our accomplishments, but none of that is important. What really matters is what we give to others, how we influence others. It's about our willingness to use our ex-

periences to serve others and give other people a hand up in life. When we decide we're going to focus on influencing others instead of focusing on ourselves, we begin to display real character."

Moms and Dads Can Be Heroes

Tom Shea is the resident golf pro at Fox Hollow Golf Club in New Port Richey, Florida. "My birth mother died when I was six years old," he told me. "My birth father was an alcoholic and abusive at times, but he did struggle to provide for his four children. I was the youngest. My oldest sister moved out after graduating from high school, my brother was ready to leave home during his senior year, and my other sister moved in with her best friend's family when she was thirteen.

"My father realized he couldn't take care of me, so he let the state have custody of me when I was eight. Years later, I realized that, in spite of his personal demons, my father had shown enough character to realize that his alcoholism was harming me. He decided to put my well-being ahead of his own life, and that's why he gave me up. I'll forever be grateful that he had the wisdom to do so.

"I was in foster care for several years, and when I was thirteen, my foster family adopted me. My new mother had five children of her own, plus she brought numerous foster kids into the home. My parents taught us all about values and character. Because there were so many kids in the house, we all had to learn teamwork as a family, and love was the basis of our teamwork. Mom taught us right from wrong, and that we needed to take a stand against the bad influences of the crowd. She shaped all of her kids into people of character.

"My father introduced me to football, basketball, baseball, and golf. I fell in love with the game of golf, and he used the game to shape my character. On one occasion, Dad and I were playing and I got angry and broke a club. He said, 'Son, the next time you break a club in anger, you won't be playing golf again.' Well, that quickly righted the ship of my character, and it was a great lesson in self-control.

"His most important influence on my life comes from his

example. As a golfer, he's shot in the nineties and hundreds as long as I can remember—but he knows it's a game and he simply enjoys playing the game and being in the company of his buddies. If he shanks one into the trees or misses an easy putt, he just laughs. I learned from his example. When I hit a bad shot, I don't break clubs—I just laugh. I know what I did wrong, I know how to fix it, and I know how to enjoy the game as it was meant to be enjoyed.

"My mother and father have had a great influence on me, and I try to be an influence on the young people I meet through the game of golf. I work with kids on a daily basis, and I try to pass along the values and character qualities I've learned.

"Golf is an individual sport, but it's a sport where you have to be aware of your surroundings and your fellow players. You have to manage the golf course together and finish the game in a manner that is respectful to everyone else. Golf is a patient sport, and it teaches kids to listen, take turns, work together in groups, and respect each other. They have to learn to leave the course as they found it and take responsibility for actions. You have the most fun when you play the game in a responsible way.

"My greatest influence on kids has more to do with teaching character than teaching golf skills. It has given me great pleasure to watch kids make progress in their own game, then turn around and help other kids, giving them encouragement and helping them improve their game.

"I run a junior golf tour in Pasco County, Florida, and I have kids from ages seven to sixteen playing. One young man has worked hard to improve his game and follow the rules. He lost tournaments to kids he knew were playing dishonestly. Despite his disappointment, he kept his integrity and kept improving until he started winning. He continues to win honestly even when his opponents fudge the numbers.

"It's so important to be a person of influence. My foster parents adopted me and became the greatest influence of my life. And, of course, the most important influence we can have on others is

to impact the people around us for Jesus Christ. Faith in Him as Lord and Savior is the basis for living a life of character and influence every day of our lives."

Erik Schmudde is a young man who interned at Walt Disney World in Orlando and now lives in Los Angeles. "I'm going after my dream in the motion picture industry as an aspiring writer," he told me. "I'm working at the Walt Disney Studios in California, seeking to inspire people through entertainment."

Erik told me his character has been shaped by the influence of his parents. "One event especially stands out in my mind," he said. "When I was fifteen, my father became very sick and had to undergo a series of surgical procedures. As he faced one of those surgeries, he believed he probably wouldn't make it, so he wrote each person in the family a personalized letter. I've never shared this letter with anyone before, but I think it's typical of the kind of positive influence my father has always had in my life."

Here's the letter Erik's father wrote to him:

> Dear Erik,
>   You are my youngest and most creative child. Your creativity and sensitivity will guide you through your future. I never want words to come out of your mouth like, 'I'm not good at anything,' or, 'I can't do that.' You must believe in yourself like I believe in you. You already have great things in you. You have a personality where people like you. You make friends easily and you can see things others can't. These are gifts from God. Use them wisely. Planning your future is not easy, but never be afraid. Life is an adventure and it's full of turns, but with your gifts you'll be on the right road.
>   Love, Dad

The happy ending: the surgery was successful and Erik's father continues to have a positive influence in his life. Here's a father

who's a hero to his son—and he's showing his son how to be a hero to others. Facing the possibility of his own death, he urged his son to live the adventure and to make an impact on the world.

That's a great legacy for a father to leave to his son.

Teachers Can Be Heroes

After more than three decades in the classroom, Kathy Megyeri is retired and living in the Washington, D.C., area. She told me about an inspirational teacher who was a hero in her life. "One of the most treasured and lasting gifts I received from my St. Olaf College education," she said, "was my acquaintance with associate professor of English Emeritus Graham S. Frear. During his career at St. Olaf, from 1962 to 1986, Professor Frear taught eighteen different courses to over two thousand students. He calculated that he had administered 6,308 exams and evaluated at least 9,533 papers. But at least as important as the academic education he imparted was the character education he instilled.

"Professor Frear was a part of St. Olaf as a student, alumnus, faculty member, and emeritus for almost sixty years. St. Olaf is a Lutheran liberal arts college in Northfield, Minnesota. When he enrolled in 1940, the campus consisted of eight buildings; today there are forty-three. When he was a student, folk dancing was accepted, but social dancing was not. He recalls how character education was imparted by one professor who told students in the freshman hygiene class that 'dancing was the vertical expression of a horizontal desire' and that students should be wary of 'cigarette suckers, cosmetic users, and those boozers who were losers.'

"While I was his student, Professor Frear exemplified character as he taught me the craft of teaching. He convinced me that teaching is the profession that most benefits society and impacts most positively on youth. Once, when I asked him his philosophy of teaching, he wrote me the following statement: 'Teaching was always my way of attempting to impact attitude and dedication more than skills. I became a teacher largely through attempting to do what I would

have wanted done with me as a student. The teachers I remember were the ones who conveyed a sense of purpose and enthusiasm more than those who were centered on subject matter.'

"During my own thirty-four-year career of teaching secondary English, I attempted to follow Professor Frear's example and convey the importance of good character, an upbeat attitude, and an enthusiasm for life—all in addition to teaching the subject matter. Whether or not I was as successful as Professor Frear remains to be judged, but I tried to follow his example. I wish all students could have such a life-affirming teacher, mentor, and role model as Professor Frear."

Perhaps the reason Kathy Megyeri has been a hero to her own students is that she was mentored by a true hero. Kids need heroes, and what better hero to have than a great teacher of excellent character.

There's a man in the pro basketball business who has made heroes out of teachers. Retired NBA star Allan Houston, who spent most of his career as a shooting guard for the New York Knicks, served as the spokesman for a city-wide contest called "My Teacher Is My Hero." Each year, students from New York City's fourteen hundred public schools were invited to write an essay about why their teachers are heroes.

"Teachers don't get the recognition they deserve," Houston told a press conference when the program was announced. "They shape the future—our children—and they often work under difficult conditions. Yet, society as a rule looks at others to emulate—athletes such as myself, show-business figures, and so forth. To say that teachers are under-appreciated is merely stating the obvious. Besides parents, teachers have the greatest impact on the children."

Each year, the "My Teacher Is My Hero" program received thousands of essays, and the three students whose essays were judged the best (one each from elementary school, middle school, and high school) were invited to watch a Knicks game from a

luxury box at Madison Square Garden. They were also honored at halftime by Mayor Michael Bloomberg.

Invariably, the teachers who were praised as heroes by their students were those who exemplified character. Let me just quote from one winning essay from 2002, written by student Jessica Cardona from Steinway Intermediate School, describing her teacher, Mrs. Tzimas:

> A hero is someone who is always there for you, an inspiring person, someone who helps you in whatever you need. Someone who is understanding, a good role model, someone who encourages you, a person that is willing, an admirable person, but most of all, a hero is someone who cares for your well-being.
>
> My hero would have to be my Language Arts teacher Mrs. Tzimas because whenever I needed help in something she has always been there for me. I've had Mrs. Tzimas for two years, once in sixth grade and in eighth grade and she has always asked me if I understand something and if I didn't then she would take time from her busy schedule to help me.
>
> I remember in sixth grade when I first got to this school and I was slacking off because I thought I was cool. Mrs. Tzimas opened my eyes and made me realize that thirty years from now it's not going to matter how many friends I had or how cool I was, but what was going to matter was my education. I was about to make a very bad decision and Mrs. Tzimas made me stay in her class until I promised her that I wasn't going to do what I knew was the wrong thing.
>
> Mrs. Tzimas may give us a lot of work, but she does it for our own good not for her amusement. Right now we might hate doing all the work but in the future we will thank her for giving us such a good education.

To me Mrs. Tzimas is the definition of a hero. I thank her for what she has done for me, and for not letting me slack off or make wrong decisions. I hope to see her thirty years from now so she could see what I have become and be happy to know that she has made a great impact in my life.

For most teachers, the education profession often seems like a thankless and under-rewarded job. But occasionally a teacher like Mrs. Tzimas gets to hear those five words that make it all worthwhile: "My teacher is my hero."

Coaches Can Be Heroes

Born in 1916, Danny Litwhiler is a living legend of major league and college baseball. In a career that lasted from 1940 to 1951, he was a great outfielder for the Philadelphia Phillies, St. Louis Cardinals, Boston Braves, and Cincinnati Reds. While playing with Cincinnati, he appeared beside Jackie Robinson in a publicity photo to show the world that the formerly all-white team welcomed the first Black player in Major League Baseball history. Though Litwhiler took a lot of flack from small-minded fans and players about that photo, he was proud of the long friendship he enjoyed with Jackie Robinson.

Danny credits his family and one great coach for shaping his early character. "One of the outstanding mentors in my life," he said, "was my coach at Bloomsburg State, Dr. E. H. Nelson. He's the man who got me into professional baseball. He actually gave me the money so that I could go to my first professional team, and he insisted that I go.

"The reason he gave me money to play pro ball was that I was already playing semi-pro ball for eighty dollars a month while living at home. If I took the position with the Tigers farm club in Cherleroi, Pennsylvania, I would only be paid seventy-five dollars a month, out of which I'd have to pay room and board plus transportation. So going pro was a step backwards financially.

"But Dr. Nelson had faith and confidence in me. He believed I had the character qualities—the work ethic, perseverance, and commitment—to become successful in the major leagues. He believed in me more than I believed in myself, and he invested in me."

From Coach Nelson, Danny Litwhiler learned a lot about the importance of exemplifying character as a coach. After his major league playing career ended, Danny coached and managed in the minors for several years. Then, in 1955, he was hired to coach baseball at Florida State University. During his time there, he compiled a record of 189-81. In 1964, he signed on as baseball coach at Michigan State University, racking up another impressive record, 488-363. He became known throughout his college coaching career as a teacher who developed his players not merely as athletes but as well-rounded men of character.

"As a college coach," he told me, "I stressed academic achievement, good character, and proper dress. Long hair, mustaches, and beards were coming into style. I insisted on haircuts and clean-shaven faces. My barber was a great baseball fan, and he came out to one of our indoor workouts and gave free haircuts to the entire team. On road trips, I insisted that players wear a sport coat and dress slacks in the hotel, but could dress comfortably on the bus. Everyone on the team conformed to the dress code.

"At rest stops, I told the team before they left the bus, 'Don't take home anything you haven't paid for.' Years later, I got a letter from a former player, now a teacher and coach. He said, 'Remember when you used to say, 'Don't take anything you haven't paid for'? Well, my senior year I went to the bookstore as I had for three years and I stole all my books for the semester. I went to my room and looked at the books and your words came to my mind. So I returned the books to the store and I never stole again. Thank you for teaching me a lesson in integrity.'

"Over the years, many of the players I coached came back and told me how much I had helped them get a good start in life—not only as baseball players but as men. It brought tears to my eyes to

hear them thank me for playing a part in their training and character growth. I could never repay my coach, Dr. Nelson. But I think he'd be pleased to know how I repaid his influence in my life by influencing other young men over the years."

Danny Litwhiler's legacy as a coach is very much Dr. Nelson's legacy as well. Danny may have been a famed sports hero during his illustrious playing career, but as a coach he became something even greater—a hero and a shaper of young souls.

Todd Peterson shared another story of a coach-hero. Todd Peterson is an NFL place kicker who has played with the New York Giants, the Seattle Seahawks, and the Atlanta Falcons. He also shared with me a story of a coach-hero. "I recall a significant moment early in my NFL career," he said, "when I was confronted with the importance of character. My first year in the NFL, I signed a form acknowledging that I wouldn't sell Super Bowl tickets for more than face value. But just a couple of days after I signed that form, a man came into our locker room with over a hundred thousand dollars in cash. He was buying up Super Bowl tickets for four times their face value.

"I was tempted. I rationalized that I could do great things with the extra money. But God used one of our coaches, Dave Brown, to remind me of my integrity. He said something to me at just the right moment about how money has a way of tarnishing people and their character. I realized how important it is that what we say and what we do should be totally aligned."

You may have heard of the coach Todd is talking about. Dave Brown was a Pro Bowl cornerback before becoming a defensive backs coach with the Seattle Seahawks, and later an assistant coach for five seasons at Texas Tech. He was active in the Fellowship of Christian Athletes and led Bible studies for the student athletes at Texas Tech, and he was well known among his colleagues as a man whose way of life spoke so loudly that he never had to preach character with words.

In January 2006, just six days before his fifty-third birthday,

Dave Brown was playing basketball with his son when he suffered a fatal heart attack. It's always a tragedy when the world loses a role model of character, but the good news is that such people always leave behind a legacy of character in the lives of those they have influenced.

Mentors Can Be Heroes

What is a mentor? More even than a teacher, counselor, or coach, a mentor is a person who invests his or her life in another person in a profound and personal way. A mentor's function is not merely to dispense knowledge or skills. A mentor focuses primarily on encouraging the growth of strong character traits in another person.

Lamell McMorris is founding principal and CEO of Perennial Strategy Group, a consulting firm. I asked him if he had a mentor when he was growing up. "Absolutely," he said. "My pastor, the Reverend William J. Vance. His deeds matched his words, and he was a true friend and mentor.

"Reverend Vance would pick me up from school or from my home and take me to lunch. He'd spend time with me—not because he had to but because he wanted to. He saw something inside me that he wanted to encourage and cultivate. We talked for hours. He always talked straight across to me. He never talked down to me. Whether he affirmed or admonished me, I always felt that he believed in me.

"Funny thing was he never called me by name. Reverend Vance always called me 'Doctor,' because that's what he thought I should become. I didn't become a doctor, but I did internalize the fact that he believed I could succeed in life. I learned about character just from observing his life. He was what I wanted to become. In fact, he was the kind of man I *still* want to be.

"I absorbed his example so much that, when I was in college, I was involved in youth ministry at my church. I worked mostly with high school kids. Their attention span is next to zero—but

they will let you know right away if you do anything wrong. You're never quite sure if you're getting through to them.

"Almost ten years later, I heard from one of the young men who had been in my class at this church. He thanked me for my influence in his life and told me that our talks together had convinced him to go on to college. I remembered those sessions, and how I encouraged him to view college as a challenge—and the toughest part of the challenge was not just making it *to* school, but making it *through* school. At the time, it looked like he could never afford college, but he persevered and made it through school.

"Today, this young man is a high school teacher and a basketball coach. He was a student; now he's a mentor. What Reverend Vance instilled in me, I passed on to him, and he passes it along to others."

Lamell's experience shows how the values of good character go on and on, a legacy that never ends. The student becomes the mentor, and the mentor instills these traits in more and more students. That is how we influence and impact each succeeding generation.

How to Be a Hero

Young people need heroes. They need parents, teachers, coaches, pastors, youth leaders, and mentors who will teach them what it means to be people of character. In my hundreds of interviews with people across the country and in all walks of life, I have gathered a treasury of insights on how to be a hero to the next generation:

1. Continually express unconditional love, acceptance, and forgiveness. To be a hero of influence, let young people know you're on their side, not on their back. If they fail, correct them— but make sure they know you're correcting them in love. Tell them you forgive them, you believe in them, and you expect great things of them in the future. Give them a clean slate and a fresh start.

Kirsten Gillette is the junior high youth pastor at Walnut Hill Community Church in Bethel, Connecticut. "When I was a young

teenager, I was at a camp for our annual church family picnic," she told me. "The camp was owned by Mr. McGowan, my Sunday school teacher. He was also a high school math teacher, and I was hoping to be in his ninth-grade class in the fall.

"Some friends and I were walking around the camp when we spotted the soda machine. We had no money, so we thought we'd try to reach up into the machine and snag a soda for free. I was the daring one, so I got down on my knees and put my arm into that slot all the way up to my elbow. I told my friends, 'I've almost got one!'

"We were so engrossed in our effort to rob the vending machine that we didn't notice Mr. McGowan approaching. I heard his voice behind me: 'What are you doing?'

"I turned and saw Mr. McGowan's disappointed expression. My heart sank. I was ashamed and embarrassed. I had been caught trying to steal from my Sunday school teacher—a man I respected and admired! I had let him down and made a fool of myself.

"Without another word, Mr. McGowan turned and walked away. I hung my head for a couple hours, trying to figure out what to do. Finally, I couldn't take it anymore and I went looking for him. I found him sitting alone on the dock by the lake. I approached him timidly and said, 'Mr. McGowan, I don't know what I was thinking. I'm really sorry.'

"He had me sit down and as we talked, I felt his forgiveness wash over me like a wave. He not only forgave me, but he told me he was looking forward to having me in his math class next year! I couldn't believe the grace he showed me after what I had done to him—and after setting such a terrible example to my peers.

"Now that I'm a youth pastor and teacher, I share this story with my students. I tell them, 'People are always watching your character, even when you think no one sees.' But this story is also a lesson in forgiveness. When someone hurts me, fails me, or lets me down in any way, I remember the example of Mr. McGowan, and I make a decision to express the same level of love, acceptance, and forgiveness that he showed me."

2. Be consistent and keep your word. Whether you promise rewards or consequences, make sure you deliver. Few things threaten a young person's sense of security as a parent, teacher, or mentor who behaves in an unpredictable and capricious manner.

John N. Howell, associate head basketball coach at Oviedo High School in Seminole County, Florida, told me, "Several years ago, one of my starters kept getting in trouble in a particular classroom. The teacher approached me for help in the matter, so I sat down with the young athlete and got his side of the story. I reminded him that student athletes are leaders, so his behavior had to be above reproach. Another complaint from his teacher, I said, would result in a one-game suspension.

"Unfortunately, during the JV District Championship Week, the teacher again wrote him a referral to the office. The school turned it over to me. I met with him and told him that—as I had promised—he would not participate with us in the upcoming championship game. Then I sent him home from practice.

"We were already hurting because we had lost our point guard to the varsity team. When this young man was benched for a game, we lost our second-best guard as well. We went into the championship game and the team fought valiantly, but in the end, we lost, 53–51.

"The young man cried as much as anyone in the locker room that night. He knew his season was over and he didn't get to participate in the final battle. He also knew that he alone had let his team down. It wasn't my fault or anyone else's.

"Some would say that I punished the whole team—but what do you do? How do you show kids that they must do what's right? You have to keep your word. Would I do it again? Yes—because it was the right thing to do. You hope that it doesn't come to that. You give warnings and second chances, but some kids don't respond unless there's a promise of consequences. When you make that promise, you have to keep it.

"A friend of mine faced a similar situation. He had two players

in a game who broke the rules of conduct. He punished the less talented player but gave the more talented player a pass. I asked my friend why he didn't punish both. He said, 'If I punished the more talented player, it would have hurt the whole team and we might have lost the game. Winning is important.'

"Yes, winning is important—but character is more important. The proof of this principle is that, the very next week, the kid who escaped being corrected had to be warned by an official for his foul language on the floor.

"Kids who learn that their talent gets them favorable treatment grow up to become arrogant and disrespectful. We need to be consistent and keep our word—even when it means we may lose games. If our players learn skills but don't learn character, we may win the battle but lose the war."

3. *Always be aware of your influence.* You are under scrutiny at all times, even when you aren't aware of it. Young people are learning what it means to be a person of character by watching how you make decisions, deal with opposition, overcome adversity, and respond to criticism. Make sure you never let them down.

Dr. Roy E. Yarbrough, director of sports management studies at the California University of Pennsylvania, told me, "Seventy percent of how we communicate is non-verbal. I demonstrate my character to my students by being on-time for class, by responding to student email within twelve hours, by learning their names, and by taking time to listen to them. These may sound like simple, inconsequential acts, but I've found that these small actions give me credibility with my students. My life is under scrutiny, and I have to prove my character by the way I live.

"Senior students have come to me and said, 'I've been in college four years and you're the only professor who knows my name.' It's so easy to take note of a student and have an influence in that young person's life. My goal is not only to impart knowledge but to instill character, and you can only do that by showing students you care about them as people."

4. Continually preach character and virtue. Take time to have honest, meaningful talks with your kids, and share your views and experiences about character. Mom or Dad, post sayings about character by the bathroom mirror, on the dashboard of the car, or by the family computer. Coach, post character quotations in the locker room and around the gym. Teacher, place character sayings around the classroom. Surround your kids with constant reminders of the importance of good character.

Coach Mary "Kissy" Walker is head coach of women's basketball at Husson College in Bangor, Maine. In twelve years as a head coach, she has compiled a career record of 236-100, and has coached Husson to four NAIA National Tournaments, including a Final Four appearance.

"My mission statement is posted in our locker room, my office, and in our media guide," Coach Walker told me. "I constantly stress honesty, responsibility, hard work, and attitude. Every game we play has a word that expresses a character theme, such as 'courage,' 'believe,' 'pride,' or 'heart.' Sometimes we wear motivational sayings on our shooting shirts, like, 'There's only one way to play: Hard.' We expect character and good behavior at all times, and there are some things—such as swearing—that we do not tolerate. We constantly preach and teach character."

5. Talk to your kids about heroes. Tell your kids or students who your own personal heroes are and the character qualities you admire in them. Tell the stories of their lives and how they have impacted the choices you've made over the years.

Ask, "Who are your heroes? Why is that person your hero? What admirable qualities does that person possess?" Don't let kids off with an answer like, "He's cool," or, "She's famous." Make kids think about heroes in terms of genuine character qualities, not talent, image, or attitude. Show them how *real* heroes of character have a positive effect on the lives of other people. Show them what the character of a real hero looks like.

Dr. Pamela M. Brill is senior vice president of learning solutions

at Linkage, Inc. A licensed psychologist, she is also the author of *The Winner's Way: A Proven Method for Achieving Your Personal Best in Any Situation* (McGraw-Hill, 2004). "When I was a young girl," she told me, "my parents were influential in forming my ideas about character. They exemplified character by the lives they lived, and they taught character in many ways, including telling me stories of heroes of character.

"My dad was orphaned at four and was raised on the farm of his foster parents on Long Island during the Great Depression. He had to do his chores before going to school, and he also worked in a local movie theater. His foster father was strict and demanding. Still, my dad got to play baseball when he was a boy, and he also learned to fly the crop-dusting planes.

"A stellar shortstop, Dad was approached by a pro baseball scout while he was in high school, but the scout decided he was too young. After graduating from high school, Dad traveled in a series of primitive planes to China with a bunch of other young mavericks, and they became the Chinese Air Force—the original 'Flying Tigers.'

"The Flying Tigers played a key role in World War II. They defended China against attack by Japan before America officially entered the war. The pilots and planes of the Flying Tigers were absorbed into the U.S. Army Air Corps in 1942, and Dad continued flying as an Army Air Corps fighter pilot. After the war, he went to college in New Jersey on the GI Bill. There he played baseball and was again approached by a scout. This time they rejected him because, in his early twenties, he was 'too old.'

"I also grew up with stories of my beautiful Italian-American mother, Rita DeDominicis. Raised in Haverhill, Massachusetts, she wanted to serve our country when World War II broke out. So she took a train to Washington, D.C., and landed a job as an assistant to the Quartermaster General. She lived in a boarding house for young women and enjoyed living in the nation's capital.

"After the war, she returned home. One weekend, my dad and

his buddies took a train from New Jersey to Haverhill, just to go to a dance spot there. Dad saw my mother and it was love at first sight. They danced all night, and my mom invited him to family dinner the next day. Dad accepted the invitation—and that's how my orphan-turned-flying-hero father married into a clan of emotional Italian-Americans.

"Mom and Dad had a wonderful life together. But just when Dad was getting ready to retire and travel with Mom, she was diagnosed with early onset Alzheimer's. So I watched Dad lovingly take care of her at home until she became so ill that she was a danger to herself. At that point, he sold their home, found a nursing home he trusted, moved her in, and lived in a mobile home nearby. He visits her every day, cooks for her, and even though she no longer knows people or even speaks English anymore, he's sure she knows him. There's so much more to that story, but the important thing is that my dad exemplifies true self-sacrificing love.

"Throughout my life, my parents told me story after story, and most of those stories had to do with virtue, values, and character. I constantly heard such statements as, 'Time is life—don't waste it,' and, 'Follow your heart but use your head.' I learned the importance of hard work, family loyalty, self-sacrifice, courage, and living with passion and purpose.

"When I was twelve, Dad gave me two books to read, and both had to do with character: One was *PT 109*, the story of John F. Kennedy's heroism in World War II. The other was Dale Carnegie's *How to Win Friends and Influence People*—about how to authentically connect with other people. I'm grateful that I've had parents who were true heroes and role models, and who pointed me to other heroes to admire and follow."

6. *Support your kids as they take on tough challenges.* Encourage young people to dare great things—then stand with them as they persevere through obstacles and opposition.

Kimberly Waltmire teaches second graders in Manchester, Connecticut—and she doesn't just teach reading, writing, and arith-

metic. She's a hero to her kids because she involves her students in real-life experiences that teach character and values. One of Kim Waltmire's most famous exploits could be called "The Tale of the Lobster"—an adventure in character education that resulted in a feature story in *USA Today* (November 18, 2006) and an appearance on *Oprah*.

It began when one of Kim Waltmire's students told her he wanted to liberate a six-pound, twenty-year-old lobster that was imprisoned in a glass tank at a local supermarket. She said, "Well, let's make it a class project!" In order to free the lobster, her students would have to use their math, science, and writing skills—and more importantly, they would have to learn new depths of character qualities such as courage and perseverance.

A big part of the project involved a letter-writing campaign—which meant the kids needed to use their English language skills. "We often give children a blank piece of paper," Mrs. Waltmire told *USA Today*, "but we don't give them the tools to write. Time and time again, their writing is dull and unimaginative, and the kids are so stressed that they can't write. So I allow kids to experience things first, and the writing comes last."

The save-the-lobster campaign was sparked by one student's compassion. "The lobster was too big for the tank," Mrs. Waltmire told me. "The boy wanted to do something about that. Our class wasn't looking for a cause or publicity. The cause found us, and these kids responded with compassion. The entire class came together to reach a common goal. The children wrote eloquent, passionate letters to the store manager and they worked hard to raise the money to purchase the lobster.

"Even the store manager was touched by the effort. He knew it wasn't merely about saving one lobster. It was the act of an entire classroom of young people standing up for what they believed in, working together, and persevering no matter what others might think.

"The effort got a lot of media attention. First there were the

headlines. Then people in the community wrote letters to the editor or to our class. Some letters were very supportive and cheered the kids on. Others ridiculed what the class was trying to do. Many of the comments people made were very hurtful to the children and to me.

"But the opposition and criticism we received was a lesson in character. As a class, we learned to persevere through the adversity together, and were glad we had the faith to endure and keep doing what we believed was right. In the end, the children could say, 'People laughed, but we stood up for our values—and the lobster went free.'"

Kimberly Waltmire is more than a teacher. She's a hero who stood by her students while they took on a grown-up–sized challenge. She showed them how to make a difference in the world.

Steel for Your Soul

Elbert Hubbard was a writer, publisher, and founder of the Roycroft movement (an arts community in New York). He once wrote an essay about the last moments of Macy's department store magnate Isidor Straus and his wife Ida, who perished aboard the *Titanic* in 1912. As the ship was going down, Straus refused to take a place in the lifeboat ahead of other passengers. Ida refused to go if her husband stayed behind. "We have been together for many years," she said. "Where you go, I go. Our fate is one."

In his essay, Hubbard concluded, "Mr. and Mrs. Straus, I envy you that legacy of love and loyalty left to your children and grandchildren. The calm courage that was yours all your long and useful career was your possession in death. You knew how to do three great things—you knew how to live, how to love and how to die."

Three years after the *Titanic* sank, Elbert Hubbard and his wife, Alice, boarded the ocean liner *Lusitania* in New York and sailed for Europe, where they planned to gather stories for a report on the First World War raging at the time. Six days out of port, the *Lusitania* was torpedoed without warning by a German submarine.

A survivor of the *Lusitania*, Ernest Cowper, reported that the Hubbards came out on the boat deck after the ship was torpedoed. They stood arm in arm together, looking out to sea. When Cowper asked them what they were going to do, Elbert Hubbard calmly shook his head, saying nothing. Alice said, "There doesn't seem to be anything to do."

A few minutes later, Elbert and Alice Hubbard went back to their cabin and closed the door behind them. They chose to die together in their cabin, where the Atlantic waters would not pull them apart. The character qualities of peace, love, and courage that Elbert Hubbard admired in Isidor and Ida Straus were the same qualities he and his wife Alice displayed in their last moments. They, too, knew how to do three great things. They knew how to live, how to love, and how to die.

People of character know how to live.

They live with integrity, making sure every room in their lives is clean. The tongue in their shoes is pointed in the same direction as the tongue in their mouths. They live courageously and humbly. They persevere. They shoulder their responsibilities without complaint. They work hard. They are self-controlled.

People of character know how to love.

They love unconditionally. They forgive freely. They lift up all people without prejudice or discrimination.

And people of character know how to die.

Their faith in God has brought them safely through the refining fires of this life. It will take them securely through the shadow of death.

People of character are tested and proven. They are unshakeable and unbreakable. Their souls have been forged from tempered steel. A soul made of steel may be hammered and torched, flexed and stressed—but a soul made of steel can't be destroyed.

Steel endures. Character abides.

Notes

3. Integrity: Every Room Is Clean

1. Mortimer B. Zuckerman, "Our Cheating Hearts," *U.S. News & World Report*, November 6, 2006, 88.
2. Gay Jervey, "Cheating: 'But Everybody's Doing It,'" *Reader's Digest*, March 2006, retrieved at http://www.rd.com/content/openContent.do?contentId=25419.
3. John Wooden with Steve Jamison, *The Essential Wooden* (Columbus: McGraw-Hill, 2006), 179.

5. Self-Control: Secure Against Attack

1. John Eldredge, *Wild at Heart* (Nashville: Thomas Nelson Publishers, 2001), 164.
2. Kathryn Wilson, *Stone Cold in a Warm Bed* (Camp Hill, PA: Horizon Books, 1998), vii.
3. Dr. Bruce H. Wilkinson, *Experiencing Spiritual Breakthroughs* (Sisters, OR: Multnomah, 1999), 111.
4. Dr. James Dobson, excerpt from *Complete Marriage and Family Home Reference Guide*, retrieved at http://www.family.org/docstudy/solid/a0005855.html.
5. Pam Stenzel with Crystal Kirgiss, *Sex Has a Price Tag: Discussions about Sexuality, Spirituality, and Self Respect* (Grand Rapids: Zondervan, 2003), 124.
6. "Dannah Gresh Bio," retrieved at http://purefreedom.org/dannah.htm.
7. Courtney Lee, "Interview: Vicki Courtney: Bringing Teenage Girls Closer to Christ," ChristianToday.com, July 27, 2006, retrieved at http://www.christiantoday.com/article/interview.vicki.courtney.bringing.teenage.girls.closer.to.christ/7065.htm.

6. Courage: Doing the Thing You Fear

1. Kristin Harty, "Students Learn Courage from Mother's Example," *The News Journal*, May 23, 2006, retrieved at http://www.delawareonline.com/apps/pbcs.dll/article?AID=/20060523/NEWS/605230361.

11. Faith: The Engine of Character

1. C. S. Lewis, *Mere Christianity* (New York: Macmillan, 1952), 109–110.

Contact

You can contact Pat Williams at:
Pat Williams
c/o Orlando Magic
8701 Maitland Summit Boulevard
Orlando, FL 32810
phone: (407) 916-2404
pwilliams@orlandomagic.com

Visit Pat Williams's Web site at:
www.PatWilliamsMotivate.com

If you would like to set up a speaking engagement for Pat Williams, please call or write his assistant, Andrew Herdliska, at the above address or call him at 407-916-2401. Requests can also be faxed to 407-916-2986 or emailed to aherdliska@orlandomagic.com.

We would love to hear from you. Please send your comments about this book to Pat Williams at the above address or in care of our publisher at the address below. Thank you.

Rolf Zettersten
Hachette Book Group USA
10 Cadillac Drive, Suite 220
Brentwood, TN 37027
Fax: 615-221-0962